SYMPATHY FOR THE DEVIL

SYMPATHY FOR THE DEVIL

NEUTRAL EUROPE AND NAZI GERMANY IN WORLD WAR II

Christian Leitz

New York University Press
Washington Square, New York

First published in the USA in 2001 by
New York University Press
Washington Square
New York, NY 10003

New York University Press edition published by special arrangement with
Manchester University Press, Manchester, UK

Library of Congress Cataloging-in-Publication Data
Leitz, Christian.
    Sympathy for the devil : neutral Europe and Nazi Germany in World War II /
       Christian Leitz.
          p. cm.
    Includes bibliographical references and index.
    ISBN 0-8147-5175-x (alk. paper)
       1. World War, 1939–1945—Germany. 2. World War, 1939–1945—
    Diplomatic history. 3. Neutrality—Europe. 4. Neutral trade with belligerents.
    I. Title.
    D749.L45 2001
    940.53'43—dc21   00-051979

Printed in Great Britain

CONTENTS

LIST OF TABLES

ACKNOWLEDGEMENTS

The completion of this book has benefited from the much appreciated help of colleagues at Auckland University, former colleagues at the University of the West of England, Bristol, friends here and there, and the staff of various libraries and archives in Britain, Germany, Sweden, Spain, New Zealand and the United States. I am, of course, grateful to Manchester University Press and Vanessa Graham and Louise Edwards in particular for having given me the opportunity to pursue work on this fascinating subject. I hope that I did not overstretch their patience when the completion of the project took longer than anticipated. Finally, my deepest gratitude goes to my family, Anja, Barnaby and Emmeline, who had to bear the brunt of our move from England to New Zealand (one, though not the only, reason for the delay in completing the book). For their constant reminders that there is a life outside research and teaching I dedicate this book to them.

1

INTRODUCTION

Germany's war effort depended significantly upon its imports of raw materials and goods from the neutral nations. Switzerland was Nazi Germany's banker and financial facilitator, taking and transferring German gold – most of it looted – and providing Germany with Swiss francs to purchase needed products. Switzerland also supplied Germany with key war materials such as arms, ammunition, aluminum, machinery and locomotives. Moreover, Germany was able to mitigate slightly the effect of Allied bombing by moving some arms production to safety beyond the Swiss frontier. Sweden was a critical trading partner of Nazi Germany. Its wartime exports of ball bearings to Germany were vitally important, and for a time Sweden supplied Germany with 40 percent of its iron ore until other European sources reduced that dependency. Spain and particularly Portugal provided Germany with invaluable supplies of wolfram (tungsten) required in the steel-hardening process. Spain also supplied iron ore, mercury, and zinc. Turkey exported very scarce chrome ore to Germany, where the valuable mineral was in short supply.[1]

During the Second World War, Nazi Germany gained vital services from the five European neutrals, Portugal, Spain, Sweden, Switzerland and Turkey.[2] Even though important political, ideological, economic and military differences distinguished the five countries, their economic contribution to the war effort of the Third Reich provides an important rationale for a joint examination. Obvious questions arise. What precisely was this contribution and how important was it? Can a link be established between the services provided and the survival of the five countries as independent and peaceful entities in the midst of war and occupation? Were each country's supplies and services to Germany simply means to assure its independence – or were the countries also guided by motives that went beyond ensuring their survival?

During the Second World War, neither the existence of internationally recognised laws of neutrality nor the adoption of neutral policies was sufficient to save European countries from being affected by the war or, worse, from getting dragged into it. Commentators from both belligerent camps were often scathing about the attitude of the neutrals. Winston Churchill, who at other times was quite sympathetic towards neutral states, commented in September 1944 that the war against Nazi Germany was a morally justifiable crusade, and that 'neutrals who have played a selfish part throughout ought to be made to suffer in the post-war world'.[3] During the war, the Allies occasionally violated the rights of the neutral states[4] – though they clearly stopped short of forcing any of the European neutrals to alter their status. As Cordell Hull remarked in his last major foreign policy address on 9 April 1944, 'we have scrupulously respected the sovereignty of these nations; and we have not coerced, nor shall we coerce, any nation to join us in the fight'.[5]

In stark contrast, not only did Hitler virulently despise the concept of neutrality, but in many cases his policies went beyond limited violations of the neutral status of a particular country and put an outright end to its independence. This ruthless approach should, however, not surprise us in view of the fact that insistence on neutrality and neutral rights greatly contradicted National Socialist ideology. According to Nazi commentators, in the 'New Order'

> the whole pattern of relations between the individual states would radically change. International law would inevitably go by the board. .... Nor could the principle of neutrality be admitted. ... [I]t was inconceivable that any individual states ... should 'take no part in such wars, particularly in Europe'.[6]

In a world view based on the notion of the struggle between nations and the survival of the fittest, the adoption of a neutral stance amounted to nothing more than a cowardly 'cop-out', and as such it was usually treated with disdain. In its most extreme form, of course, this disdain resulted in a complete disregard for a country's recognised neutrality, a policy 'perfected' by Nazi Germany in 1940. In quick succession, Denmark, Norway, Holland, Luxembourg and Belgium fell victim to German aggression. Official pronouncements made by Hitler before the war, in which he had expressed his respect for the neutrality of certain European countries, had obviously been a ruse.[7]

Hitler's views on neutrality were clearly not at all benign. In fact, he did not alter his views even when, after the defeat at Stalingrad, others in the regime, including Joseph Goebbels, found it necessary to strike a more conciliatory note towards the remaining neutrals. Hitler openly detested the lack of courage and commitment of those states that remained neutral in the face of his own crusade. He firmly believed that, once the war had been won, there would be no space in the 'New Order' for such outsiders. There was no doubt in Hitler's mind that a victorious Germany would ultimately not permit the continued existence of independent states in Europe. In May 1943, Goebbels recorded Hitler as saying that `the small state junk which, today, is still in existence in Europe will have to be liquidated as quickly as possible. ... The aim of our struggle must be the creation of a unified Europe.'[8]

Hitler's comments were echoed in the views expressed by other Nazi leaders. Heinrich Himmler and his SS, for instance, planned for the resurrection of a Greater Franconian-Germanic Reich in which a German Reich commissioner would take charge of Switzerland while central and southern Sweden would be incorporated into Germany.[9] When economic experts both in the Reich economic ministry and in private companies discussed and planned the *Großwirtschaftsraum* (Greater Economic Space), they firmly anticipated some control over neutral countries such as Sweden, Switzerland and Spain.[10]

During the war disdainful comments about the five neutrals highlighted the threat that hovered over their independence. None of the five neutral countries had been a target of Hitler's expansionist plans as discussed in the 1920s, in particular in *Mein Kampf* and the so-called 'Second Book'. With the exception of Spain during that country's civil war, the five states also received little attention in the years before the war. However, as the experience of Sweden's neighbours Denmark and Norway was to demonstrate, such a lack of interest on the part of Hitler did not necessarily save countries from Nazi aggression. In fact, after 1 September 1939, even among the five surviving neutrals only Sweden and Turkey did not become the objects of concrete invasion plans.[11]

Nonetheless, in contrast to Denmark and Norway and those other unfortunate victims of the Wehrmacht, the five neutral states under consideration did not fall prey to Hitler's insatiable expansionism. A number of factors combined to ensure their survival. As already indicated, respect by the Nazi regime for the rights of a neutral was certainly not one of these factors – nor did the neutral states themselves survive by scrupulously respecting the legal obligations demanded by their status. The history of the relations between the five neutral states and the Third Reich is littered with violations of the then most important international guidelines on the rights and obligations of neutral states during war, the Hague Conventions, specifically Conventions V and XIII of 18 October 1907.

These Conventions did in any case not completely cover all areas of war. Most obviously, while the 'Rights und Duties of Neutral Powers and Persons' were outlined both 'in Case of War on Land' (Convention V) and 'in Naval War' (Convention XIII), no such guidelines were produced for the air war. To give one example, the frequent violations of the air space of neutral countries by the belligerents were not officially prohibited by a particular article – though it may be argued that a neutral state was protected by Article 1 of Convention V concerning the inviolability of its territory.[12]

Despite their incompleteness and outdatedness, the Hague Conventions acted as the main legal reference point for both neutrals and belligerents during the Second World War. Neutrality clauses were brought into play by neutral governments to fend off 'unneutral' demands by belligerent governments. More frequently, and usually even more unsuccessfully, the Conventions were cited in protest by one belligerent party if a neutral state had violated them in favour of the other belligerent party.

To demonstrate the level of deliberate contravention of the Conventions, a few examples should suffice at this point. As will be shown, Article 2 of Convention V (prohibiting the movement of 'troops or convoys of either munitions of war or supplies across the territory of a neutral Power') was clearly, but not solely, violated in the case of Sweden. Franco Spain actively supported Nazi Germany's violation of Articles 3 (prohibiting the establishment of wireless telegraph stations 'for the purpose of communicating with belligerent forces on land or sea') and 4 (the formation of 'corps of combatants ... on territory of a neutral Power to assist the belligerents') of Convention V and Article 5 (prohibition of use of 'neutral ports and waters as a base of naval operations') of Convention XIII. The demand for internment of 'troops belonging to the belligerent armies ... as far as possible, at a distance from the theatre of war' (Article 11 of Convention V) was violated on various occasions by various neutrals. Turkey, Spain and Portugal violated Article 9 of Convention XIII, which demanded the impartial application 'to the two belligerents the conditions, restrictions, or prohibitions ... in regard to the admission into its ports, roadsteads, or territorial waters, of belligerent war-ships'.

These examples show that, despite their obvious shortcomings, the pre-First World War Hague Conventions continued to cover important military aspects of the Second World War. Yet they were a woefully deficient guide on how to deal with the most significant aspect of the relationship between the neutral and the belligerent states during the Second World War, the conduct of economic affairs. The Swiss historian Linus von Castelmur has neatly summarised this particular problem:

> The international laws of neutrality defined and regulated the economic aspect of war in a totally inadequate manner. As a concept, the economic duties of the neutral during a war on land were outlined in such broad terms that almost any action or omission could be regarded as conforming with neutrality as long as it was not applied onesidedly.[13] In other words: almost anything could slip through the coarse-meshed net of the 'violation of neutrality grid'.[14]

Not only did the Conventions not set strict parameters for the economic aspect of war, they provided, in fact, a major loophole to any neutral state intent on giving a helping hand to Nazi Germany's (and indeed the Allied) war effort. Article 7 of Convention V stated very clearly that 'a neutral Power is not called upon to prevent the export or transport, on behalf of one or other of the belligerents, of arms, munitions of war, or, in general, of anything which can be of use to an army or a fleet'. This allowed the neutrals to enter into deals which, while not necessarily outside the boundaries of their neutral obligations, were without any doubt highly reproachable in moral terms. A particularly good example concerns the export of war material. The fact that this was explicitly not prohibited in Article 7 provided the Swiss government in particular with a welcome rationale for its vigorous sales of war material, initially to the Allies and, for most of the war, to the Axis powers. Article 7 thus became *carte blanche* for entering into an intense economic exchange with the Third Reich.

The Nazi regime, on the other hand, also exploited the glaring absence of a clearly defined framework on the economic aspect of neutrality. At the outbreak of the war hollow promises were made to the neutrals, with the German government issuing an official assurance to all neutral governments about its respect for their economic neutrality. 'In the economic sphere', the regime announced, 'Germany's position towards the neutrals is clearly defined to conform with international law.'[15] Precisely because international law was not clearly defined, this promise was, in fact, of little use to the neutrals.

The Nazi regime was interested in international law only if it could be cited against Germany's military opponents or used to put pressure on the neutral states. Eventually, it would, of course, 'go by the board'.[16] As Werner Best, one of the leading constitutional theoreticians of the Third Reich, pointed out, '*Großraumordnung* and *Großraumverwaltung* constituted a new legal charter of coexistence to which the terms 'international law' and 'constitutional law' of the former liberalistic era no longer applied.'[17] In Axis Europe, different rules applied which very rapidly from mid–1940 affected the policies of the surviving neutrals.

My interest in the wartime relations between neutral Europe and the Third Reich was awakened while I was working on my doctoral thesis (and subsequently book) on Nazi Germany's economic relations with Franco's Spain. The more documents I perused the more details pointed to a conclusion which should be quite obvious even to a casual reader (though still disputed by Franco apologists): Spain's neutrality/non-belligerence was transparently onesided in favour of Nazi Germany. The particular issue of Spanish wolfram (tungsten) supplies to Germany, which I explored in depth, allowed me to gain some insight into the dealings of a second neutral state, Portugal. Finally, with various documents referring to neutral Sweden's and neutral Switzerland's transactions with Spain via Germany or German-occupied France, I had virtually arrived at the circle of countries examined in this book.

Although very conscious of the contentious nature of my project (part of the attraction, of course, for commencing it in the first place), little could I have foreseen, when I first started my preparations, that its subject matter would assume such intense topicality. At regular intervals a new article or book on the extremely dubious wartime role of Switzerland's ruling circles and financial institutions would find its way on my desk. Damning reports on other states also appeared, though they were clearly not of the same intensity as those on Switzerland.

Nonetheless, the so-called Eizenstat report, instigated by the US President and based on a vast number of previously classified documents, put the emphasis not just on 'neutral' Switzerland's relations with Nazi Germany, but also to a lesser degree on the role of other European neutrals. Yet while the dark history surrounding Jewish gold deposits in Swiss (and other) banks and secret Nazi gold transfers into neutral countries undoubtedly constitutes one facet of the relations between the Nazi regime and neutral European countries, it is not the most significant compared with the magnitude of other services provided to the German war effort.

It is those latter services, largely of an economic and, to a lesser extent, military nature, which lie at the heart of this study of international history. The rationale for my approach is simple: my intention has been to focus on those aspects which had an impact on the development of the war in general and of Nazi Germany's war effort in particular. Economic and financial issues are absolutely central to our understanding of the neutrals' contribution to the war and, as such, also demonstrate the nature of the neutrality of the five countries. The book highlights that, while the overall share of Germany's total imports from the five neutral European countries was fairly modest – including Finland, it grew only from 11 per cent in 1938 to 18 per cent in 1943[18] – each country made a vital contribution to the German war economy.

Readers looking for socio-cultural aspects of the relations will unfortunately be disappointed; even so, given their diversity, such aspects undoubtedly deserve examination. There is clearly work to be done on, to name only a few, the role of German schools in neutral countries, the experience of students and workers from neutral countries in Germany, the dissemination and influence of German films and propaganda material, and the role of sports competitions.[19] Few authors have as yet grappled with these issues with reference to the relations of all, as a comparative study of two or more, or even of one neutral country with the Third Reich.

Still, for such a study (or studies) to make sense, the reader would first need some solid background information on the relations between the Nazi regime on the one side and each neutral government on the other. To cite a random example: why were Spanish workers, whose experience in Germany is being researched, sent there in the first place? Or, as a second example, why was Sweden, whose football matches with Nazi Germany are the subject of research, permitted to remain neutral when all its Scandinavian neighbours became embroiled in the war? This book will provide this kind of essential background information. Its purpose is to focus on those issues which determined and dominated the relations as they unfolded during the Second World War. An analysis of such crucial aspects of Germany's relations with the neutrals as, for instance, the supply of Spanish and Portuguese wolfram (tungsten), Turkish chrome and Swedish iron ore as well as military transport agreements with Sweden and Switzerland is essential in understanding the stance of the five neutrals and the benefits which Germany drew from it. It should also help the reader make sense of the question of why, of all the countries of Continental Europe, Nazi Germany permitted precisely those five to remain outside the war.

If recent media coverage of the attitude of the neutrals *vis-à-vis* Nazi Germany has made one thing clear to the general public, it is the extent to which these countries acted 'unneutrally'. This book, based on a wide range of secondary sources in English, German, French, Swedish, Spanish and Portuguese, augmented by archival material from various German archives, examines the extent to which the five countries lived up to announcements of neutrality made at the beginning of the war. In this context, a number of questions receive particular attention. What was the motivation behind policies in support of Nazi Germany, and how important were such contributions to the German war effort? Can one detect any similarities between supportive actions of the five neutrals? How did the development of the war affect German–neutral relations? What role did the Allies play?

My intention has been to provide succinct and focused information on the central aspects. Quite a few of the topics discussed in this book have been the subject of journal articles and full-length monographs containing considerably more detail than is presented here. However, owing to the varied nature of the sources, including the diversity of languages in which they are written, it would be an arduous task for most interested readers to gain an overview of the subject area – indeed, more so as even the more broadly oriented secondary sources usually cover only the relations of one (or exceptionally two) of the neutrals with Nazi Germany. This book, in contrast, brings together for the first time analyses of the relations between the Third Reich and all five Continental European states which retained their neutrality throughout the Second World War.

Notes

1 *US and Allied Efforts to recover and restore Gold and other Assets stolen or hidden by Germany during World War II*, preliminary study co-ordinated by Stuart E. Eizenstat, prepared by William Z. Slany (Washington DC, May 1997), V (hereafter referred to as 'Eizenstat Report'), xxi–xxii.

2 The sixth European neutral, Ireland, is not examined in this book. When the Nazi regime referred to Germany's economic relations with the 'neutral European states', it did not include Ireland for two related reasons. First, the country did not provide valuable services to the Third Reich and, secondly, it was seen as firmly within the Allied sphere of influence. The latter point is reflected in a comment Winston Churchill made on Ireland's neutrality. Britain's wartime leader firmly stated that, if it had become necessary, the British would 'fast and violently have obtained what they wanted' from Ireland; Churchill's comment in *New York Times*, 14 May 1945, cited in Nils Ørvik, *The Decline of Neutrality 1914–1941* (London, 2nd edn, 1971), 217. See also John P. Duggan's not entirely convincing *Neutral Ireland and the Third Reich* (Dublin, 1989).

3 Bernd Martin, 'Deutschland und die neutralen Staaten Europas im zweiten

Weltkrieg', in Louis-Edouard Roulet (ed.) with Roland Blättler, *Les états neutres européens et la seconde guerre mondiale* (Neuchâtel, 1985), 374.

4 Violations included, for instance, the passing over neutral air space and the bombing of neutral territory by mistake (most notably, but not exclusively, in the case of Switzerland). A summary of such so-called *de facto* violations is provided by Jürg Martin Gabriel, *The American Conception of Neutrality after 1941* (Basingstoke, 1988), 42–5.

5 Cordell Hull, *The Memoirs of Cordell Hull*, vol. II (London, 1948), 1322.

6 Werner Best, 'Großraumordnung und Großraumverwaltung', *Zeitschrift für Politik*, June 1942, and Hans Ballreich, in *Die Bewegung*, 19 September 1942, both cited in Arnold Toynbee and Veronica M. Toynbee (eds), *Hitler's Europe*, Survey of International Affairs 1939–1946 (London, etc., 1954), 53.

7 See, for instance, Reichstag speech, 28 April 1939, in Norman H. Baynes (ed.), *The Speeches of Adolf Hitler, April 1922–August 1939*, vol. II (New York, 1969), 1608.

8 Entry in Goebbels's diary, 8 May 1943, cited in Markus Heiniger, *Dreizehn Gründe. Warum die Schweiz im Zweiten Weltkrieg nicht erobert wurde* (Zürich, 2nd edn, 1989), 39–40.

9 Josef Ackermann, *Heinrich Himmler als Ideologe* (Göttingen, 1970), 178 ff. and 191, cited in Martin, 'Deutschland und die neutralen Staaten Europas', 375 and 388 n. 66.

10 See, for instance, BA (German Federal Archive) R25/53, memo Möglichkeiten einer Großraumwehrwirtschaft unter deutscher Führung, August 1939.

11 A military operation against Turkey was suggested as early as September 1940 as part of Admiral Raeder's plan to push the British out of the Mediterranean region. A proper operational plan was, however, never put together. Although Portugal did not become the subject of a separate invasion plan, it was included in Germany's plans for Spain, most notably in Operation Felix.

12 This and all subsequent references to the Hague Conventions cited from James Brown Scott (ed.), *The Hague Conventions and Declarations of 1899 and 1907* (New York, 3rd edn, 1918); see also Roderick Ogley, *The Theory and Practice of Neutrality in the Twentieth Century* (London, 1970), 36–7.

13 See, in particular, Article 9 of Convention V, which states that 'every measure of restriction or prohibition taken by a neutral Power ... must be impartially applied by it to both belligerents'.

14 Linus von Castelmur, *Schweizerisch-Alliierte Finanzbeziehungen im Übergang vom Zweiten Weltkrieg zum Kalten Krieg. Die deutschen Guthaben in der Schweiz zwischen Zwangsliquidierung und Freigabe 1945–1952* (Zürich, 1992), 409.

15 Georges-André Chevallaz, *Le défi de la neutralité: diplomatie et défense de la Suisse 1939–1945* (Vevey, 1995), 235.

16 See above.

17 Best, 'Großraumordnung und Großraumverwaltung', 53.

18 Willi A. Boelcke, *Deutschland als Welthandelsmacht 1930–1945* (Stuttgart, 1994), 159.

19 See, for instance, Gunnar Richardson, *Beundran och fruktan; Sverige inför Tyskland 1940–1942* (Stockholm, 1996) which includes, *inter alia*, useful sections on sports contests between Swedish and German teams.

2

SWITZERLAND

THE PROFESSIONAL NEUTRAL

Gold was a strong, possibly the strongest, link in the chain which held the German giant and the small state of Switzerland in mutual dependence. Other links in the chain – Swiss arms, Swiss war material, Swiss credits – helped to firmly tie together the odd neighbours. The German Reich required not only gold and foreign currency, but also part of Switzerland's highly developed armaments production.[1]

Two particular factors make Switzerland the obvious choice for starting off this book on the relations between neutral European states and Nazi Germany. First, Switzerland boasts a special kind of neutrality to which it (and the international community) has been committed longer than any other nation. The nature and longevity of Switzerland's neutral status have made it an example to other states proclaiming neutrality. Second, and of more specific significance to this chapter (and book), neutral Switzerland provided various economic and financial services to Nazi Germany. These were of vital importance not only in their bilateral relationship, but also in the Third Reich's relations with the other four neutral states. Did the 'indispensability' of the Helvetian Republic, the small peaceful state, to Nazi Germany, the aggressive military power, ensure its survival? Was Switzerland's neutrality ultimately only a myth to which its leaders constantly appealed, but which they often conveniently ignored when they dealt with the Nazi regime?

Recent revelations about the shameful role of various Swiss banks in the 'administration' of Jewish accounts have considerably dulled the carefully tended patina of the country's neutrality. The intense media attention surrounding the investigations has highlighted the fault lines running through Switzerland's long-standing neutral status. Yet to the informed observer, such cracks have long been apparent. During the Second World War it was already clear that Switzerland's leaders were conducting the country's foreign affairs in a fashion not truly befitting its strictly neutral status – hence the growing frequency of Allied protests and warnings. In the immediate aftermath of the war, the Allied–Swiss Washington accord of May 1946 bore evidence of the problematic nature of Switzerland's wartime conduct. The accord required Switzerland to transfer US$250 million into the Allied Gold Pool in recognition of the fact that it had received looted gold from the Nazi regime during the war.[2]

Nazi gold and currency transfers into Switzerland constituted one hugely important aspect of the multi-faceted story that made up German–Swiss war-time relations.[3] During the war, and in its aftermath, its true history was only partially revealed. A much more thorough examination of the relations, and more generally of Switzerland's role during the Second World War, did not take place. A few publications in the 1950s and 1960s aside,[4] the first major studies did not appear until the early to mid–1970s. In his multi-volume seminal work on the history of Switzerland's neutrality, Edgar Bonjour devoted three volumes to the Second World War.[5] Bonjour's major study was followed, in 1974, by Werner Rings's *Schweiz im Krieg 1933–1945*, a critically acclaimed publication in its own right.[6]

Bonjour's and Rings's works ushered in a series of more specialist publications on Switzerland's foreign relations during the Second World War. Aspects as wide-ranging as Switzerland's defensive preparations and activities,[7] its military and intelligence contacts with both the Axis and the Allies,[8] its attitude towards refugees, in particular from Germany,[9] Swiss pro-National Socialist and pro-Fascist movements,[10] and last, but certainly not least, the country's economic relations to the belligerents,[11] have been under intensive scrutiny.[12] Switzerland's role during the Second World War has been truly dissected. The following sections provide a synthesis of this 'dissection'. Naturally, the particular focus of this chapter will be economic and financial – not only because this book is specifically concerned with this subject matter, but, more important, because it constituted the central plank of Nazi Germany's relations with Switzerland as well as with the other four countries under consideration.

Swiss neutrality – the background

Neutrality is part of the Swiss identity, it is like a myth. Every country and every people needs a common myth, especially Switzerland, where there is no such thing as a Swiss nation in cultural terms. Swiss identity is based on a common history, values and experience, but not a common culture or language. Neutrality is one of the few things we have in common.[13]

The origins of Switzerland's neutrality go back as far as the fifteenth century.[14] Then, 'slowly, empirically, a policy took shape, which was the distant ancestor of the policy of neutrality'.[15] After 1515, from a case-by-case 'standing aside' in European conflicts, the status of the Confederation gradually evolved into one of permanent neutrality. Stepping stones on the way were the official prohibition of the transit of foreign troops in 1638 and the recognition of the Confederation's neutrality by various powers in 1713. However, even more than in the case of Sweden, the decisive moment came during the period in which Napoleon Bonaparte's drive for hegemony in Europe was finally derailed.

In broad terms, Switzerland today is the Switzerland which emerged from the period 1813–15. As Antoine Fleury put it, in their present form 'its territory, its borders, its cantons were established at that time. Since then Switzerland has not seen invasion, expansion or amputation of its territory.' To underline this very special experience Fleury concludes that 'this is without doubt unique in Europe, indeed in the world.'[16] This uniqueness extends to the establishment of Switzerland's present state of neutrality. In 1815, the signatories of the Acts of the Congress of Vienna arrived at a joint decision to guarantee Swiss neutrality. It has not been breached since. The signatories to the Acts acknowledged that 'the neutrality and inviolability of Switzerland and its independence from all foreign influences are in the best interests of the political structure of all of Europe'.[17] The official international recognition of Switzerland's neutrality was eventually followed by its domestic, though not explicit, affirmation in the Federal Constitution of 1848.

Closer to the period under consideration, Switzerland followed the wording of 1815 when, upon the outbreak of war in 1914, it declared its strict neutrality. After the First World War, Swiss neutrality was reconfirmed by the League of Nations on 13 February 1920 as a condition of the country's membership of the organisation. The Council of the League of Nations, in fact, again highlighted Switzerland's 'unique position ... due to its centuries-old tradition, which has been expressly recognised in international law'.[18] In Switzerland's own terminology the country's admission to the League of Nations marked a switch from 'integral' to 'differential' neutrality. The country was now subject to nearly all membership obligations. It was not, however, required to participate in military sanctions, nor was it obliged to participate in the preparation of military operations in its territory. The passage of foreign troops through Switzerland continued to be prohibited.

While Switzerland enthusiastically participated in the League of Nations during the 1920s, the dramatic foreign policy steps of Hitler's Germany and Mussolini's Italy in the 1930s eventually led the Swiss government to modify its position. Two months after the *Anschluss*, on 14 May 1938, Switzerland informed the Council of the League of its decision 'to completely cease to participate in the implementation of the regulations on sanctions'.[19] Although still a member, and the host country of the League, Switzerland returned to 'integral neutrality'. Just over a year later, on 31 August 1939, Switzerland asserted its strict neutrality in anticipation of the military conflict which was about to break out. In a statement very similar to that made at the outbreak of the previous World War, the country reiterated the historic roots of its international status:

> With all the means available to it, the Swiss Confederation will maintain and preserve the inviolability of its territory and its neutrality, which the treaties of 1815 and supplementary agreements have shown to be in the true interest of European policy as a whole.[20]

Nazi Germany and Switzerland in the 1930s

Switzerland's declaration of neutrality was as much an assertion of its traditional status as an appeal to the belligerents to affirm the importance of the country's neutrality to them. It required no such appeal for Britain and France to accept Switzerland's neutrality. Italy, which promised to keep its ports open to Swiss imports,[21] and Germany also affirmed the declaration. Yet it is extremely doubtful whether the Nazi regime truly accepted Switzerland's announcement. When the Swiss emphasised their neutrality as being in 'the true interest of European policy', this cannot but have fallen on barren ground with a regime whose interpretation of 'European policy' was so radically different from that of the Western democracies.

During the years preceding the war, the Swiss had received sufficient warning signs to make them feel extremely apprehensive about the intentions of Hitler and his fellow Nazi leaders. As shown in Chapter 1, there were the comments, speeches and proclamations in which Hitler and his cronies had openly expressed their disdain for neutrality. Officially, however, Hitler assured Swiss officials about his respect for their country's international status. In February 1937, he announced to the Swiss federal councillor Edmund Schultheß that 'at all times, whatever happens, we will respect the inviolability and neutrality of Switzerland'. And only weeks before Germany's attack on Poland Hitler reiterated that Switzerland had nothing to worry about, that he would respect its neutrality.[22]

Despite the seemingly reassuring tone of Hitler's statements, they were, however, almost certainly part of his usual game of deception. On various other occasions Hitler expressed quite a different view of Switzerland. A conversation Hitler held with Mussolini and Ciano in June 1941 should be regarded as more typical of his true feelings. According to Hitler, Switzerland

> possessed the most disgusting and miserable people and political system. The Swiss were the mortal enemies of the new Germany. ... On the Duce's query whether Switzerland, as a true anachronism, had any future, the Reich foreign minister [Ribbentrop] smiled and told the Duce that he would have to discuss this with the Führer.[23]

It can be assumed that Ribbentrop's enigmatic reply was a direct allusion to a potential carving up of Switzerland between the two Axis partners. Sinister references to the future of Switzerland had, in fact, preceded the outbreak of war. Had not the original programme of the NSDAP included the demand for the unification of *all* Germans into a Greater Germany? And did this particular demand therefore not also apply to the Swiss Germans even if Hitler deemed them 'the wayward branch of the German people'?[24] In the Third Reich, maps of Europe frequently did not show Switzerland and included its area instead as part of the Greater Germany, as a German *Gau*.[25] This approach, which deliberately ignored Switzerland's status as a sovereign state, was reflected in the planning of Himmler and his SS. One of their major objectives was the resurrection of a Greater Franconian-Germanic *Reich* in which, among other radical 'changes', a German *Reich* commissioner would be in charge of Switzerland.[26]

Obviously, Switzerland had very good reason to be concerned about the intentions of a regime which had no qualms about determining the fate of a growing number of countries. Particularly worrying was the fact that various pro-German and Nazi groups within Switzerland were working against the country's political stability. After Hitler's appointment in

January 1933, those organisations in Switzerland which openly imitated Hitler's Nazis (and Mussolini's Fascists), in particular the so-called Fronten, rapidly expanded their activities. A special notoriety was enjoyed by the Nationale Front, a direct copy of the SA. Mass meetings and marches were held, swastikas appeared in windows, buildings were damaged and broken into, Jews, Social Democrats, Freemasons and other 'enemies' were attacked. The methods used by the Nazis in Germany were openly applied in Switzerland, albeit on a much smaller scale.[27] In contrast to Germany, however, the political and legal system of Switzerland continued to function in a democratic and *rechtsstaatlich* fashion. An increasing number of the Nazi perpetrators ended up in Swiss courts or had to take refuge in the Third Reich.

Although the anti-Communism (and, to a lesser extent, antisemitism) of the Nazis was applauded by many members of the Swiss bourgeoisie, the Swiss authorities did not tolerate the criminal activities committed in their country. Frequently, however, their efforts were undermined by the protection and support that the perpetrators enjoyed in neighbouring Germany. In a number of cases, crimes were committed in Switzerland by German Nazi agents on direct orders from Berlin. In one of the most notorious examples, the abduction of Berthold Jacob in 1935,[28] the Gestapo enticed the said Jacob, refugee from Nazi Germany and fierce critic of the regime, to leave his *refugium* in France for Basel. Once there, he was abducted and taken to Berlin.

This was, in fact, not the first time a political opponent of the Nazis had been abducted from Swiss territory. More than any other case, Jacob's fate revealed, however, the extent of the Gestapo's criminal activities in Switzerland. The Swiss authorities did not tolerate this obvious violation of the country's sovereignty and a major diplomatic initiative was commenced against the Nazi regime. Eventually, it was crowned with success. Jacob was released and was able to return to France. Despite the release the case as a whole proved, however, to be an early indication of the appeasing approach the Swiss government was adopting towards its mighty neighbour. Although the case had given Guiseppe Motta, at the time in charge of Switzerland's Department of Political Affairs (i.e. foreign ministry), a strong lever to humiliate the Nazi regime, he decided to offer a compromise solution which, in essence, tried to hush up the sinister activities of the Nazis. Not surprisingly, Motta's solution was eagerly accepted by the German government.

Why did Motta act in this manner? In Rings's words, Motta's motivation can be explained as follows:

To ensure the cherished peace and its survival, the small state has no other option but to make concessions. It cannot afford to, indeed must not overstep the mark. The highest principle of its foreign policy must be to avoid, to defuse, and to get rid of conflicts in as generous a manner as possible. Motta showed himself to be a master of such a policy.[29]

However, by endorsing Motta's policy, Switzerland's Bundesrat (Federal Council)[29] 'entered a path which it would not leave until the end of the war'.

That Hitler had grudgingly permitted the release of Jacob did not indicate a change of his regime's policy *vis-à-vis* Switzerland. On the contrary, Swiss and German Nazis continued to expand their activities in Switzerland. This became blatantly obvious even while the 'Jacob case' was still going on. The murder of Wilhelm Gustloff, *Landesgruppenleiter* of all German National Socialists in Switzerland, on 4 February 1936 demonstrated the extent of the 'Nazi network' in the country.[31] One Basel newspaper noted how 'hard it was to believe that so many swastika organisations existed in Switzerland'.[32]

As if the spread of the Nazi organisation across Switzerland was not in itself a worrying sign to the Swiss, they were given even more reason for concern by the hostility expressed by many Nazi commentators upon Gustloff's murder. While Hitler mentioned Switzerland only briefly and without any apparent hostility in his funeral speech, others were more forthright. The Nazi press had a field day inundating their readers with reproaches of Switzerland. On a diplomatic level, Ernst von Weizsäcker, Germany's minister in Berne since 1933,[33] passed on a serious warning to the Federal Council.

In contrast to most of Switzerland's newspapers and most of its citizens, both of which reacted with outrage to the Nazi comments, the Bundesrat adopted a policy of appeasement towards Hitler and his regime. While more energetic steps were (eventually) taken, including a ban on all NSDAP leadership offices (from *Landesgruppenleiter* downwards), this showed little effect. The Nazis persevered with their activities.[34] Switzerland continued to be exposed to the Nazi menace.

In view of the Jacob abduction, the Gustloff murder and other related events it was not surprising that both sides saw their political relations with each other in a very negative light. In March 1936, Weizsäcker stated that they had not been so bad for a hundred years.[35] His comment to the editor of a Berne newspaper cannot be discarded as an intimidatory threat, but needs to be seen as a true assessment of the problematic relationship between the two countries. After 1933, political relations between the neighbouring states became increasingly tense. In the economic sphere, Germany remained, however, 'what it had been for years, by far the most important trading partner of Switzerland'.[36]

At the end of the 1920s Switzerland imported nearly 70 per cent of its machinery from Germany while 45 per cent of its coal and over 40 per cent of its iron and steel requirements were filled by Germany.[37] Although the latter import item declined to about a quarter in 1937, German coal supplies continued to make up about half of Switzerland's requirements. Switzerland's economy was also dependent on Germany as its major export market. During the years preceding the war (1937–39), over 15 per cent of all Swiss exports went to Germany.[38] At the outbreak of the Second World War, Switzerland was clearly more dependent upon the economic relationship with the Third Reich than vice versa. While, during the war, Switzerland became even more reliant upon trade with Germany, the latter also came to depend increasingly upon certain services provided by Switzerland.

Switzerland and the threat of a German invasion

> Only an intellectually limited 'superpatriot' can ascribe our survival to our military strength or a Helvetian miracle. Instead, it can be explained by a combination of fortunate, benevolent and undoubtedly also morally unsound factors.[39]

Any discussion of Switzerland's relationship with Nazi Germany during the war would be incomplete without emphatic reference to the country's unique position during the war. From June 1940 to autumn 1944, Switzerland was a neutral island surrounded by Axis or Axis-friendly countries. In fact, after the Wehrmacht took control of Vichy France in November 1942 and of much of Italy in the summer of 1943, Switzerland was completely encircled by German forces. More than any other neutral European country, Switzerland was directly exposed to the pressures and threats of the Nazi regime. Not surprisingly, Switzerland's exceptional position has consistently been highlighted by those seeking to explain why the country was forced to make economic and financial concessions to the Third Reich. Before, however, taking a more detailed look at the economic and financial aspect, a brief summary will follow on how Switzerland came to end up in its enclosed position, and how concern about Hitler's military intentions continued to have an impact upon the country after June 1940.

Nazi Germany's attack on Poland came as a major shock to Switzerland, not only because the Wehrmacht overcame Polish resistance so speedily but also because the outbreak of war focused the attention of Switzerland's political and military authorities on their woefully inadequate defence preparations. In Poland, and before that during the Spanish Civil War, the Luftwaffe had shown itself to be a ruthless destroyer of civilian and military targets. How were the Swiss expected to defend themselves against German air attacks with only a very limited number of anti-aircraft guns and fighter aircraft?[40] The state of the other components of Switzerland's armed forces was at least as worrying. Owing to the absence of stocks of fuel, tyres and parts, army vehicles, for instance, were even dependent upon private petrol stations for supplies.[41]

In September 1939, Henri Guisan, newly elected by the Swiss Federal Assembly to the rank of general and leader of all Switzerland's troops,[42] put together a report on the state of the armed forces. It made extremely grim reading. Not surprisingly, it was not made public until after the war. In 1939, it would undoubtedly have caused widespread panic. Enough was, in fact, known by the public of the report's conclusions to create a heightened level of anxiety. Was there, however, anything to worry about? How likely was an attack by Germany?

From Switzerland's perspective, invasion was extremely likely. With Germany's eastern front secured after the Non-aggression Pact with the Soviet Union and the defeat of Poland, Hitler was sure to turn his attention towards the west. In France, however, the Wehrmacht was faced with the seemingly impregnable Maginot line, which made a direct advance unworkable. Two obvious alternatives for a German attack on France offered themselves to the north-east and south-west of the Maginot line. As neither Belgium nor Switzerland was a match for the Wehrmacht's overwhelming might, they constituted inviting options for Germany's strategic planners.

The Swiss certainly feared so – as did the French government. Yet Poland's defeat was initially followed by a pause in Germany's aggressive drive. Still, during the so-called 'Phoney War', Swiss concerns were raised by the successful deception tactics of the Wehrmacht command. *Fall Gelb* cleverly created the impression of an imminent attack upon northern Switzerland and western France. Neither the Allied nor the Swiss intelligence services recognised the troop movements in Baden as a ruse. Only hours before the actual German offensive against Holland, Belgium and Luxembourg, thirty-seven French divisions, nearly a third of the Allied forces, were tied down behind the Maginot line and along the border with Switzerland by nineteen mediocre German infantry divisions.[43] The deception had worked, in fact it intensified over the coming days.[44]

Although Switzerland's minister in Berlin, Hans Frölicher, did not detect any signs of troop movements when he travelled to south Germany on 10 May 1940 (the day of the offensive in the west),[45] the Swiss authorities ordered the general mobilisation of the country on 11 May. Frölicher's sounding of the all-clear got drowned in the flood of alarming messages which reached Berne. The overall picture clearly indicated an impending attack on Switzerland. On 13 May 1940, Goebbels even announced in a speech that no neutral states would continue to exist within Europe after the next forty-eight hours. An attack was expected to take place during the night of 14–15 May, then during the night of 16–17 May.[46]

In the end, however, nothing at all happened – or, more precisely, nearly nothing. Fighting between Swiss and German military units did, in fact, take place, albeit only in the air. Ironically, the aerial combat involved German planes on both sides. From December 1938 to April 1940 the Swiss air force had taken delivery of ninety Messerschmitt Bf 109s.[47] These planes were to carry the main burden of Switzerland's defence effort during subsequent months. And, as various incidents were to show, the Swiss were forced to make good use of their improved air force.

During the Wehrmacht's military campaign in the west, the Luftwaffe showed extraordinary disdain for Switzerland's neutrality. The country's air space was repeatedly violated, in most cases deliberately.[48] The most notable event took place on 8 June 1940 when Göring ordered thirty-two German fighter aircraft into Switzerland's air space in a deliberate attempt to punish the Swiss air force for its previous shooting down of German planes. Yet in the ensuing battle the Swiss did not suffer any losses and managed to force the superior German contingent out of Switzerland's air space. In response, a furious Göring ordered the sabotaging of Swiss airports and a munitions factory, though the attempt was comprehensively foiled.[49]

There is no evidence that the various aerial tussles over Swiss territory were preparatory moves for an invasion. German and Swiss pilots were not engaged in a 'Battle of Switzerland'.[50] By deliberately engaging in battle with Swiss aircraft, Göring's Luftwaffe attempted to intimidate the Swiss authorities into tolerating German breaches of Switzerland's neutrality, including the violation of its air space. In contrast to the courageous response of the Swiss air force, Switzerland's political leadership, and in particular Marcel Pilet-Golaz, successor of the recently deceased Motta at the Department of Political Affairs and Federal President in 1940, reacted with a display of timid obsequiousness.

By not only releasing all German aircraft and pilots interned in Switzerland, but also offering to pay for the losses suffered by the Luftwaffe,[51] Pilet-Golaz gave a first example of the kind of attitude which soon made him the most controversial figure among Switzerland's wartime leadership. Pilet-Golaz settled the matter to the advantage of the Third Reich only days after the armistice with France had made Hitler master of continental Europe. Yet the concessions were not the outcome of a solo effort by the man in charge of Switzerland's external affairs. Pilet-Golaz's fellow political, and military, leaders had all agreed on this course of action.

Their belief that Switzerland had only narrowly escaped falling prey to the victorious Nazi war machine led them to adopt a position amenable to Nazi demands. According to the Swiss historian Klaus Urner, the prospect of a German invasion did indeed loom over Switzerland once German troops had reached Switzerland's western border on 16 June 1940. Urner argues that, if Mussolini's offensive in southern France had failed, Hitler would have given the go-ahead for an invasion of Switzerland.[52] As it turned out, Hitler had no need to send the Wehrmacht into Switzerland. Other comments which Hitler made about Switzerland in mid-June show, in fact, that he did not see it necessary to order an invasion of the country.[53]

Nonetheless, at the end of June 1940, Switzerland could not afford to be obdurate towards the Nazi regime. The country had been spared from getting dragged into the war, yet it had no reason to feel at ease. With the Axis powers in control of western and central Europe, how long would powerless, isolated Switzerland be allowed to hold out? And even if it was permitted to retain its independence, did it have any choice but to reach an accommodation with the Axis powers, or, as Pilet-Golaz declared on 25 June 1940 in a speech to the Swiss people, to 'adapt to the new conditions'?[54]

More will be said on 'adapting to the new conditions' or, in the words of the Federal Council, 'co-operating in the new Europe'. First, it needs to be examined to what extent a military threat continued to hang over Switzerland after Germany's defeat of France. Even while Pilet-Golaz was granting various concessions to the Third Reich, Hitler instigated the operational planning of an attack against Switzerland. An invasion plan was produced on 24 June and General von Leeb, commander of Army Group C in the south of Germany, was given orders to prepare for the military occupation of neighbouring Switzerland.

Despite Leeb's preparations, the likelihood of an actual invasion was, however, remote. In practice, the operational planning of late June proved to be only one version of a number of studies on which Germany's military leadership continued to work until October 1940. These planning studies, which became known under their code name Tannenbaum, did not translate into a serious threat to Switzerland. One German officer, Bernhard Lossberg, who was closely involved in the planning activities, referred to the studies as 'sketches produced for the drawer'.[55]

Despite various operational plans, the Wehrmacht never attacked Switzerland, either in 1940 or, as will be shown, later. Why? On 12 July 1940 General Guisan had argued that Switzerland's defensive efforts needed to be such that an attack on the country would be 'drawn out and costly, and that it would create an unnecessary and dangerous battle-ground at the heart of Europe which would interfere with the execution of their [the Nazis'] plans'.[56] Switzerland was, it seems, not entirely unprepared.

Both the Swiss historian Walther Hofer and a former Swiss chief of staff, Hans Senn, have emphasised the importance of Switzerland's military preparedness in putting both Germany and Italy off any hostile plans. For Senn, it is not sufficient to refer simply to Switzerland's moun-tainous terrain as the main obstacle to a military intervention by the Wehrmacht.[57] Hofer concurs. Refuting the claims of 'some historians of the younger generation', he acidly maintains that 'it is really naive to believe that it had nothing to do with Switzerland's defensive preparedness if all these plans ultimately came to nothing'. Hofer instead points at the roughly SFr 200 million which the Swiss government had allocated to the defence of the country in June 1938. He also highlights the speed with which 630,000 men were mobilised in September 1939. And finally, though Switzerland would not have been able to keep the enemy out, Hitler would have found it extremely difficult to crack the Swiss *Réduit* in the Alps. In Hofer's words, the *Réduit* strategy 'definitely made sense, indeed it was the only solution which promised success'.[58]

As implied by Hofer, other historians do not share his (and Senn's) convictions.[59] In theory, Switzerland's defence strategy sounded undoubt-edly promising. In brief, it was anticipated that, upon being attacked, the Swiss army would destroy all installations, including roads, bridges and factories, useful to the Axis and retreat to a fortified zone (the *Réduit*) in the Alps. From there, the Swiss troops would continue the struggle against the invaders. In reality, however, the *Réduit* existed, at least initially, on paper only.

As Werner Rings reminds us, the strategy did not automatically translate into an actual defence capacity. It was expected to be at least a year before the *Réduit* was sufficiently serviceable. In the meantime, Goebbels later boasted, 'Switzerland ... could have been taken care of in three to four weeks.'[60] Instead of a stubborn display of opposition, the Swiss government chose to grant more concessions as the best response to the perceived threat. On 15 September 1940, the Federal Council acted upon Germany's demand for strict radio silence to be observed after 10.00 p.m. This was to make it more difficult for British aircraft to find their way to targets in southern Germany and northern Italy.[61] Shortly afterwards, on 7 November, an additional German demand was again heeded. All Swiss citizens were ordered to black out their homes from 10.00 p.m.[62]

The black-out order, which was not lifted until September 1944, led to a number of mistaken attacks, resulting in some casualties and damage exceeding SFr 40 million. To argue, however, as Hans Senn has done, that the casualties and damage were responsible for the eventual rescinding of the order,[63] plainly ignores the fact that it was cancelled only after Allied troops had reached Switzerland's western border. For four years, the daily black-out was a reminder to the many Swiss hostile to the Nazi regime that the Swiss authorities were willing to appease their German counterparts.

Yet it is also true to say that for much of those four years most of Switzerland's people and its government and military continued to believe in the possibility of a German attack. From time to time news reached Switzerland, either openly or via the country's intelligence service, about apparent plans to 'deal with Switzerland'. In May 1941, for instance, according to one source from within Himmler's entourage, the Nazi regime was expected to act during the course of the coming summer. German–Swiss negotiations, if unsuccessful, were to be followed by the use of arms.[64]

Fear continued to mingle with the hope that Switzerland would be spared the fate of other European countries. The Nazi regime cleverly played on these anxieties. Only two months before the May 1941 news about a likely German attack, Goebbels had declared that Germany had no intention of occupying Switzerland. As usual, however, such a 'calming' comment was followed by a threat. On this occasion, Goebbels picked on a major bone of contention between the two countries, the attitude of the Swiss press. As was the case with many Swedish newspapers, the Nazi regime simply could not accept that pockets of critical reporting continued to exist in Europe. In a scathing attack, Goebbels threatened the Swiss with 'Germany's reply' should they continue to offend National Socialism.[65]

Gesinnungsneutralität ('moral neutrality'), not simply *Staatsneutralität* (neutrality of the state) was repeatedly demanded by the Nazis. In other words, the Nazi regime did not accept that Switzerland's neutrality was simply confined to the state and that citizens of the neutral state, and in particular its media, should not be required to demonstrate a 'sufficiently' neutral attitude. Even though the Swiss authorities frequently intervened against 'anti-German' reports and comments in the press, Switzerland's critical voices did not subside.[66] These voices, in fact, took courage from the position Switzerland's leadership had itself adopted in 1940. Shortly after Motta, a fervent supporter of the Staatsneutralität concept, had died, the members of the Federal Council endorsed his views in the Federal Assembly:

> Switzerland must be allowed to express freely its opinions about the events which are occurring around the world. With regard to public mani-festations of views, for instance in the press, criticism is permitted as long as it remains objective and is expressed in moderation.[67]

Even though Germany's military victories of summer 1940 led to the adoption of a more restrictive approach by the Swiss political leadership, the free expression of (critical) opinion was never curbed to the extent to which the Nazi regime would have liked. In any case, complying with German demands of this kind would have only marginally eased the pressure on the country.[68] It would certainly not have removed the threat of attack and occupation.

After 1941, concern about a potential German invasion continued to occupy the Swiss even though, in military terms, Germany's attack on the Soviet Union severely reduced the likelihood of a military strike against Switzerland. While an enormous (and rapidly growing) number of Wehrmacht units remained engaged in the east, an attack on Switzerland would have meant a totally unnecessary diversion of troops. Swiss worries, however, lingered on and continued to be fuelled by further disquieting news. Frequently, hostile reports appeared in the German press.[69] Scathing comments by Nazi journalists about the protection Germany's war against the Soviet Union provided to Switzerland's 'petty shopkeepers' and the repeated written and verbal attacks by the regime's 'megaphone', Goebbels,[70] against the 'filthy state' kept the Swiss on edge.

The Swiss were also kept on edge by disquieting intelligence reports from Germany. In this context, the so-called *Märzalarm* of March 1943 provides the outstanding example. On 18 March 1943, a report arrived from Berlin which warned that discussions at the highest level indicated hostile intentions against Switzerland. The shock value of the news was enhanced when it was confirmed by Walter Schellenberg, chief of the SS foreign intelligence service (part of the SS-Reichssicherheitshauptamt), who, at the time, was in direct contact with Roger Masson, chief of Switzerland's military intelligence service.[71]

The Schellenberg–Masson communication link constituted the most infamous example of the intense intelligence operations conducted by both sides. Constantly concerned about German intentions, the Swiss authorities constructed a wide network of intelligence-gathering activities (one of which, the so-called Wiking line, was to provide the initial *Märzalarm* warning).[72] As has been shown in detail, most recently by Braunschweig, information was collected from various sources and by various organisations, including in particular Masson's intelligence service.[73] On the German side, Admiral Wilhelm Canaris's Abwehr and Schellenberg's SS foreign intelligence service used neutral Switzerland as a major source of information.

In particular Berne, the capital, very conspicuously experienced the intelligence war between the Germans and the Allies, in fact increasingly so as the war progressed. In 1942, only Lisbon among the other neutral or non-belligerent capitals saw as many Abwehr agents actively engaged in intelligence work as Berne (twelve in each case). Significantly, however, the Abwehr ceased all espionage activities against Switzerland in mid–1943 after Canaris had emphasised Switzerland's lack of military usefulness and warned about the political repercussions of continuing such activities. Schellenberg concurred with Canaris's assessment.[74]

While activities against Switzerland were scaled down, Switzerland's importance as a 'centre for the procurement and exchange of information' continued to increase. With the development of the war reducing Germany's access to other sources, the Swiss '"turntable" of international espionage'[75] spun ever faster. In contrast to the Franco regime in Spain, however, which actively assisted Nazi officials in their intelligence operations, the Swiss authorities endeavoured to take a strictly neutral approach (though it appears that the Nazi regime drew part of the monies needed for its espionage activities in Switzerland from the credits granted by that very country[76]). In summer 1944, Allen Dulles, Office of Strategic Services (OSS) representative in Berne from November 1942 to July 1945, reported to the head of the OSS, William J. Donovan, that 'the *Swiss counter-espionage is extremely wide awake* and any mistake we made would eliminate the section of our organization which was involved.'[77]

Dulles clearly made very few mistakes – quite in contrast to his Nazi counterparts. Throughout the war German espionage efforts were frequently undermined. *In toto*, 865 spies working for Germany were arrested and convicted;[78] seventeen (of thirty-three spies condemned to death) were executed.[79] Of the neutral countries, Switzerland proved to be most successful in countering Germany's espionage efforts. Despite such setbacks, however, for the Germans (and the Allies) the conclusions of the US military attaché in 1920 still held true during the Second World War:

> Switzerland is *the whispering gallery of Europe*; and although unquestionably much of the political information to be gained is second-hand and in the nature of political international gossip, it has, if properly evaluated, great value as corroborative data.[80]

On the particular issue of the Schellenberg–Masson link the Allies did not, in fact, have to draw on gossip, as they appear to have been reliably informed about the meetings between the two 'spy masters'.

In contrast, the information gathered by Swiss agents, which led to the *Märzalarm* of 1943, proved to be far less reliable. As it turned out, the warnings were not followed by any military activities. In fact, in March 1943, a military operation against Switzerland was not even under consideration. Instead, as various historians have concluded, the Nazis deliberately created the rumour to force Switzerland to grant economic concessions during the ongoing negotiations (see below).[81]

In hindsight, Swiss fears about a potential attack always surpassed the real intentions of the Nazi regime. Despite various Wehrmacht planning studies, the country was never a serious target of Nazi aggression. Owing to the outcome of the military developments of summer 1940, Hitler had no need to take the final step of ending the country's independence. Not only did an invasion of Switzerland offer no strategic advantages, it would, in fact, have endangered important supplies and services on which the Third Reich had come to rely. It even appears that the Nazi regime used the threat of invasion deliberately to enforce the continuation of these economic and financial concessions vital to the war effort. By trading with the Third Reich, Switzerland contributed, in fact, to its own potential downfall. It is clear that, once the Nazis had achieved final victory (with the help of Swiss products and financial assistance), Switzerland would have fallen into their hands like an overripe fruit. While the war continued, it was, however, 'preferable for the Axis powers to make use of the services of the Swiss economy than to occupy [the] country.'[82]

Switzerland's economic and financial wartime 'partnership' with Nazi Germany

Switzerland has become a German war arsenal which Britain is not allowed to bomb.[83]

For almost the entirety of the war Nazi Germany benefited from the importation of vital goods from its southern neighbour, including armaments and related material. It benefited from huge shipments of gold to Switzerland (valued at between SFr 1.6 billion and 1.7 billion) which allowed the Nazi regime to pay for vital purchases not only in Switzerland but also in other neutral or allied countries. And, last but not least, it benefited from the generous credit facilities Switzerland made available through the bilateral clearing. By the end of the war, these credits amounted to a total of SFr 1,119.6 billion.[84]

In the early 1980s, in a brief examination of these three aspects of Switzerland's wartime relations with the Third Reich – the supply of important goods, the receipt of substantial quantities of gold, the provision of credit facilities – the Swiss historian Philippe Marguerat arrived at a very 'clean' conclusion. Switzerland, though 'exploiting the whole margin permitted by international law', remained within the confines of neutrality by striking a balance in particular between the financial services it rendered to the Allies and those it made available to the Axis. In terms of international law and in purely economic and financial terms, Switzerland acted as neutrally as was possible under the special conditions created by the war.[85]

A cynic may argue that 'striking a balance' is a rather weak argument to defend Switzerland's commercial and financial wartime activities. Not only were its dealings with Nazi Germany of a different moral 'quality', but, viewed in practical terms, they also had a much greater impact upon the development and duration of the war than the country's transactions with the democratic western Allies. In terms of both the quantity and the variety of the products, a huge gap opened up after 1940 between the level of Switzerland's exports to the Axis powers and its meagre trade with the Allies.[86] For four years, the Third Reich remained the main beneficiary of Switzerland's foreign trade. How did the Swiss–German economic relationship pan out in detail during the Second World War?

In September 1939, the wartime economic relationship between the two countries started off on the basis of friendly mutual respect. The Federal Council was encouraged by the accommodating tone adopted by the German negotiators during initial discussions in Berne. The German

26

delegation assured its Swiss counterpart of Germany's respect for Switzerland's neutrality in the economic field. It also promised to attend to Germany's clearing debt of SFr 80 million and, most important, it guaranteed the continuation of vital supplies of coal and iron. During the first few months of the war, supplies arrived on a regular basis.[87]

These encouraging early signs were, however, of only a temporary nature. With the war in Europe in the balance, the Nazi regime pretended to treat Switzerland as an equal while trying to prevent it from moving too close to Britain and France. The true attitude of the Nazi regime was revealed during the spring and summer of 1940 when the Wehrmacht was successfully demolishing the *status quo* in Europe. While Switzerland's neutral status remained untouched, it received its first forceful economic reminder of the newly emerging 'order' in Europe. The target chosen by the German government was one of the most vulnerable areas of Switzerland's economy, its need for supplies of German coal.

Before the war, Germany had been Switzerland's largest supplier of coal. In 1938, 54 per cent of the 3.336 million mt of coal imported into the country originated in Germany.[88] Although supplies declined after the outbreak of war, Germany continued to be an indispensable source of the raw material. During the first half of 1940, about 700,000 mt of German coal were exported to Switzerland. Eventually, the Nazi regime decided to make use of Switzerland's obvious dependence on German coal. On 27 May 1940, AA official Karl Ritter threatened the Swiss delegation with an embargo on coal supplies because, he argued, they were being used in the production of war material for the Allies. Switzerland, Ritter complained, was like 'a major armaments workshop which worked almost exclusively for England and France'.[89] Ritter's warning was followed by action. In June 1940, the threat of a coal embargo became reality.[90]

In view of the development of the war, the reaction of the Swiss government was predictable. A week before the signing of France's armistice with Germany, Johannes Hemmen, the Reich's economic envoy, reported triumphantly to Berlin:

> Federal Council prepared to supply as much war material as possible for Switzerland. ... already accepted supplies ... amount to SFr 35 million plus SFr 8 million Oerlikon orders. ... All war material supplies to the enemy powers have been stopped until our negotiations are concluded. The same ban also applies to arms supplies to Holland, Belgium, and Norway. It has been agreed that these will not be sent to London. We can take over those arms already manufactured and the [production] capacity intended for these countries.[91]

In June 1940, Switzerland was forced to cut its armament supplies to the Allies and redirect them to the Axis powers. This radical shift was, in fact, evidence of a complete refocusing of the country's production towards the economic and military needs of the Axis. The coal embargo provided the Swiss with a first taste of the kind of methods the Nazi regime was to apply at various points during the war. At this particular juncture, when the rise of the Axis seemed unstoppable, Switzerland succumbed to the pressure – though it successfully opposed German demands for all trade with Britain and its colonies to be terminated. Hemmen's report on the progress of the negotiations was followed by the conclusion of an economic agreement which reflected Germany's hegemonic role in Continental Europe.

Under the agreement of 9 August 1940, Switzerland granted Germany a clearing credit of SFr 150 million.[92] German buyers were given the right to use the credit on any strategically vital goods.[93] In addition, Switzerland agreed to pay a certain proportion of their clearing obligations in Swiss francs (nearly 12 per cent in 1940), that is, money which the Nazis could freely use in other markets. Moreover, the Swiss accepted in principle the policy of buying gold, again in exchange for valuable francs. Thus started the upward spiral of Germany's gold sales to Switzerland. By even taking gold confiscated, plundered or looted from its rightful owners, the Swiss banks offered the Nazis an invaluable source of foreign currency. It would, in fact, become so important to the Nazi regime that, in June 1943, the German economics minister and Reichsbank president, Walther Funk, was forced to make his now well known comment that not even for two months could he do without Switzerland's help in converting gold into foreign currency. In more detailed terms, a report by Switzerland's Independent Commission of Experts: Switzerland – Second World War, the so-called 'Bergier Commission',[94] has highlighted the importance of the Swiss banks:

> During World War II, Switzerland was the most important conduit for gold originating from countries occupied or controlled by the Third Reich. Roughly 79 percent of all gold shipments from the Reichsbank to other countries was routed through Switzerland. In terms of volume, the SNB accounted for 87 percent of this bar, with Swiss commercial banks handling the remaining 13 percent. Although there are differences in the figures, the value of the gold delivered by the Reichsbank to the SNB was between SFr 1.6 and SFr 1.7 billion. Of this sum, the SNB purchased SFr 1.2 billion on his own account, the rest was placed in deposits held with the SNB for other central banks and the BIS. Large quantities of gold bought by the SNB were sold to third countries, most notably Portugal (SFr 452 million), Spain (SFr 185 million), and Romania (SFr 102 million).[95]

Table 2.1   *Reichsbank gold exports to Switzerland, 1940–45*

Year	Million SFr
1940	125.9
1941	269.0
1942	458.4
1943	588.9
1944	258.1
1945	15.8
Total	1,716.1

Source: Rings, *Raubgold aus Deutschland*, 197, table I. All the gold transferred to the SNB between January 1939 and 30 June 1945 would today amount to a value of US $3.9 billion; Eizenstat Report, iv.

Germany's gold transactions with Switzerland were indispensable not only to its acquisition of strategically important raw materials, but also 'for its foreign intelligence service, its worldwide use of agents, for the purchase of radio programmes and press notices, for financing overseas operations of the Kriegsmarine and much more'.[96] In neutral Turkey, for instance, Germany's foreign currency requirements for propaganda, intelligence gathering and press subsidies were calculated at about RM 4 million monthly in November 1943. To cover this expenditure the German government needed to tap into the monies gained through its sale of gold to Switzerland.[97]

By late 1943, the SNB had adopted a more cautious attitude in its dealings with the Nazi regime. Guarantees were demanded that the gold it received from Germany was 'of impeccable provenance', that is, not confiscated, plundered or looted. In practice, however, little changed. The verdict of the Bergier Commission is clear:

> The SNB Governing Board was extremely slow in recognizing that the Nazi regime was systematically operating a policy of theft and plunder and the murder of individuals and entire segments of the population. Although it was plain for all to see that Germany was acquiring gold by illegal means, the SNB authorities appear to have remained wedded to 'business as usual'. Despite their awareness of the dubious provenance of the gold that was being shipped and of the warnings issued by the Allies, the official representatives of Swiss banks and insurance companies continued to pressure the SNB to continue taking gold from Germany even as the war was entering its final stages. Indeed, the gold transfers persisted as late as April 1945.[98]

Table 2.2   *German coal exports to Switzerland, 1938–45*

Year	Million mt	% of total Swiss coal imports
1938	1.783	54
1940	1.565	
1941	1.985	90
1942	1.830	96
1943	1.632	86
1944	1.168	83

Source: Chevallaz, *Le défi de la neutralité*, 263, table II.

Table 2.3   *Total German exports to Switzerland, 1938–45*

Year	Million SFr	% of total Swiss imports
1938	373.1	23.2
1939	440.4	23.3
1940	411.3	22.1
1941	656.2	32.4
1942	660.3	32.2
1943	532.2	30.8
1944	433.4	36.5
1945	54.3	4.4

Source: Bourgeois, 'Les relations économiques', 61 n. 74.

In hindsight, the concession on gold purchases granted to the Nazi regime in August 1940 was to have a marked effect for the entirety of the war. In return for its concessions, Switzerland received guarantees that Germany would continue to supply vital goods. As a whole, however, the treaty weighed heavily in favour of the Third Reich. In other words, it reinforced in economic terms the military reality in Europe. More than ever, Switzerland was dependent upon trade with Germany for the health of its economy and its work force.[99] During the second half of 1940, 870,000 mt of German coal made their way to Switzerland while, in late 1940, Germany promised 2.4 million mt of coal for 1941. Although, as usual, the German government failed to fulfil its promise and Switzerland, in fact,

Table 2.4   *Total Swiss exports to Germany, 1938–45*

Year	Million SFr	% of total Swiss exports
1938	206.1	15.6
1939	191.5	14.7
1940	284.8	21.6
1941	577.0	39.4
1942	655.6	41.7
1943	598.4	36.7
1944	293.6	25.9
1945	11.2	0.75

Source: Bourgeois, 'Les relations économiques', 61 n. 74; see also Kamber, *Schüsse auf die Befreier*, 365. Owing to a rapid increase in prices, changes in the actual quantities imported and exported were far less dramatic. By 1942 Switzerland's total imports (in quantity terms) had actually fallen to about half, by 1944 to not even a third, of their 1939 level. Total exports also decreased substantially after 1941; Urner, 'Neutralität und Wirtschaftskrieg', 256.

received less than 2 million mt, this still constituted 90 per cent, that is, almost the whole, of Switzerland's imports.

German supplies of coal were vital to the Swiss economy, satisfying its basic needs. German purchases of Swiss products, on the other hand, were essential to the survival of Switzerland's important export trade. Between 1939 and 1942, Germany's share of Switzerland's total exports increased from 14.7 per cent to 41.7 per cent. In view of Nazi Germany's total dependence upon trade within Europe, it was, of course, not surprising that imports from Switzerland increased during the war. From mid-1940, when the development of the war marginalised Germany's main competitors for Swiss goods, Nazi officials set their eyes firmly on Switzerland's production, in particular of armaments and armaments components. During the decisive month of June 1940, the Sonderstab HWK (Special Staff for Trade and Economic Warfare) of the OKW hinted at the future course of German–Swiss trade when it concluded that, individually, the goods imported from Switzerland were not of decisive importance to the war effort, but 'the potential supplies as a whole [were] of great interest'.[100]

Soon it became obvious that Germany's political and military leadership was intent on turning potential into real supplies. By February

1941, the chief German negotiator with Switzerland, Seyboth, asserted that Switzerland had become the supplier of 'important armaments in substantial quantities'.[101] In the intervening period since June 1940, Switzerland had thus moved from being a virtually non-existent to a useful source of armaments for the Third Reich. In October 1940, the three branches of Germany's armed forces had placed new orders to a total value of SFr 261 million, while, in January 1941, the Luftwaffe announced that it alone intended to make purchases for the whole of 1941 which would require SFr 344 million.[102] In view of this interest in Switzerland's arms production, it was not surprising that the Nazis demanded, and received, an expansion of the clearing credit of August 1940.

A provisional German–Swiss economic protocol was signed on 7 February 1941. It provided Germany with an additional clearing credit of SFr 165 million over and above the previously agreed SFr 150 million. Yet as soon as the Swiss government had given in, new demands were made. Within weeks, the German negotiatiors were demanding a further substantial increase of the credit ceiling. Not only that, but they also pushed the Swiss delegation to accept an increase in the value of war material exported to Germany. In fact, during negotiations which took place in Berlin in April, the Swiss negotiators, Jean Hotz and Heinrich Homberger, were confronted with even higher demands, first and foremost among which was the demand for the credit facility available to Germany to be allowed to grow to SFr 850 million.[103]

As on previous occasions, the first reaction of the Swiss delegation was to immediately reject the demand. Very quickly, however, Swiss annoyance at such an outrageous request again gave way to resigned recognition of the reality of Switzerland's relation to the Third Reich. After more than six months of negotiations, a new agreement was eventually signed on 18 July 1941 which permitted an increase of Germany's debt to SFr 850 million in the period to 31 December 1942. For its concessions, which also included increased restrictions on exports to Britain,[104] Switzerland was 'rewarded' with guarantees on urgently needed supplies of coal, iron, lubricating oil and petroleum.

In summer 1941 the direction of Switzerland's external economic relations was again set most firmly towards the Axis. The country's trade figures bear out this conclusion. While, during August 1941, SFr 40 million and SFr 14 million of goods were exported to Germany and Italy,[105] the value of Britain's imports amounted to SFr 894,000.[106] More important, Germany's imports included a range of products of crucial strategic value. The Nazi negotiators had forced the Swiss government delegation to accept

SWITZERLAND: THE PROFESSIONAL NEUTRAL

Table 2.5 *German clearing credit level in Switzerland, 1940–43*

Year	Million SFr
August 1940	150
February 1941	315
July 1941	850
April 1943	1,150

that Germany was to be the recipient of all Switzerland's exports of precision engineering products. Britain, which was particularly keen to secure supplies of Swiss micro-precision parts for its war production, was forced to resort to smuggling them out of Switzerland.[107]

Although Britain's smuggling operations helped to satisfy the needs of its arms industry, their effect could not compare with the much greater benefit Germany's war economy enjoyed from the open importation of Swiss high-quality products. During the first half of 1942, Switzerland exported SFr 250 million of goods of 'very great importance to the war effort' to Germany while the value of similar goods exported to the Allies (Britain and the United States) was given as only SFr 1.7 million.[108] During the whole of 1942, over SFr 350 million of war material (arms, munitions, fuses) and related goods (ball bearings and machinery) were supplied to Germany while the Allies received only SFr 13.8 million. In 1943, the gap increased even more markedly.

Since the fall of France, Switzerland's foreign economic relations had experienced a total transformation or, more precisely, reorientation towards the Third Reich (and to a lesser extent Fascist Italy). Reflecting bitterly upon this radical change, a deputy of the Ständerat wrote on 1 September 1941:

> We supply arms ... only to Germany. We supply textiles only to Germany. We supply Swiss timber ... only to Germany. We open a credit facility of SFr 850 million only to Germany, and an additional 150 million only to Italy. We put our north–south transport system at the disposal of Germany's military interests. Financial relations between Switzerland and Germany are governed in accordance with Germany's interests.[109]

Even though this comment conveys the impression that Switzerland was completely at the mercy of the Nazi regime, the country's negotiators did not, in fact, simply make concessions without putting up a fight. Swiss and Nazi officials were both aware of the significance of Switzerland's

NAZI GERMANY AND NEUTRAL EUROPE

Table 2.6   *Swiss exports of war materials and related goods to Germany, 1938–44*

Year	Million SFr
1938	66
1940	126
1941	316
1942	375 (or 353[a]) (13.8 to the Allies)
1943	409 (or 425[a]) (17.8 to the Allies)
1944	42

Note: [a] Urner, 'Neutralität und Wirtschaftskrieg', 272.
Source: Chevallaz, *Le défi de la neutralité*, 263, table III. During its negotiations with the Allies in late 1944, the Swiss government presented lower figures, SFr 258 million for 1942 and SFr 289 million for 1943; Kamber, *Schüsse auf die Befreier*, 279–80.

Table 2.7   *German arms exports to Switzerland, 1937–43 (contracts only)*

Year	Million SFr
1937	0.1
1938	7.4
1939	16.6
1940	2.7
1941	5.0
1942	3.5
1943	2.1

Source: Boelcke, *Deutschland als Welthandelsmacht*, 136.

industrial output to the German war effort. This fact gave Switzerland's negotiators some bargaining power in their discussions with the German government, in particular after the invasion of the Soviet Union and the American entry into the war.

On numerous occasions, Nazi officials admitted as much when they discussed the value of Switzerland as an independent state. Despite his many scathing comments about Switzerland, Goebbels recognised the importance of the country as a trade partner and supplier of valuable arms products.[110] The same view prevailed even more clearly within the AA. In

August 1942, Germany's minister in Berne, Köcher, appealed to his predecessor, Ernst von Weizsäcker, to help ensure the trouble-free continuation of Switzerland's war material production. It was, after all, 'so significant' to the needs of the Wehrmacht.[111] This verdict was confirmed by the OKW. In July 1942, its Economic Office warned that losing 'Switzerland's armaments capacity would prevent the execution of certain programmes'.[112] At the end of September 1943, Field Marshal Wilhelm Keitel even ordered that no steps should be taken which might in any way upset Switzerland.[113]

This appreciation of Switzerland's contribution to the Axis war effort was not solely founded upon its supplies of war material. Repeatedly, German officials emphasised the need to keep open the transit routes via Simplon and the Gotthard which proved to be vital to the Axis. During the war years, 34.8 million mt of goods were conveyed by the transit routes.[114] In contrast to Sweden, however, Switzerland never permitted the passage of military personnel. Nonetheless, some Swiss citizens were convinced that troops hidden in sealed railway wagons made their way through the country. Frequently, this belief derived from reports of voices coming from the wagons.[115] Yet the voices were, in fact, not German but Italian, the voices not of soldiers but of Italian workers sent to work or returning from work in Germany. By permitting a final transport of forced Italian labour in September 1943, the Swiss authorities became part of the shameful history of Germany's ruthless exploitation of Italy.

While military personnel were not routed via Switzerland, the carriage of war material was condoned until October 1941. Even after the Swiss stopped the transit of war material, the Nazis continued to benefit from Switzerland's transport links with Italy. 'Ordinary' merchandise traffic through the St Gotthard tunnel continued until February 1945 while the Simplon route was closed to such traffic slightly earlier, at the end of October 1944. The Swiss government was well aware that it eased the pressure on Germany's other transport routes south, most notably on the Brenner, by allowing the transit of large quantities of civilian products. Moreover, while the Brenner was repeatedly the target of Allied air attacks, the Swiss route was protected by the country's neutrality. Among the goods making their way through Switzerland, coal was particularly important. In 1940, Johannes Hemmen told the Swiss delegation bluntly that an end to the coal traffic would mean an end to Switzerland.[116] Wagon after wagon rolled through Switzerland, according to a German government report of mid–1943 a monthly average of 470,000 mt.[117]

Switzerland thus possessed certain means by which it could influence the course of its relations with the Third Reich. Yet the importance of

Switzerland's services did not stop the Nazi regime from repeatedly failing to keep to its side of various economic agreements. In one instance, soon after the Soviet counter-offensive of December 1941, the Swiss were warned of a reduction in petroleum supplies. In mid-July 1942, a reduction in the monthly iron supplies from 14,000 down to 6,500 mt was announced and, even more important, coal too failed to arrive in the quantities guaranteed in July 1941.[118] By December 1942, Germany's arrears in the agreed supplies amounted to 960,000 mt of coal, 130,000 mt of iron and 78,000 mt of petroleum and oil.[119]

In response to Swiss protests, the Nazi regime showed its usual verbal contempt for Switzerland's neutrality. From the regime's point of view, Switzerland, in contrast to many other European countries, deliberately avoided giving any support to the fight against the Soviet Union.[120] In the eyes of the Nazi leaders, the only official, though in fact privately organised, contribution, the dispatch of a Swiss medical mission to the eastern front on 15 October 1941, was obviously not regarded as of any significance.

The mission, which comprised thirty-seven doctors and thirty nurses, was proposed by the Swiss minister in Berlin, Frölicher, and was led by the germanophile Colonel Eugen Bircher. On his orders, the mission was permitted to treat German soldiers only.[121] Despite having been officially sworn to secrecy, Dr Rudolf Bucher, a member of this, the first of four missions, broke the silence and went public about the atrocities he had witnessed in the German-occupied east. Faced by this and other disclosures about the mass killings in the east, the Federal Council made every effort to keep the information from the public view by applying a policy of strict censorship. In 1943, however, one Swiss newspaper reported that five million Jews had already been murdered, while the *Neue Zürcher Zeitung* stated that 'the Jewish question has become a Jewish slaughter'.[122]

While it maintained its pressure on Switzerland to make a more whole-hearted contribution to the 'anti-Bolshevik campaign', the Nazi regime also decided to bring the trade gap with Switzerland into the discussions. When confronted about the shortcomings in German supplies, the Nazis presumptuously argued that they should be regarded as Switzerland's contribution to a rapid conclusion of the anti-Bolshevist campaign.[123] Not surprisingly, the Swiss delegation, which had brought up the issue in Berlin in August 1942, did not want to see Germany's supply difficulties resolved in the way suggested. Instead of being able to get the German negotiators to stick to the agreement of July 1941, however, the Swiss were faced with threats of more reductions in supplies and demands for an increased credit limit.

The events in North Africa and Stalingrad hung heavily over the talks, which continued unresolved. No new economic accord replaced the July 1941 agreement when it came to an end on 15 January 1943, though the bilateral economic relations continued informally on the same basis. The military situation, while making an invasion of Switzerland less likely, increased the importance of the country to Germany's (and Italy's) war effort. More than ever the Wehrmacht desired Swiss military hardware, the Nazi war economy required various Swiss products, the Reichsbank was desperate to maintain the Swiss banking connection and the Axis powers needed to keep the through route via Switzerland open. Switzerland, however, was seemingly intent on penalising Germany for the failure to keep to its supply obligations. How could the Nazi regime make sure that the Federal Council did not alter its policy to the detriment of the Axis?

As outlined by Bourgeois,[124] one option considered at a meeting of various high-ranking Nazi officials in February 1943 was to engage in an economic war with Switzerland. By cutting the country off from vital supplies, it was hoped that the Swiss would be forced to give in. Yet the idea was rejected because of its likely repercussions on Germany. Hitler was sceptical about the idea, not only because he did not trust Italy to enforce it in a similar manner,[125] but also because he had come to accept the significance of Switzerland's supplies and services. On 11 March 1943, Emil Wiehl noted that

> the Führer stated that the conflict with Switzerland should not be taken to extremes, but that instead the option of a compromise solution should be kept open even if German requests for new armaments supplies had to be reduced.[126]

The discussions surrounding the economic war option, and its eventual rejection, undermine the position of those historians who have downplayed Switzerland's role in the German war effort. Admittedly, shortly before the resumption of bilateral negotiations and the subsequent conclusion of the German–Swiss Protocol of 23 June 1943, Albert Speer had announced that RM 300 million of armaments orders placed in Switzerland were not as indispensable as had previously been maintained. Nonetheless, Speer's comment did not lead to economic warfare. (It was, in any case, very probably never an option favoured by Hitler's armaments minister.) Instead, the stance adopted by the AA in June 1943 reflected the prevailing position in the German government. By arguing that the war material supplied by Switzerland 'consisted of specialist products of particular importance'[127] the AA urged against economic war and for a new economic agreement with Switzerland.

Ironically, this comment by an AA official highlighting the significance of certain Swiss products is stood on its head by the Swiss historian Georges-André Chevallaz. Chevallaz's conclusion is clear. After stating categorically that 'in quantitative terms, Switzerland's contribution to Germany's war effort was negligible', Chevallaz also denies that the supply of certain products was 'qualitatively indispensable'. He rejects it simply by arguing that 'it is in any case unlikely that German technology ... would not have been capable of providing these products in the absence of Swiss ones'.[128]

Chevallaz's book, in particular the chapter on Switzerland's neutrality and its war-time economy, represents one of the most recent examples of publications firmly written as a defence of the country's war-time record[129] and, at the same time, as an indictment of those historians who have dared to attack it.[130] In purely quantitative terms, Chevallaz has a point. On average, the total value of Swiss war material and war material-related exports to Germany amounted only to a maximum of about 1.6 per cent of Germany's own production.[131]

Chevallaz's outright denial of the importance of Swiss products and services, however, does not stand up to closer scrutiny. The significance of various industrial activities has already been highlighted. Apart from generous supplies of war material and related products, Switzerland also exported about an eighth of its electricity production to the Third Reich, most notably to German factories in southern Germany. In fact, about 40 per cent of the total power supplies of southern Germany (0.5 billion kW annually) was imported from Switzerland.[132] Switzerland's financial services, finally, were clearly indispensable to the Nazi regime.

The Allies certainly did not regard Switzerland's contribution to the German war economy as negligible. Although all the neutral countries under consideration were criticised by the Allies for their contribution to the German war effort, Switzerland's economic and financial relations with the Third Reich were of particular concern to the British and US administrations. When, in February 1944, a total of fifty governments were formally warned by the Allies about taking 'German' gold,[133] Switzerland was the foremost Allied target. Yet the threat of forced restitution of the gold to its rightful owners did not immediately have an effect on Switzerland.

During the summer of 1944, the Swiss still stubbornly refused to follow Allied demands to stop receiving gold from Germany. Not until 2 March 1945 did the Allies achieve the desired result, and then only after protracted negotiations.[134] Two months before Germany's capitulation, the Federal Council finally agreed to end all purchases of gold from the Third Reich except for the expenses of the German legation, the Red Cross, and for Switzerland's services as protecting power.[135] Having these exceptions cleverly included in the agreement enabled the Swiss Federal Council to permit the receipt of a final 3 mt to 3.5 mt of gold (about SFr 15.8 million) from the Reichsbank in April 1945.[136]

Apart from the transfer of gold, mention has also been made of the generous credit facilities the Nazi regime gained from Switzerland. In May 1942, the Swiss government admitted that its 'credit undertakings' and the 'intimate ties between the two economies' created a relationship between Switzerland and Germany that was 'fundamentally different from that of Germany and its other European partners'.[137] The Nazi regime undoubtedly made good use of the availability of credit. When, on 12 April 1943, Switzerland decided to resume the economic negotiations with the German government, the latter had already exceeded the credit ceiling of SFr 850 million by around SFr 300 million. Despite this obvious violation of the agreed terms, Berne decided to bring the negotiations to a successful conclusion.

On 23 June 1943, a provisional accord was signed which was eventually followed by the new economic agreement of 1 October 1943. Both the provisional and the final agreement were largely concerned with the usual issues. Switzerland's concerns were addressed by German promises of regular supplies of coal, iron and oil while the Nazi regime managed to persuade the Swiss to agree to a further (and final) extension of the credit.[138] By then, the Swiss credits exceeded the total of those granted to Germany by the other four neutrals by four times.[139]

As the agreement of 1 October was only short-term, new negotiations were under way in spring 1944. Yet it appeared that the German delegation was not unduly concerned about the conclusion of a comprehensive new economic accord. As shown by the delegation's plan of negotiation, it sought, however, to achieve agreement on individual points. While the supply of Swiss goods and electricity was not regarded as essential, 'the transit [was] so important that, for economic reasons, one could not do without it even if it was restricted'.[140] Since Italy's entry into the war in June 1940 this particular assistance provided by Switzerland had proved to be of great usefulness to the Axis. After the fall of Mussolini in July 1943 and the subsequent occupation of large parts of Italy by German troops, the transalpine transport facilities had taken on an even more crucial role.

A short-term agreement was finally reached on 24 March 1944. As a result, Germany was able to retain significant Swiss services, including the continuation of the transit traffic. Between February and May 1944, a monthly average of about 400,000 mt of goods were transported south while about 50,000 mt reached Germany from Italy. During the same period, Switzerland also maintained its purchases of gold from the Third Reich. A monthly average of about 5 mt was transferred into foreign currency.[141]

In June, the March accord was eventually replaced by a new agreement. Under increasing pressure from the Allies, the Swiss negotiators achieved the inclusion in the agreements of a reduction in Switzerland's supplies to Germany. According to Bonjour, this meant that instead of a monthly average of SFr 55 million (as had been the case in 1942), the value of exports to Germany, including mainly war material and war material-related goods but excluding agricultural products, decreased to about SFr 23 to 24 million.[142]

While the trade between the two countries continued uninterrupted, it clearly followed a downward trend. When reducing its trade with Germany, Switzerland made use of the fact that Germany proved to be unable to fulfil its contractual supply obligations.[143] Yet despite the ban on exports of ball bearings, arms and related material on 1 October 1944[144] and the blocking of German assets in Switzerland on 16 February 1945, the economic relationship with the Third Reich was not completely abandoned. On the contrary, both sides even signed a further economic protocol on 28 February 1945 which covered the reduced remainder of German–Swiss commercial relations. Despite the openly expressed annoyance of the British and US governments, Switzerland insisted that its neutral status precluded a forced rupture of relations with one belligerent side. While imports from Switzerland faded almost completely in the last months of the war, the country continued its economic and diplomatic relations with Nazi Germany to the end.

Notes

1 Werner Rings, *Raubgold aus Deutschland. Die 'Golddrehscheibe' Schweiz im Zweiten Weltkrieg* (Munich, 2nd edn, 1996), 123.

2 On the creation of the Gold Pool in November 1945 and its subsequent history, see Eizenstat Report, 56–7 and 181–5.

3 While the Swiss have always insisted that a total of RM 1 billion was transferred, much higher estimates have been made. According to a report to the Allies by Dr Landwehr of the Third Reich's foreign exchange department, 'the sum of German assets which passed into Switzerland amounted to at least 15 billion reichsmarks'. In his interview, Landwehr apparently 'dismissed

with an ironic smile the Swiss estimate of 1 billion reichsmarks'; Johanna McGeary, 'Echoes of the Holocaust', *Time*, 24 February 1997, 19. Referring to figures in the ledgers of the Reichsbank, Bower arrives at the same amount; Tom Bower, *Blood Money: The Swiss, the Nazis and the Looted Billions* (London, 1997), 48.

4   See, for instance, Hans Rudolf Kurz, *Die Schweiz in der Planung der kriegführenden Mächte während des Zweiten Weltkrieges* (Biel, 1957).

5   Edgar Bonjour, trans. Charles Oser, *Histoire de la neutralité Suisse: quatre siècles de politique extérieure fédérale*, vols. IV–VI (Neuchâtel, 1970).

6   Werner Rings, *Schweiz im Krieg 1933–1945* (Zürich, 9th edn, 1997). 1974 also saw the publication of Daniel Bourgeois's *Le Troisième Reich et la Suisse 1933–1941* (Neuchâtel, 1974), a suitable lead-in to the period examined in this book.

7   See, *inter alia*, Peter Kamber, *Schüsse auf die Befreier. Die 'Luftguerilla' der Schweiz gegen die Alliierten 1943–1945* (Zürich, 1991).

8   Although the German intelligence services were already active in the neutral European countries prior to the entry of the United States into the war, this consequential event increased substantially the importance of the remaining neutral countries to Germany's intelligence-gathering activities. In this context, Switzerland came to play a particularly significant role. See, in particular, Hans Rudolf Kurz, *Nachrichtenzentrum Schweiz. Die Schweiz im Nachrichtendienst des Zweiten Weltkriegs* (Frauenfeld, 1972); Hans Rudolf Fuhrer, *Spionage gegen die Schweiz. Die geheimen deutschen Nachrichtendienste gegen die Schweiz im Zweiten Weltkrieg 1939–1945* (Frauenfeld, 1982), and Pierre-Th. Braunschweig, *Geheimer Draht nach Berlin. Die Nachrichtenlinie Masson-Schellenberg und der schweizerische Nachrichtendienst im Zweiten Weltkrieg* (Zürich, 3rd edn, 1990).

9   Jacques Picard, *Die Schweiz und die Juden 1933–1945. Schweizerischer Antisemitismus, jüdische Abwehr und internationale Migrations- und Flüchtlingspolitik* (Zürich, 2nd edn, 1994). See also Jean-Claude Favez, *Das internationale Rote Kreuz und das Dritte Reich* (Zürich, 1989).

10 Arnold Jaggi, *Bedrohte Schweiz. Unser Land in der Zeit Mussolinis, Hitlers und des Zweiten Weltkrieges* (Berne, 1978).

11 Again, Werner Rings has been the 'pacesetter'. In 1985, his *Raubgold aus Deutschland* already detailed many controversial aspects of Switzerland's financial dealings with the Third Reich which have since been at the centre of public attention. Other writers have added important facets to Rings's original examination. See, in particular, Robert Urs Vogler, *Die Wirtschaftsverhandlungen zwischen der Schweiz und Deutschland 1940 und 1941* (Zürich, 1983); Marco Durrer, *Die schweizerisch-amerikanischen Finanzbeziehungen im Zweiten Weltkrieg. Von der Blockierung der schweizerischen Guthaben in den USA über die 'Safehaven'-Politik zum Washingtoner Abkommen 1941–1946* (Berne, 1984); Oswald Inglin, *Der stille Krieg. Der Wirtschaftskrieg zwischen Grossbritannien und der Schweiz im Zweiten Weltkrieg* (Zürich, 1991); Gian Trepp, *Die Bank für Internationalen Zahlungsausgleich im Zweiten Weltkrieg. Bankgeschäfte mit dem Feind. Von Hitlers Europabank zum Instrument des Marshallplans* (Zürich, 1993, here 3rd edn, 1997).

12 A very useful summary of the various strands of investigation (focusing on

the reasons why Switzerland was not invaded) is provided by the journalist and historian Markus Heiniger in *Dreizehn Gründe*.

13 Peter Burkhard, member of the Swiss government task force set up to investigate Swiss–German relations during the Second World War, in Adam LeBor, *Hitler's Secret Bankers: How Switzerland profited from Nazi Genocide* (London, 1997), xviii.

14 For a brief summary of the historical development of Switzerland's neutrality see Rudolf L. Bindschedler, 'Die schweizerische Neutralität. Eine historische Übersicht', in Rudolf L. Bindschedler *et al.* (eds), *Schwedische und schweizerische Neutralität im Zweiten Weltkrieg* (Basel and Frankfurt, 1985), 149–54.

15 Jean Freymond, 'Neutrality and Security Policy as Components of the Swiss Model', *Government and Opposition* 23 (1988), 54.

16 Antoine Fleury, 'La neutralité suisse à l'épreuve de l'Union Européenne', in Jukka Nevakivi (ed.), *Neutrality in History* (Helsinki, 1993).

17 Antoine Fleury, 'The Role of Switzerland and the Neutral States at the Genoa Conference', in Carole Fink, Axel Frohn and Jürgen Heideking (eds), *Genoa, Rapallo, and European Reconstruction in 1922* (Cambridge, 1986), 201.

18 Cited in Walther Hofer, 'Neutraler Kleinstaat im europäischen Konfliktfeld. Die Schweiz', in Helmut Altrichter and Josef Becker (eds), *Kriegsausbruch 1939. Beteiligte, Betroffene, Neutrale* (Munich, 1989), 209.

19 Cited in Hofer, 'Neutraler Kleinstaat', 215.

20 Cited in Hans Senn, 'Militärische Aspekte der Neutralität', in Roulet (ed.), *Les États neutres*, 70. For the complete text of the declaration see, for instance, the inside cover of Bonjour, *Histoire de la neutralité*.

21 A transit agreement with Italy was signed on 4 November 1939. Italy's ports remained open to Swiss trade until September 1943.

22 Cited in Horst Zimmermann, 'Die "Nebenfrage Schweiz" in der Außenpolitik des Dritten Reiches', in Manfred Funke (ed.), *Hitler, Deutschland und die Mächte. Materialien zur Außenpolitik des Dritten Reiches* (Düsseldorf, 1976), 814.

23 Andreas Hillgruber (ed.), *Staatsmänner und Diplomaten bei Hitler. Vertrauliche Aufzeichnungen über Unterredungen mit Vertretern des Auslandes*, vol. I: *1939–1941* (Frankfurt, 1967), 573. Hitler also referred to Switzerland as a canker of Europe; see Jürg Fink, *Die Schweiz aus der Sicht des Deutschen Reiches 1933–1945* (Zürich, 1985), 236.

24 Fink, *Die Schweiz*, 233. The process by which Switzerland severed its links with the Holy Roman Empire of the German Nation started in 1291 and was formally concluded in 1648. About three-quarters of the Swiss population are German-speaking.

25 See, for instance, a map of *Großdeutschland* of 1935, reproduced in Rings, *Schweiz im Krieg*, 65. In a further example, Bonjour mentions a map of Europe in a UFA film of mid–1941 in which Switzerland appeared within the borders of the Third Reich; Bonjour, *Histoire de la neutralité*, vol. V, 249.

26 Martin, 'Deutschland und die neutralen Staaten Europas', 375 and 388 n. 66.

27 In electoral terms, the Fronten were a very marginal force. In federal elections, they achieved their best result in 1935 when they received fewer than 14,500 votes (1.5 per cent of the total vote); Chevallaz, *Le défi de la neutralité*, 21.

28 On the Jacob case and its outcome see Rings, *Schweiz im Krieg*, 32–46.

29 *Ibid.*, 45.

30 Switzerland's government consisting of seven members.

31 In early 1936, the Nazi network in Switzerland led by Gustloff consisted of forty-five local groups (*Ortsgruppen*) and twenty-one party bases (*Stützpunkte*).

32 Cited in Rings, *Schweiz im Krieg*, 50. The scale of the organisation in Switzerland was demonstrated by the fact that fifty NSDAP leaders of the Swiss *Landesgruppe* attended Gustloff's funeral.

33 Otto Karl Köcher succeeded Weizsäcker in 1937 when the latter was promoted to permanent state secretary in the AA. Köcher remained in charge of the German legation in Berne until 1944.

34 Their leaders in Switzerland, including Gustloff's successor, Baron Siegmund von Bibra, were given diplomatic status and thus enjoyed immunity.

35 Rings, *Schweiz im Krieg*, 137.

36 Traditionally, Switzerland has enjoyed a close economic relationship with Germany. In 1913, Switzerland imported more goods by value from Germany than from France, Italy and Britain combined; Hofer, 'Neutraler Kleinstaat', 211.

37 *Ibid.*

38 Daniel Bourgeois, 'Les relations èconomiques germano-suisses 1939–1945', *Revue d'histoire de la Deuxième Guerre Mondiale* 121 (1981), 50.

39 Hans Tschäni, 'Die Frage der Verhältnismässigkeit', *Tages-Anzeiger Magazin*, 19 April 1980, 3, in Heiniger, *Dreizehn Gründe*, 124.

40 In September 1939, Switzerland only possessed just over thirty anti-aircraft guns.

41 Heiniger, *Dreizehn Gründe*, 153.

42 The Federal Assembly (Bundesversammlung) consists of the two chambers (Nationalrat and Ständerat) of the Swiss parliament. In peacetime the Swiss militia do not have a commander-in-chief or the rank of general. They are instead led by a defence commission consisting of the most senior military commanders, with the chief of the Military Department (the Swiss defence ministry) at its head.

43 Despite urgent appeals by the British government, Paul Reynaud's government refused to move troops stationed on the border with Switzerland to the northern flank of the Maginot line.

44 On *Fall Gelb* and Switzerland's response to it, see Janusz Piekalkiewicz, *Schweiz 39–45. Krieg in einem neutralen Land* (Stuttgart and Zug, 2nd edn, 1979), 51–65.

45 For Frölicher's report see *ibid.*, 61. On Frölicher's role as Swiss minister in Berlin, and in particular on his many pro-German comments, see Bonjour, *Histoire de la neutralité*, vol. IV, 239–56. Frölicher was 'well regarded' by the higher echelons of the Nazi regime, a 'plus factor' for Switzerland. Many Swiss, on the other hand, criticised Frölicher for his seeming deference to the Nazis. A particularly scathing *résumé* of Frölicher's pro-German conduct, especially in deliberately ignoring German atrocities, is Fred David, 'Ein furchtbar neutraler Diplomat', *Die Zeit*, 29 May 1992, 78.

46 Piekalkiewicz, *Schweiz 39–45*, 63–4.

47 *Ibid.*, 228.

48 See *ibid.*, 229–31. During the first four weeks of the war in the west Switzerland's air space was violated 197 times, mostly by German aircraft; Rings, *Schweiz im Krieg*, 188.

49 The sabotage attempt was given the code name Wartegau; see Piekalkiewicz, *Schweiz 39–45*, 231–3; Senn, 'Militärische Aspekte', 71; Braunschweig, *Geheimer Draht*, 412–13 n. 156.

50 Guisan had, in fact, conducted secret negotiations with the French military leadership before the war. It had been agreed that, in response to a German attack and Switzerland's call for help, French troops would march into the north-west of Switzerland. The Nazi regime was, however, not aware of this violation of Switzerland's neutrality at the time of the air attacks.

51 Piekalkiewicz, *Schweiz 39–45*, 233.

52 See Neville Wylie, '"Life between the Volcanoes": Switzerland during the Second World War', *Historical Journal* 38 (1995), 761.

53 See Heiniger, *Dreizehn Gründe*, 42–3.

54 Rings, *Schweiz im Krieg*, 176.

55 Heiniger, *Dreizehn Gründe*, 49.

56 Rings, *Schweiz im Krieg*, 235.

57 Hans Senn's comment originally in Walter Schaufelberger (ed.), *Sollen wir die Armee abschaffen? Blick auf eine bedrohliche Zeit* (Frauenfeld, 1988), 42, here paraphrased from Hofer, 'Neutraler Kleinstaat', 208.

58 Hofer, 'Neutraler Kleinstaat', 222–3 and 228.

59 See, in particular, Heiniger, *Dreizehn Gründe*, chapter 11 (164–81).

60 Cited in Marco Durrer, 'Die Beziehungen zwischen Schweden und der Schweiz im Zweiten Weltkrieg aus schweizerischer Sicht. Informelle Solidarität', in Bindschedler *et al.* (eds), *Schwedische und schweizerische Neutralität*, 169.

61 Rings, *Schweiz im Krieg*, 244.

62 Piekalkiewicz, *Schweiz 39–45*, 235.

63 Senn, 'Militärische Aspekte', 72.

64 Bonjour, *Histoire de la neutralité*, vol. V, 240–1.

65 *Ibid.*, 244–5.

66 On *Gesinnungsneutralität* and the attitude of the Swiss government, see Rudolf Bindschedler, Hans Rudolf Kurz, Wilhelm Carlgren and Sten Carlsson, 'Schlußbetrachtungen zu den Problemen der Kleinstaatneutralität im Großmachtkrieg', in Bindschedler *et al.* (eds), *Schwedische und schweizerische Neutralität*, 432–3.

67 The announcement was made on 21 February 1940; Bonjour, *Histoire de la neutralité*, vol. VI, 150.

68 In arguing that 'every new concession leads to new pressure' Albert Oeri, editor-in-chief of the *Basler Nachrichten*, correctly interpreted the approach of the Nazi regime; Bonjour, *Histoire de la neutralité*, vol. VI, 161.

69 For a summary of the views on Switzerland expressed in the *Völkischer Beobachter* and *Das Reich*, see Fink, *Die Schweiz*, 237–8.

70 See, for instance, Bonjour, *Histoire de la neutralité*, vol. V, 254 drawing on comments in the October/November 1942 issue of *Das Reich*.

71 See Braunschweig, *Geheimer Draht, passim*.

72 See Rings, *Schweiz im Krieg*, 347.

73 *Ibid.*, 65–158.

74 Heiniger, *Dreizehn Gründe*, 148–9.
75 *Ibid.*, 145.
76 *Ibid.*, 153–4.
77 Braunschweig, *Geheimer Draht*, 445 n. 130. On Dulles's activities in Switzerland see Neal H. Petersen (ed.), *From Hitler's Doorstep; The Wartime Intelligence Reports of Allen Dulles 1942–1945* (University Park PA, 1996).
78 Five hundred and twenty-three of the 865 were Swiss citizens.
79 Rings, *Schweiz im Krieg*, 348.
80 Braunschweig, *Geheimer Draht*, 248, 250. Emphasis in original.
81 See, *inter alia*, Heiniger, *Dreizehn Gründe*, 48–9, and Rings, *Raubgold aus Deutschland*, 152.
82 Bonjour, *Histoire de la neutralité*, vol. VI, 232.
83 John G. Lomax to an unknown Swiss official, 7 December 1941, in Kamber, *Schüsse auf die Befreier*, 248.
84 Bourgeois, 'Les relations économiques', 61.
85 Philippe Marguerat, 'La Suisse et la neutralité dans le domaine économique pendant la Seconde Guerre Mondiale: 1940–fin 1944', in Roulet (ed.), *Les états neutres*, 56.
86 In the period 1941–44 Britain accounted on average for about 1 per cent of Switzerland's total imports and about 2 per cent of its exports. The figures for the United States were 6 per cent and 9 per cent, respectively; see Klaus Urner, 'Neutralität und Wirtschaftskrieg. Zur schweizerischen Außenhandelspolitik 1939–1945', in Bindschedler *et al.* (eds), *Schwedische und schweizerische Neutralität*, 258.
87 Bonjour, *Histoire de la neutralité*, vol. VI, 197–8.
88 Chevallaz, *Le défi de la neutralité*, 263, table II.
89 From Switzerland's lifting of its self-imposed arms export ban in September 1939 to March 1940, France ordered SFr 142.7 million of war material and Britain SFr 121.2 million, while Germany's orders amounted to a negligible SFr 150,000; Urner, 'Neutralität und Wirtschaftskrieg', 270–1.
90 During the same month, Germany also blocked the routes between Switzerland and the Scandinavian and Baltic states, Hungary and Slovakia.
91 Urner, 'Neutralität und Wirtschaftskrieg', 271–2.
92 On the economic agreement of 9 August 1940 and its implications see Bourgeois, 'Les relations économiques', 53–4; Bonjour, *Histoire de la neutralité*, vol. VI, 218–20.
93 The Swiss hoped that the credit would support Germany in making additional purchases of arms and munitions (SFr 100 million), aluminium (SFr 20 million), and machinery and agricultural products (SFr 40 million); Urner, 'Neutralität und Wirtschaftskrieg', 279.
94 The commission was created by the Swiss parliament on 13 December 1996. It is chaired by Professor J.-F. Bergier and consists of eight historians and one legal expert; see http://www.switzerland.taskforce.ch and http://www.uek.ch.
95 Conclusion to Interim Report on Gold Transactions, 'Independent Commission of Experts: Switzerland – Second World War', May 1998; available at http://www.uek.ch/e/m1/gold_ez.htm.
96 Willi A. Boelcke, personal statement to Werner Rings, in Rings, *Raubgold aus Deutschland*, 8.

97 BA 09.01/68765, memo by Süßkind-Schwendi (RWM), 8 November 1943. It is likely that the AA hid almost a ton of gold from its so-called Ribbentrop Gold Fund in Ankara. The fund consisted of about 15 mt of gold which was apparently employed by the AA for the use of its diplomatic missions; see Eizenstat Report, 127 n. 5 and 144 n. 1.

98 Http://www.uek.ch./e/m1/gold_ez.htm. On 5 April 1945, the SNB bought a final 3 mt of gold.

99 Exports to Britain continued to be permitted, though only in limited quantities and only if they were of non-strategic value.

100 Bourgeois, 'Les relations économiques', 51.

101 Urner, 'Neutralität und Wirtschaftskrieg', 255.

102 Ibid., 279.

103 Bonjour, Histoire de la neutralité, vol. VI, 226.

104 Switzerland agreed not to use aircraft for its trade with Britain. Exportation by land through Vichy France was permitted only via Geneva Bellegarde which meant that, for a few kilometres, the goods had to travel through occupied France. German officials were even permitted to check goods destined for Britain at a Swiss railway station; Bourgeois, 'Les relations économiques', 54–5.

105 In 1941 Switzerland's trade with Italy reached its highest war-time level, with SFr 185 million of Swiss goods exported to Italy and SFr 244 million of Italian goods imported by the Swiss. For a full set of figures of Switzerland's trade with Italy, France, Spain and Portugal see Chevallaz, Le défi de la neutralité, 265, table IV.

106 Bourgeois, 'Les relations économiques', 55.

107 See Piekalkiewicz, Schweiz 39–45, 279–88.

108 Bonjour, Histoire de la neutralité, vol. VI, 241.

109 E. Löpfe Benz to Gustav Däniker, in Bonjour, Histoire de la neutralité, vol. VI, 233.

110 Fink, Die Schweiz, 236–7.

111 Rings, Raubgold aus Deutschland, 124.

112 BA/MA RW19/433, report by Troitzsch, 31 July 1942.

113 Rings, Raubgold aus Deutschland, 162.

114 Ibid., 219 n. 269.

115 See Kamber, Schüsse auf die Befreier, 292–3.

116 Cited in Heiniger, Dreizehn Gründe, 59.

117 Kamber, Schüsse auf die Befreier, 291. According to the Swiss customs authorities, up to 1,200 wagonloads of coal crossed Switzerland daily in 1941; Heiniger, Dreizehn Gründe, 56–7.

118 During the first year of the agreement less than three-quarters of the guaranteed supplies were exported to Switzerland; Bourgeois, 'Les relations économiques', 56.

119 Urner, 'Neutralität und Wirtschaftskrieg', 280.

120 A very limited number of Swiss citizens – at the last count, on 1 September 1944, the SS had 661 Swiss members; thirty-four Swiss fought in the German army and the Luftwaffe – fought as SS volunteers. More worryingly for the Swiss authorities, about 1,500 Swiss were involved in clandestine activities for the Third Reich in Switzerland; see Bonjour, Histoire de la neutralité, vol. V, 262, and Georg Kreis, 'Die schweizerische Neutralität während des Zweiten

Weltkrieges in der historischen Forschung', in Roulet (ed.), *Les états neutres*, 40.

121 As National Councillor, Bircher continued to play a shameful role by stirring up resentment among the Swiss population against internees and refugees; see Kamber, *Schüsse auf die Befreier*, 172–3. On the Swiss medical mission, see Luzius Wildhaber, 'Neutralität und Gute Dienste', in Roulet (ed.), *Les états neutres*, 84, and Anne-Françoise Praz, *Du Réduit à l'ouverture; la Suisse de 1940 à 1949* (Prilly, 1995), 68–9.

122 Bower, *Blood Money*, 66. On the restrictive attitude of the Swiss government see Picard, *Die Schweiz und die Juden*, 407–9, and Kamber, *Schüsse auf die Befreier*, 38–40.

123 Bonjour, *Histoire de la neutralité*, vol. VI, 241.

124 Bourgeois, 'Les relations économiques', 57–8.

125 Boelcke, *Deutschland als Welthandelsmacht*, 125.

126 Heiniger, *Dreizehn Gründe*, 79.

127 Chevallaz, *Le défi de la neutralité*, 249 (based on Marc Hofer, 'Die Schweizerischen Kriegsmaterialexporte nach Deutschland während des zweiten Weltkrieges', seminar paper, University of Fribourg, 1992, 18).

128 Chevallaz, *Le défi de la neutralité*, 248–9.

129 One of the earliest examples was an article by one of Switzerland's main wartime economic negotiators, Jean Hotz, 'Handelsabteilung und Handelspolitik in der Kriegszeit', in *Die schweizerische Kriegswirtschaft 1939–1948* (Berne, 1950), 53–107.

130 Werner Rings, for instance, is singled out for the highly critical views of Switzerland's financial relations with Nazi Germany expressed in his 'pamphlet' (Chevallaz) *Raubgold aus Deutschland*; Chevallaz, *Le défi de la neutralité*, 254.

131 *Ibid.*, 247, using figures produced by Philippe Marguerat and Marc Hofer. See also Marguerat, 'La Suisse et la neutralité dans le domaine économique', *passim*.

132 Eizenstat Report, 24; Kamber, *Schüsse auf die Befreier*, 280 and 283. Swiss electricity was particularly vital to the production of aluminium in Rheinfelden, just across the border from Switzerland.

133 In the Declaration on Gold Purchases of 22 February 1944, Britain, the United States and the Soviet Union separately announced that they would not recognise 'the transference of title to looted gold which the Axis at any time held or had disposed of in world markets'; Eizenstat Report, 10.

134 In summing up his mission to Switzerland, Lauchlin Currie, the chief US negotiator, reported on 5 March that 'after three weeks of continuous negotiation with our exerting the strongest pressure against strong resistance and a stalemate yesterday, the Swiss delegation capitulated today ...'; quote in Castelmur, *Schweizerisch-Alliierte Finanzbeziehungen*, 24 n. 27.

135 In the agreement with the Allies of 8 March 1945, the Swiss also agreed to block the assets of all European countries, except the neutrals, and of Japan, to prevent the cloaking of enemy assets, to assist in the restoration of looted property and to conduct a census of German assets in Switzerland; see Eizenstat Report, 32.

136 A further 1.5 mt of gold destined for the BIS had to remain in Germany. On

these final gold transactions see Trepp, *Bankgeschäfte mit dem Feind*, 156–9, and Rings, *Raubgold aus Deutschland*, 110–11.

137 BA R901/68743, Köcher to AA, 8 May 1942.
138 On the agreements, see Bonjour, *Histoire de la neutralité*, vol. VI, 252–4.
139 Individually, Switzerland's credits to Germany were six times larger than Spain's, thirty-five times larger than Portugal's and Sweden's and 190 times larger than Turkey's; Rings, *Raubgold aus Deutschland*, 138, citing a RWM statistic of April 1944.
140 BA/MA RW19/438, copy of negotiation programme *Switzerland*, January 1944.
141 BA/MA RW19/440, war diary 8 (appendix) for the period 1 April–30 June 1944.
142 Bonjour, *Histoire de la neutralité*, vol. VI, 262–3.
143 As usual, coal, iron and oil supplies did not match the quantities agreed in June.
144 See IWM Speer Docs. Reel 25, FD3045/49, Sc. 324, 26 September 1944.

3

SWEDEN

THE COMMITTED NEUTRAL

> Iron ore and neutrality are what Hitler demanded of Sweden – and what he got.[1]

During the Second World War, Sweden remained a 'safe haven' in the turmoil which embroiled its three Scandinavian neighbours. While Norway and Denmark were occupied by Nazi Germany from the spring of 1940 until the end of the war, Finland first had to defend itself – ultimately unsuccessfully – against an attack by the Soviet Union in the Winter War of 1939/40 and later fought on Germany's side – again in the end unsuccessfully – against the same opponent. Between April 1940 and June 1941, Germany's conduct of the war removed the buffer function which these three states had held in Sweden's strategic considerations.[2] Yet despite such an early and severe weakening of Sweden's position, the country remained at peace throughout the war.

In view of the fate of its neighbours, it is without doubt astounding that Sweden retained its neutrality, and that the Nazi regime did not put an end to its exceptional position. Why should Hitler have spared a country which was economically most attractive to the German war effort and which, owing to its central location among the Scandinavian countries, also offered obvious strategic benefits? One short answer is that Sweden, whilst neither occupied nor belligerent, nonetheless played an important role in the development of the war and, more precisely, in Germany's war effort.

Introductory comments

Although Sweden is, in contrast to Switzerland,[3] now part of the European Union and a long-standing member of the United Nations, it nevertheless adheres to a policy of neutrality which its governments have consistently applied for over 100 years. In fact, Sweden has avoided involvement in any wars for an even longer period, since 1814.[4] In contrast to Switzerland, however, Sweden's neutrality is of a less rigid nature, as it is neither 'laid down in the Constitution or otherwise proclaimed as a permanent state doctrine' nor confirmed or guaranteed by any international agreement.[5] However, while there may not be any 'permanent state doctrine' on neutrality, 'freedom from alliances in peace aiming for neutrality in war' has long been Sweden's guiding 'doctrine' in foreign policy.[6]

Acts of hostility against Sweden did not occur, either in the First or in the Second World War. That Sweden did not share the fate of other neutrals between 1939 and 1945 cannot, however, be put down to relying simply on the tenuous protection offered to the neutral state by the Hague Conventions. Instead, successive Swedish government representatives have consistently emphasised that there is no contradiction at all between military strength and the preservation of neutrality. Very much like Switzerland, military preparedness was – and continues to be – regarded as a guarantor of neutrality. In a semi-official pamphlet on Swedish neutrality, Sverker Åström, a former official in the Swedish Ministry of Foreign Affairs, makes this point very clear:

> Our defence ... must be strong enough to make resistance worthwhile. ...
> It must be organized and equipped in such a way that it is self-supporting, without help from abroad, for a certain length of time. ... This is one of the motives behind the support given to domestic production of military equipment.[7]

During the Second World War, the same attitude was apparent. In May 1940, Gösta Bagge, the leader of Sweden's conservative party, revived a metaphor which first appeared in a liberal newspaper in 1865: 'May Sweden be the armed hedgehog which confronts with the tips of its bayonets every attacker from coast to coast.'[8] Bagge's comment reflected the attitude of the Swedish government at large. Although, at the outbreak of the Second World War, Sweden's military preparations had not reached a satisfactory level,[9] by early 1940 they compared favourably with the military position of imminent victims of Nazi aggression such as the Netherlands and Denmark (and the Baltic States, neutral victims of Soviet aggression).[10] Hitler's comment of August 1941 that Sweden was only 'playing at soldiers'[11] detracts from the fact that Germany's military leadership did not see Sweden's defence forces as a 'quantité négligable'.[12]

Keeping defence forces does not constitute a contravention of the Hague Conventions. A neutral state is, in fact, encouraged to resist, 'even by force, attempts to violate its neutrality'.[13] While defence against a belligerent power is thus encouraged by the Fifth Convention, support of the military campaign of a belligerent is discouraged. Neutral states are clearly dissuaded from permitting or even assisting the transit of belligerent 'troops or convoys of either munitions of war or supplies'.[14] As will be shown, it is in this context that certain policies adopted by Sweden in favour of the Third Reich came under sustained criticism.[15] Arguably the most crucial policy of the Swedish government, the supply of vital goods to the Third Reich, will also receive particular attention.

German–Swedish relations from the outbreak of war to Operation Weserübung

On 1 September 1939, after Germany's attack on Poland, the Swedish government declared the country's 'complete neutrality', a decision which it reiterated after the British and French declarations of war on Germany. To the Nazi regime (and the Allies) the announcement by the Swedish government came as no surprise – indeed, in view of the government's political composition, Sweden's adoption of the status of neutrality was the best Hitler could have hoped for.[16] Sweden was, after all, led by a Social Democratic prime minister, Per Albin Hansson, who had voiced his opposition to the methods of the Nazis as early as spring 1933 and who instigated intensified rearmament efforts after Nazi Germany's annexation of Austria in 1938.[17] With democracy firmly rooted among the Swedish people – the extreme right and left both played a totally insignificant role – the vast majority of the population favoured the Allies.[18] Such obvious sympathy for the Allies did not, however, translate into taking sides openly. In fact, the closest Sweden would get to involving itself in the war was not against Nazi Germany, but rather against the Soviet Union after Stalin's attack on Finland on 30 November 1939.

Although Sweden never took the final step towards outright belligerency, the so-called Winter War had a direct impact on the running of the country.[19] In December 1939 Hansson decided that the situation demanded a grand coalition government incorporating all democratic parties (the three non-socialist parties and the Social Democrats, but not the Communists) to face the growing crisis. The most important change was the replacement of Foreign Minister Rickard Sandler, a leading Social Democrat, by a non-party career diplomat, Christian Günther. This, in Stig Hadenius's words, 'political statement' was a clear indication of Hansson's endeavour to keep Sweden out of the war. Instead of Sandler, who had favoured a more active foreign policy in favour of Finland, Sweden's foreign policy was now in the hands of a much more cautious – indeed as Erik Lönnroth put it, 'conveniently colourless but competent' – man.[20] Günther, who was to remain in charge of the Utrikesdepartementet (UD) for the duration of the Second World War, was utterly committed to not letting Sweden become a combatant, an aim he clearly shared with Hansson.[21] Two months after his appointment Günther emphasised the central aim of Sweden's policy for the years to come: 'Sweden's primary goal must be to avoid entanglement in the World War, and all questions must be regarded with that overriding consideration in mind.'[22]

To an extent, Sweden's position was favoured by the fact that the country did not figure in Hitler's expansionist plans. No mention of Sweden was made in *Mein Kampf*, or in the so-called 'Second Book',[23] and it received little attention in the years before the war. However, as the example of Sweden's neighbours Denmark and Norway was to demonstrate, such lack of interest on the part of Hitler did not necessarily save countries from Nazi aggression. Various comments made by Nazi officials during the war show very clearly that a total subordination of Sweden to the Third Reich's 'New Order' was considered.

In 1940, Hermann Göring suggested that, in a future, even larger, *Großdeutschland*, Sweden would occupy a position much like Bavaria.[24] In a similar vein, Heinrich Himmler, when planning for the resurrection of a Greater Franconian-Germanic Reich, looked forward to the incorporation of central and southern Sweden into Germany.[25] The AA was more 'generous' in its views on the future role of Sweden. Werner von Grundherr, head of the Northern Department of the AA, compared Sweden's position-to-be to that of Hungary and Slovakia.[26]

Himmler's views reflected a strong interest in Sweden for racial and ideological reasons. Nazi officials even argued that, for the German Volk, 'the Swedish people were seen as the epitome of the nordic spirit and the nordic man'. The Swedes and the Germans had become, 'in terms of race and blood, allied and partly related neighbouring people'.[27] Göring's comments, on the other hand, were more influenced by pragmatic economic reasons. Sweden constituted an attractive target for the Nazis owing to its wealth of iron ore, a raw material much coveted by Germany. The cessation of vital ore imports alone could have resulted in German counter-measures. Yet although the Wehrmacht was seemingly resigned to the fact that a war with Britain would mean an end to supplies from Sweden, plans for an attack on the country were elaborated neither before nor after 1 September 1939.[28]

The planning for Operation *Weserübung*, the occupation of Denmark and Norway, which Hitler ordered on 1 March 1940, did not include Sweden, nor did the country become a victim of Nazi aggression after the commencement of Germany's military campaign in Scandinavia.[29] Yet:

> it was hardly respect for the strength of Sweden's defenses that induced the Wehrmacht in 1940 to exclude Sweden from the scope of *Weserübung*, but rather the sober calculation that, once Denmark and Norway were conquered and the Germans had established effective control of the Skaggerak, Sweden would in any case have to submit to Germany's wishes.[30]

Despite repeated reassurances by German officials, including those given by Hitler in a letter to the Swedish king, Gustav V, on 25 April 1940,[31] the Swedish government could not be sure that Nazi Germany was not intent on attacking and occupying Sweden. During the first months of the war a mood of unease thus prevailed in Sweden's relations with Germany. It was to become much heightened by Germany's military campaign in Norway.[32] At the other end, the Nazi regime, though under no military threat from Sweden, nonetheless had reason to feel uneasy about the attitude of the Swedish government, particularly in the area of iron ore supplies. Although the problem had been temporarily defused in favour of Germany by an agreement in December 1939, future Swedish iron ore exports remained a burning issue, heightened by the execution of *Weserübung* in April 1940. It is therefore not surprising that when, on 9 April, Germany's minister in Stockholm, Victor zu Wied,[33] informed the Swedish government about the need to keep strictly neutral, continued deliveries of iron ore appeared as one of the foremost demands. As it turned out, the concessions which the Nazi regime sought from the Swedish government did not remain confined to the economic sphere alone.

To avoid entanglement in the World War, Sweden made a number of concessions to Nazi Germany. Yet 'none weighed so heavily on the minds of most Swedes, and was the object of such controversy, as the permission granted Germany to transport war material and members of its armed forces on Swedish railroads to and from Norway'.[34] In contrast to the ore trade, permitting such activities meant a clear contravention of Sweden's commitment to the Hague Conventions and its position as a neutral, both in a legal and in a moral sense. After the commencement of Germany's attack on Norway high-ranking Swedish government officials, including Prime Minister Hansson, in fact publicly acknowledged the incompatibility of military concessions with Sweden's commitment to neutrality.[35]

Norwegian requests for the transit of munitions from the northern Norwegian town of Kirkenes across Sweden to Norway were forcefully rejected in mid-April with the comment that 'war material was to be neither "transited" nor exported to any of the belligerents'.[36] Shortly afterwards, advance warning was given to the Nazi regime in similiarly unambiguous terms that any demand of this kind would meet with an immediate rejection.[37] Emphatically, the Swedish government also confirmed to its British counterpart that 'Sweden would observe strict neutrality, would resist any German invasion and would reject German demands for the passage of troops and armaments across Swedish territory.'[38] Less than three months later, however, Germany and Sweden signed an agreement permitting exactly the kind of transit traffic the Swedish government had previously rejected in forceful terms. Instead of a short-term departure from strict neutrality the embarassing transit agreement remained a burden to Sweden for the following three years.

From summer 1940, Sweden violated the obligations which it had imposed upon itself – and which it had rigorously applied against the Allies during the Winter War. In fact, the slippery slope towards the transit agreement had been entered at a time when the Swedish government was making announcements to the contrary. While Germany's invason of Norway (*Weserübung Nord*) quickly succeeded in the south of the country, in the north, in the Narvik area, German troops under General Eduard Dietl were faced with severe problems. A rapid deterioration in the supply situation, intensified by successful Allied attacks against German war and supply ships and the difficulty of tranporting goods by land from southern Norway, necessitated German demands for Sweden to permit transports of supplies on its railway link to Narvik. Although the transit of goods, which the Swedish government permitted in mid-April, was of a non-military (in official terms 'humanitarian') nature, it nonetheless contravened an earlier pledge not 'to permit any belligerent to make use of Swedish territory'.

In view of Dietl's continued problems, the appetite of the Nazi regime for concessions was whetted rather than stilled by Sweden's permission of the transit. From late April 1940, leading Nazi officials, most notably Hermann Göring and Joachim von Ribbentrop, tried to persuade the Swedish government of the urgent necessity of permitting supplies of war material to pass through Sweden. Faced by Sweden's obvious reluctance to accept such a major violation of its neutrality, both Göring and Ribbentrop soon changed their tone to one of outright hostility. Their annoyance showed most distinctly in Göring's conversation with his Swedish contact, the businessman Birger Dahlerus, on 6 May.[39] In the meeting, Göring vented his anger about Sweden's opposition to the transit of military goods and offered two plans which would achieve German objectives while still allowing Sweden to preserve a patina of neutrality. Threateningly, Göring more than hinted at the possibility of a German attack should Sweden continue to remain obstructive. According to Dahlerus, Göring made it very clear 'how meaningless it would be to attempt to defend [Sweden] in the event of the Germans wishing to occupy it.'

Despite Göring's tirades, which, upon being informed of the Swedish government's negative response, he followed up with new ones on 11 May, Sweden continued to withstand while it placed its armed forces in a state of highest combat preparedness.[40] Only days later, Ribbentrop and Weizsäcker added to the pressure in consecutive discussions with the Swedish minister in Berlin, Arvid Richert. Yet again, and despite Richert urging it to reconsider, the Swedish government replied in the negative.[41] With German pressure growing all the time, Sweden was ultimately 'saved' by the withdrawal of the final contingent of 24,500 Allied troops on 8 June and the surrender of the last Norwegian troops two days later. The Swedish government had been close to failure in its overriding objective: to keep Sweden out of the war. Yet while the danger of war abated with Germany's victory, it also made future 'unneutral' steps more likely. With Germany in control of western Scandinavia and Sweden's major shipping routes to the west, Sweden found itself totally exposed to Nazi pressure.

As could be expected, the Nazi regime wasted little time applying the thumbscrews. After General Wilhelm Keitel, chief of the OKW, had urged Ribbentrop 'to enter negotiations with Sweden for the purpose of achieving unhindered transit traffic for all kinds of transport', the foreign minister immdiately presented Richert with the demand. Richert, who needed little convincing, recounted his interview with Ribbentrop to the Swedish cabinet on 18 June, the day after France had asked Germany for an armistice. This time the government was more easily persuaded and, in the words of Prime Minister Hansson, 'our precious and strictly held line of neutrality [was thus broken] by the realization of the impossibility, in the present situation, of taking the risk of war'.[42]

On 8 July 1940, Germany and Sweden arrived at an agreement to regulate the passage of German material across Swedish territory.[43] The Germans, in fact, forced the Swedes to allow the transit to Germany and back of unarmed troops on leave stationed in Norway even though Swedish negotiators had made half-hearted attempts to limit the scope of the agreement. Officially, such traffic was restricted to one train per day in each direction between Oslo, the Norwegian capital, and Trelleborg, on the south coast of Sweden, and one train a week in each direction between Narvik and Trelleborg. In addition, it was specified that the number of German soldiers per train was limited to 500 with an equilibrium between soldiers travelling north and south. Only two months later, the agreement was extended to double the quota.

Even the increased limits, however, were not set in stone.[44] From time to time, the Swedish government was forced to permit additional troop transports or only belatedly noticed that the Wehrmacht had exceeded the quota. Transport statistics for the first sixteen months of the agreement demonstrate the extent to which the Wehrmacht managed to exceed the agreed figures. According to Swedish calculations about 670,000 German troops – an average of 1,400 men a day – were transported on both transit routes. Railway wagons with goods, largely war material, for the Wehrmacht were running at a rate of about 1,000 to 1,500 a month.[45]

Repeated efforts by the Swedish government to limit the transit traffic to the agreed terms achieved only partial results. In early 1941, for instance, Hansson's administration protested strongly about the imbalance created by a heavy increase in the number of German soldiers travelling to Norway. Hitler's reasons for circumventing the transit agreement (and thus causing the so-called *Marskrisen* in Swedish–German relations[46]) were twofold: on the one hand, to strengthen the Wehrmacht's defensive capacity in Norway and, on the other, to prepare for the forthcoming attack on the Soviet Union.[47] In fact, precisely because of Operation Barbarossa, the Nazi regime came to demand further concessions during the course of 1941. By going some way towards accommodating these demands, Sweden allowed its neutrality to reach the nadir.[48]

To highlight Sweden's *de facto* abandonment of neutrality, particular reference is usually made to the transit of the so-called Engelbrecht division from Norway to Finland.[49] In July 1940, the Swedish government had interpreted the transit of German troops on leave as conforming with Sweden's neutral status and of negligible relevance to the course of the war – though, of course, both the British and the Norwegian governments strongly disagreed.[50] Such a 'refined' interpretation was not available when, on 22 June 1941, special envoy Karl Schnurre presented Nazi Germany's requirements to the Swedish government. First and foremost, Sweden was confronted with the demand for the transit of the 163rd Infantry Division (led by General Erwin Engelbrecht) to attack the Soviet military fortress of Hanko in southern Finland.[51] Schnurre's catalogue of demands meant that, as the envoy concluded, 'without actually entering the war, Sweden should interpret her neutrality to Germany's advantage'.[52]

The turmoil Germany's demand created in Sweden clearly indicated that most Swedes were strongly concerned about the effect the decision would have on Swedish neutrality. Despite strong misgivings, particularly among the Social Democrats, Per Albin Hansson's government eventually acceded to Germany's demand.[53] King Gustav's quasi-threat of abdication may well have been a decisive factor. The king, together with Foreign Minister Günther, undoubtedly favoured a positive reply. It is, however, debatable whether the king's attitude alone was sufficient to force the issue or whether it was Hansson who 'took advantage' of the king's position to force cabinet and parliament to accept. Even though no conclusive version of the events of the so-called Midsummer Crisis (*midsommarkrisen*) has as yet been established, it is in itself revealing that the 'issue of the passage of the Engelbrecht Division has been discussed in Sweden for decades by politicians and researchers'.[54] Permitting the transit of the division clearly added a different quality to Sweden's policy of 'neutrality' – despite the government's clear warning that no further concessions of such a kind would be permitted.

On 26 June 1941, the day that Finland joined Germany in the war against the Soviet Union, the first train carrying troops of the 15,000 strong Engelbrecht Division started to make its way through Sweden.[55] While the transit of the division constituted the focal point of debate during and after 1941, it should not be forgotten that the Nazi regime gained further concessions in support of Operation Barbarossa. Between 22 June and 1 November 1941, the Swedish railways carried 75,000 mt of Wehrmacht material, half of it war material, from Germany and Norway to the Finnish border. On the return journey, Swedish trains transported about 11,000 injured German soldiers to Oslo. To assist further transit activities, the

Swedish authorities set up camps fully equipped with food, horse feed and oil. From these so-called 'transit camps' Wehrmacht lorries were taking goods to German troops in Finland.[56] German unarmed military aircraft were permitted to fly across Sweden in designated air corridors[57] while German (and Finnish) ships were given preferential treatment by enabling them to enter Swedish territorial waters, a concession denied to all other foreign warships. In addition, German ships travelling through Swedish waters were escorted by the Swedish navy.[58]

When Sweden subsequently opposed a repetition of the land transit of troops to Finland, the German government grudgingly relented – at least for a while. With Operation Barbarossa seemingly heading towards a victorious conclusion, Sweden's attitude was not deemed a major problem. By the beginning of November 1941, however, it had dawned on all observers, Hitler included, that Germany's invasion of the Soviet Union would not be a walk-over. Although the decisive Russian counter-offensives of December still lay ahead, preparations for winter conditions had already become an overwhelming necessity – not least for the troops fighting on the northern section of the front.

Again, Sweden's assistance was required, and received. Not only did Sweden aid these efforts through transit arrangements for troops and material (including the escorting of German troop and war material transport ships through Swedish territorial waters), it also supplied the Wehrmacht with equipment. Apart from buying 700 lorries from Sweden and leasing a further 330 during the first four months of the campaign in the east, the Wehrmacht also benefited from the Swedish army's mobilisation stocks, from which it received 4,000 tents (with stoves) each providing shelter for twenty-five men of General Dietl's army.[59]

Desperately trying to keep Sweden out of the war, the Hansson administration thus condoned activities which were clearly outside the confines of strict neutrality. Sweden's concessions in support of the German war effort did not, however, put the country on the path to much closer collaboration with the Axis powers. The Swedish government consistently resisted German attempts to bring the country into the war.[60] 'Substantial support', as demanded by Goebbels in January 1942,[61] was not forthcoming. Even more limited demands for Sweden to participate symbolically in the 'crusade against Bolshevism' fell on deaf ears.[62] In reaction, Hitler ordered his subordinates to ignore (*links liegenlassen*) the Scandinavian neutral, which, together with Switzerland, he proclaimed to be 'nations on holiday'.[63] To the annoyance of the Nazi regime, permitting the 'Engelbrecht transit' did not signify the total capitulation of the Swedish authorities to all future German transit demands. Shortly afterwards, on 1 August, a further request for the transit of a division to the Russo-Finnish front was rejected.[64] The Swedish authorities continued, however, to provide convoy protection for German troop transport ships.

Despite the growing dissatisfaction of the Nazis with the attitude of the Swedish government, expressed most clearly by Hitler in a letter to King Gustav in early December 1941, Sweden did not suffer any serious consequences. Part of the explanation was that the intensification of precisely the war for which Sweden's help was demanded did not permit the diversion of troops. The economic importance of Sweden undoubtedly also played a significant role. In addition, even though certain Swedish circles, most notably some members of the officer corps, shared some of the Nazi hostility to the Soviet Union,[65] it was far too insignificant to effect a political change of direction in Sweden. In fact, despite repeated German demands, the Swedish government neither banned the Swedish communist party nor sufficiently scaled down the recurrent anti-German comment in sections of the Swedish press.[66]

Hitler's forceful letter to the Swedish king coincided not only with the major Soviet counter-offensive in the Moscow sector of the front but also with the entry of the United States into the war. In the Swedish context, this major development (and the British declaration of war on Finland on 6 December) added weight to Allied demands for a reduction in concessions to Germany, most notably in the transit traffic. In the first instance, the December developments strengthened Sweden's resistance to German requests for the establishment of regular troop trains between northern Finland and Germany (via Haparanda–Trelleborg). In view of the staunch opposition of the Swedish government the Nazi regime eventually gave in. No further attempts to persuade the Swedish authorities were made after February 1942 and, on 16 March, Hitler assured the king that Sweden's neutrality would not be violated.[67]

The transit traffic from and to Norway, however, was kept up. Moreover, Sweden continued to grant other concessions in favour of the German war effort.[68] It is not surprising therefore that the Allies became increasingly critical of Sweden's approach. Under the influence of the US government, Britain, whose policies had hitherto been influenced by an understanding of Sweden's 'desperate circumstances',[69] was forced to take a less magnanimous stance. This was reflected in the discussions on the so-called Göteborg traffic (*Göteborgstrafiken*). Ever since 27 November 1940 the British government had, subject to certain conditions, tolerated trade between Sweden and neutral countries overseas. The German government

Table 3.1   *Sweden's Göteborgstrafiken trade, 1941–43*

Year	Imports		Export	
	000 mt	million SEK	000 mt	million SEK
1941	206.4	222.2	127.5	115.2
1942	426.2	347.2	196.2	158.0
1943	345.6	350.2	149.9	125.3

Note: A total of 226 ships left and 222 ships reached Sweden during the duration of the Göteborg traffic. Sweden was thus able to retain about a third of its pre-war imports from overseas and about a fifth of its exports; Gruchmann, 'Schweden im Zweiten Weltkrieg', 611. See also table 3 in Martin Fritz, 'Wirtschaftliche Neutralität wahrend des Zweiten Weltkrieges', in Bindschedler *et al.* (eds), *Schwedische und schweizerische Neutralität*, 52.
Source: Wittmann, *Schwedens Wirtschaftsbeziehungen*, table B 13, 328 n. 95.

gave its consent on 7 February 1941. Although the Göteborg traffic, which allowed for a set number of monthly sailings from and to Sweden, suffered from occasional interruptions, as a whole it certainly worked to Sweden's advantage.

Sweden's keen interest in the Göteborg traffic made it more susceptible to pressure from both sides. While the British Foreign Office argued that Swedish imports coming in via this route should be used as a bargaining tool to achieve a reduction in the German transit traffic, the US administration demanded a complete cessation of supplies to Sweden. The reasoning behind the US position was simple: supplies from overseas contributed to Sweden's ability to continue trade with Germany and were thus not to be encouraged. The US assessment was not at all off the mark. As the Nazi regime's special envoy, Karl Schnurre, admitted in September 1941, 'the Göteborg traffic ... is indirectly of benefit to us. The Swedish navy, for instance, which carries out convoy duties for German transports, thus receives the necessary oil. Other Swedish industries working for us receive the necessary raw materials.'[70]

Despite Schnurre's conclusions, the German government considered curtailing the traffic during the autumn and winter of 1941 largely over the issue of fourteen Norwegian ships held in Sweden. The Swedish government had received repeated British demands for the release of the ships and their cargoes, part of a total of some forty vessels which had been stranded in Swedish ports after Germany's attack on Norway. Their release was unacceptable to the Nazi regime. With Sweden's government and its highest courts in the middle, a tug-of-war over the ships ensued which continued into spring 1942.

On 31 March 1942, ten ships finally attempted to reach Britain, yet only two succeeded in making the journey with their cargo of mainly ball bearings and ball-bearing steel. Three were sunk by German forces, three scuttled themselves and two (*Dicto* and *Lionel*) returned to Göteborg. Yet despite the dissatisfaction of both the Allies and Germany about the out-come of this long-drawn-out 'battle', the Göteborg traffic was not affected, at least not immediately. Eventually, even the US and British govern-ments arrived at a compromise on the central question of oil supplies. Under the compromise, first applied in June 1942, the British promised to supply an agreed amount of oil, though only on condition that Sweden reduced the German transit traffic.[71]

While it has been argued that the Swedish government did not react to these demands during summer and autumn 1942 for fear of German reprisals,[72] the Swedish authorities did, in fact, make an immediate attempt to curtail the transit traffic. On 14 July 1942, in a letter to the AA, the Swedish state railways gave notice of forthcoming restrictions on the transport of German troops. In a further letter of 2 August, the restrictions were then officially introduced. Attaching the utmost importance to the issue, the AA immediately dispatched its envoy, Schnurre, to Stockholm. German pressure showed immediate results. Barely a week after the Swedish announcement, Schnurre reported back to Berlin triumphantly, 'Discussions on Wehrmacht transit through Sweden have been concluded in accordance with our wishes. … As before, no reduction in the number of transports by the Swedes will take place.'[73]

The transport figures for the first and second halves of 1942 bear out Schnurre's confident assessment. In the second half of 1942, 19,409 wagons carrying German goods were to pass through Sweden both to Norway and to Finland, an increase on the 17,714 wagons for the first six months of the year – a figure exceeding, in turn, that for the second half of 1941 (16,144). As could be expected, a substantial proportion of the goods were of a military nature, though, given Hitler's insistence on fortifying Germany's defences in Norway, large quantities of construction material were also dispatched across Sweden.[74]

Although, in mid-1942, Germany's transit traffic amounted to only around 2.5 per cent of the total passenger and goods traffic on Sweden's railways, the Allies were obviously not at all happy that any transports were being run at all. Not surprisingly, Sweden's policy of treating the transports 'as a purely commercial affair' did not strike a chord with the

Table 3.2 *German payments to Sweden for transit traffic, 1940–43 (million SEK)*

Year	Million SEK
1940 (August–December)	8
1941	16
1942	39
1943 (January–July)	21

Source: Zetterberg, 'Le transit allemand', 67.

Allies. That the Germans made regular payments to the Swedish authorities did not alter the military purpose of the transit traffic. During 1942 the Allies were therefore increasingly resolved to put pressure on the Swedish government.

As Rune Karlsson has outlined in detail, written and verbal exchanges between British and Swedish (and to a lesser extent US) officials during the second half of 1942 centred on the transit question, though other Swedish concessions to the Nazi regime also received due attention, including, as usual, the supply of iron ore. In December 1942, matters developed into a temporary crisis owing to the continued detention of the two Norwegian vessels *Dicto* and *Lionel*.[75] On British pressure, the Swedish government had given permission for the two ships to take their valuable cargo of ball bearings to Britain. The German reaction was instant. On 15 January 1943, the Nazi authorities blocked the Göteborg traffic and reopened it only at the beginning of May. The two ships, in fact, never left Sweden until after the war. The incident indicated that few tangible results regarding the transit traffic had been achieved by the beginning of 1943 despite the mounting pressure on Sweden by the Allies, aided by a gradual reversal in the fortunes of war. Secretly, however, the Swedish Foreign Ministry commenced preparations for its reduction.[76]

According to Zetterberg's data, the transit of German goods on Sweden's railways started to decline at the beginning of 1943. At the same time, protests in Sweden against the transit traffic were mounting.[77] While transports of material continued to decline,[78] troop transports did not quite follow the same clear-cut downward trend. Compared with the previous year, more German soldiers left Norway by Swedish railways than returned.[79] On its own, however, this development is not conclusive evidence in deciding whether Sweden had been successful in reducing the transit traffic or whether Hitler was simply forced to divert more German troops from Norway to more pressing theatres of war.

On 29 July 1943, Sweden finally reneged on the transit agreement with all its amendments. This decision was preceded by Allied pressure on the Swedish government and the threat of economic reprisals, should the transit traffic not be stopped by 1 October. Hansson and his ministers were put in a very difficult position. On the one hand, they were keen to keep up the semblance of steering an independent course between Allies and Axis; on the other, they were faced with Allied economic pressure and Germany's military power, still considerable despite recent setbacks. Even if the Hansson government had known (which it did not) that German staff studies in spring 1943 had advised against far-reaching military steps against Sweden, such knowledge would not have allayed fears of possible military repercussions.

Despite its anxieties, the Swedish government informed the Nazi regime on 29 July that the transit traffic had to cease. Hitler's reaction was surprisingly mild in that the Swedish demand was accepted without much ado. The Führer's decision to allow the Swedes to end the transit traffic may be explained by his preoccupation with developments in Italy (Mussolini had just been deposed) and the failure of Operation Citadel on the eastern front. Closer to home, the transit traffic had almost completely lost its initial importance for the Wehrmacht's position in Norway.[80]

The cessation of the transit traffic – for material on 15 August, troops on 20 and oil on 1 October 1943 – concluded three years during which the Wehrmacht had exceeded the agreed limitations on a regular basis. In fact, according to one calculation, the transit of a total of roughly 2,140,000 German soldiers exceeded the agreed terms by about 75 per cent. In addition, 75,000 railway wagons of German war material had crossed Swedish territory.[81] The Nazi regime had undoubtedly made good use of Sweden's so-called *eftergiftspolitik*;[82] its military effort continued to benefit indirectly from the economic relationship with neutral Sweden. With the cessation of the transit traffic agreement, however, the central military aspect of the relations between the two countries ended.[83]

Keeping Germany's war machine running: Swedish iron ore

> The importation of Swedish goods is of overwhelming significance to our [Germany's] armaments production.[84]

In the second half of the 1960s, a debate took place in the *Scandinavian Economic History Review* over whether, as Alan Milward provocatively asked, Sweden could have 'stopped the Second World War'.[85] The debate evolved from an article by Rolf Karlbom in which the author gave an overview of Sweden's exports of iron ore to Germany during the period 1933–1944. While Karlbom's tables provide statistical information on the near entirety of the Third Reich's existence, he was especially concerned with the much shorter period between Germany's attack on Poland and the fall of France. For this period Karlbom arrived at his most challenging conclusion: 'If the mines of Lapland had ceased working, the blast furnaces of the Ruhr would have shut down too.'[86] It was this conclusion in particular that aroused the opposition of Milward and Jörg-Johannes Jäger.[87]

Did Karlbom have good reason to assess Swedish iron ore as 'a *sine qua non* for the continuance of [Germany's] armaments programme'?[88] The Swedish historian pointed out that, from just over half of all German iron ore imports in 1939 (already over 60 per cent in the second half of 1939), Sweden's share rose steeply to just under 85 per cent in 1940. Even more important for Karlbom, on the basis of Germany's total consumption by estimated iron content, the Swedish share consistently exceeded not only the share of all other German suppliers but also that of Germany's own production. From just over 40 per cent in 1939, it reached nearly 48 per cent in 1940.

In challenging Karlbom's conclusion, Milward criticised in particular the figures used by the Swedish historian. Milward's own calculations show that, instead of becoming more important, Germany's consumption of Swedish iron ore (by iron content) dropped considerably in the first half of 1940, from 51 per cent in the last three months of 1939 to just over 25 per cent in the first three months of 1940. Milward's main blow to Karlbom's thesis was, however, his insistence that Germany's stockpiles were sufficient 'to quite nullify the effect of any withdrawal of Swedish supply'.[89] Milward based his conclusion on his firm belief that the Nazi regime employed the *Blitzkrieg* concept not only in the military but also in the economic sphere. This meant that Germany's economy was committed to the war only to a limited extent and was thus able to make its reserves last long enough to succeed in a short conflict.

Although, in view of more recent research outcomes,[90] Milward's

Table 3.3   *German imports of Swedish iron ore, 1933–43*

Year	Million mt
1933	2.3
1937	9.1
1942	9.0
1943	10.1

Blitzkrieg thesis can no longer be sustained, his criticisms of Karlbom's statistical calculations need to be taken seriously. They are further enhanced by Jäger, who, though attacking Karlbom's thesis partly on different grounds,[91] targeted his criticism again on Karlbom's calculations. While both reject Karlbom's more daring thesis, neither Jäger nor Milward disagrees that iron ore imports from Sweden played an important role in the German war economy.[92]

In the pre-war years Germany had long established itself as Sweden's main customer, usually taking about 75 per cent of the country's total iron ore exports. From 2.3 million mt in 1933 imports of the raw material increased to 9.1 million mt in 1937.[93] In value terms, iron ore constituted nearly half of Sweden's total exports to Germany (of a trade volume of SEK 339 million in the period 1937 to 1939[94]). It is therefore not surprising that contemporary commentators put strong emphasis on the importance to Germany of imports of Swedish iron ore. As early as November 1934, Hitler acknowledged the significance of Scandinavian ore by arguing that its absence would make it impossible for Germany to go to war. In other words, the delivery of iron ore constituted the 'neuralgic point of German–Swedish relations',[95] or, as the British press in particular liked to call it, 'Hitler's Achilles heel'.[96]

In 1938, the Reich Economics Ministry again warned about the threat to Germany's rearmament drive if imports of Swedish iron ore were to be reduced.[97] A few months before Nazi Germany unleashed war upon Europe, the importance of Swedish ore had not diminished. On 29 April 1939, the economic staff of the OKW produced a detailed examination of Germany's iron ore position and needs during 1939 and 1940 in which it concluded that maintaining Swedish ore supplies during war constituted 'a principal demand of the Wehrmacht'.[98] On 1 March 1940, finally, in particularly telling circumstances, Hitler's directive for Operation *Weserübung* referred to the need 'to secure our supplies of ore from Sweden' as one of the three main reasons for the occupation of Denmark and Norway.[99]

Germany's enemies also came to believe in the crucial importance of Swedish iron ore to the German war effort. On 18 December 1939, shortly after the OKW had again emphasised how urgently Germany required Swedish goods for its war effort,[100] the British Ministry of Economic Warfare (MEW) concluded that an end to Swedish supplies would result in a standstill of Germany's production in a matter of months. It would thus have 'a profound effect on the duration of the war'.[101] On the basis of such assumptions the British government considered and eventually set into motion an unsuccessful attempt to sabotage Swedish iron ore supplies to Germany in April 1940.[102]

While no further sabotage attempts were undertaken thereafter, the Allies continued to believe very strongly in the need to reduce Germany's access to vital ore imports. The Nazi regime, on the other hand, made every effort to maintain Swedish iron ore supplies at a high level. Until well into the second half of the war, German efforts transparently succeeded over Allied counter-measures. Sweden's willingness to comply with Germany's demands was first demonstrated as early as December 1939. Only days after the MEW had commented on the crucial nature of Swedish ore supplies to the Third Reich, the Nazi regime signed a new economic accord with Sweden in which the latter agreed to increase export licences for iron ore for 1940 from 7 million mt to 10 million mt.[103]

Sweden's early commitment to what amounted to direct support of Germany's war economy was made even firmer by the Wehrmacht's subsequent military victories. Sweden's trade with the western nations, which had been around 70 per cent before September 1939,[104] declined drastically. The country rapidly adapted to the new conditions. While Germany was overcoming France, Sweden's government was already making major economic concessions to the Third Reich. According to the British press attaché at the embassy in Stockholm (and the man in charge of the Special Operations Executive (SOE) in Sweden), Peter Tennant, these virtually amounted to 'a direct act of war against Britain'.[105]

The pressure exerted by the Reich's supremacy in Europe, however, does not wholly explain why iron ore supplies in particular were maintained at a high level for a lengthy period of time. At least as important an explanation for the export of valuable goods was Sweden's sheer need to import vital products from Germany and Axis-controlled Europe. As Martin Fritz explains, with Germany's establishment of the Skagerrak blockade in April 1940,[106] German interests

Table 3.4   *German coal and coke exports to Sweden, 1940–44*

Year	Million mt	% of total imports from Germany
1940	4.7	27.3
1941	4.7	28.8
1942	3.8	23.8
1943	4.8	26.2
1944	3.5	22.4

Source: Fritz, 'Wirtschaftliche Neutralität', 57 and 59, tables 7 and 9.

coincided with primary Swedish economic interests, since German exports could meet important Swedish requirements for coal and coke, for various kinds of chemicals, for fertilisers etc. Thus Swedish exports became oriented almost exclusively towards German-controlled Europe.[107]

Oil and rubber aside, the Nazi regime was able to satisfy most Swedish needs. This was particularly true of supplies of coal and coke. From 8.5 per cent of Sweden's total imports from Germany during the period 1936–38, coal and coke supplies increased to an average of 26.5 per cent during the period 1940–43. Even in 1944, coal and coke still made up 22.4 per cent of Germany's trade with Sweden.[108] 'Without coal Sweden's economic situation immediately deteriorated, its industrial production suffered breakdowns, and its means of transport, ships and railways, were noticeably affected.'[109] Sweden's dependence on German coal offered the Nazi regime a significant bargaining tool, yet in practice coal supplies were a necessary method of paying for vital imports from Sweden.

Even supplies of coal, however, could not prevent Germany from accumulating, by autumn 1941, a deficit in its balance with Sweden. As the Nazi regime expected the deficit to be of a temporary nature, it asked the Swedish government to arrange commercial credits to permit a continuation of the exisiting trade relations. After some consideration, the Swedish government eventually agreed. By December 1942, when the practice of granting commercial credits to Germany was brought to an end, their total amount was estimated to have reached SEK 200 million, of which a large proportion had been employed in the purchase of wood, paper and cellulose.[110]

About 34 per cent of the SEK 200 million credit was, in fact, reserved as an advance payment on the purchase of German war material for the Swedish army. In real terms, war material assumed only a minor role in the Reich's financial and economic dealings with Sweden. Nonetheless, supplies, or promises of supplies, of armaments were an essential bargaining tool in the efforts of the Nazi regime to secure vital imports from Sweden. In one case, in May 1943, the German government was faced with the likelihood of an annulment of a RM 20 million arms contract. When asked whether it could cope with a reduction in supplies of Swedish iron ore, cellulose, wood, high-grade steel and ball bearings to compensate for the cancellation of the contract, the Ministry of Armaments and Munitions replied with a definite no.[111]

While, among the Scandinavian states, Sweden had been the Reich's most important pre-war customer for armaments, war material nonetheless accounted for only 0.5 per cent of Sweden's imports from Nazi Germany. It increased slightly to 2 per cent in 1939 when interest in the products of German arms manufacturers was stimulated by the fear of war stirred up by Nazi Germany. During the war, the motivation for Sweden's continued interest in arms imports remained largely the same. Sweden desired German war material to build up its defences against a possible German attack. When, in December 1939, the Swedish government enquired about purchasing about RM 100 million worth of German war material, it was, however, also strongly influenced by the aggressive behaviour of the Soviet regime, which had just commenced its attack on Finland.[112]

Although Hitler agreed to supply a substantial proportion of Sweden's request, arms supplies were subsequently discontinued during the invasion of Denmark and Norway. They commenced again on 13 July 1940 after the Swedish government had accepted Germany's transit demands (see below). Subsequently the largest annual amount of contracts in value terms was signed, at nearly RM 50 million. In 1941 and 1943, however, contracts only just exceeded RM 14 million, while 1942 saw the conclusion of contracts worth RM 40 million, precisely the amount advanced as part of the commercial credits. As was usual with German arms deals, contractual obligations were not fulfilled in the agreed time frame. In December 1942, the AA acknowledged that German deliveries were about RM 50 million behind schedule.[113] War material thus provided only limited compensation for Swedish deliveries, in particular of iron ore.

Commercial credits had indirectly assisted purchases of iron ore in 1942 by easing the pressure on Germany's finances. In 1943, this effect vanished with the cessation of credits. Other ways had to be found to safe-

Table 3.5 *German war material exports to Sweden, 1938–44 (million RM)*

Year	Contracts	Exports
1938	4.5	?
1939	19.8	?
1940	49.6	46
1941	14.4	17
1942	40.0	28
1943	14.1	28
1944	?	24 (?)

Source: Contracts in Boelcke, *Deutschland als Welthandelsmacht,* 130, exports in Wittmann, *Schwedens Wirtschaftsbeziehungen,* 292, table A 18.

guard vital supplies from Sweden. First and foremost, an obvious method was applied: Germany increased its exports of goods to Sweden. Trommer has, in fact, concluded that 'in 1943 Geman deliveries to Sweden were more extensive and regular than ever before and were sufficient both to pay for current Swedish exports to Germany and to repay earlier export credits that had fallen due'.[114]

At the same time, however, imports of iron ore from Sweden increased, to 10.1 million mt or 5,568,000 mt of iron content. This constituted about a quarter of Germany's supplies, from both domestic and foreign sources.[115] To cover the expenditure, the Nazi regime was forced to resort to methods additional to the normal exportation of goods. Thus Sweden became the recipient of 'German' gold, albeit to a smaller extent than Switzerland. In autumn 1942 and spring 1943, as part payment of the commercial credits, the Reichsbank dispatched gold to a total value of SEK 105 million to Sweden.[116]

The fact that the Nazi regime used gold in its dealings with the Swedish authorities has been highlighted during the ongoing investigations into the policies and activities of the neutrals during the Second World War. As a recent preliminary Swedish government report has shown, in the case of Sweden the focus of attention is whether the country,

fully aware of what it was doing, received gold from Nazi Germany as payment for transactions before and during the Second World War, although officials knew, or should have known, that the gold had either been appropriated from the central banks of occupied countries or stolen

Table 3.6   *Total German exports to Sweden, 1938–44*

Year	Million SEK
1938	454
1939	620
1940	769
1941	870
1942	808
1943	894[a]
1944	799

Note: [a] Fifty per cent of total Swedish imports.
Source: Fritz, 'Wirtschaftliche Neutralität', 53, table 4.

Table 3.7   *Total Swedish exports to Germany, 1938–44*

Year	Million SEK
1938	335
1939	369
1940	491
1941	558
1942	530
1943	538[a]
1944	345

Note: [a] Forty-six per cent of total Swedish exports.
Source: Fritz, 'Wirtschaftliche Neutralität', 53, table 4.

from Jews in connection with Nazi persecution of the Jews, so-called looted gold.[117]

Although the investigations had not been completed at the time of Sweden's December 1997 report, the existing evidence shows without any doubt that the country received gold from the Third Reich which the Nazi regime had looted from other countries, most notably Belgium and the Netherlands. Gold was sent to Sweden even after spring 1943; its total value exceeded the aforementioned SEK 105 million. According to official calculations undertaken immediately after the war, Sweden's Riksbank received nearly 7.3 mt of Belgian and 8.6 mt of Dutch gold between late

Table 3.8   *German imports of Swedish iron ore, 1939–44 (million mt iron content)*

Year	Million mt	% of Swedish exports to Germany
1939	6.226	50.1
1940	5.339	32.6
1941	5.027	28.3
1942	4.205	28.3
1943	5.568	34.3
1944	2.628	24.6

Source: Fritz, 'Wirtschaftliche Neutralität', 62–3, tables 10–11.

Table 3.9   *Swedish iron as percentage of German consumption, 1940–44*

Year	%
1940	39.5
1941	26.9
1942	23.2
1943	27.5
1944	23.9

Source: Wittmann, *Schwedens Wirtschaftsbeziehungen*, 243, table A 15.

1942 and early 1944. It is clear that the Nazi regime used looted gold, resmelted to disguise its origin, in order to secure valuable goods from Sweden.

It has been shown that, in 1943, Germany increased its imports of Swedish iron ore. Referring to quantities alone, however, does not suffice to arrive at an understanding of the importance of the material to the German war economy. Particular emphasis needs to be put on the quality of Swedish iron ore by comparison with domestically mined ore and ore from German-occupied Lorraine (*Minette-Erz*).[118] While the latter contained an average of only about 30 per cent iron, Swedish ore boasted about 60 per cent iron content. Using Swedish iron ore enabled German steel producers to save on labour, blast furnace capacity and coke. German officials estimated that coal and coke savings alone amounted to about 2 million mt a year. Savings in terms of labour were therefore not limited to the steel industry, they also affected the number of workers needed in the mining of coal and domestic iron ore. The importance of Swedish iron ore in terms of its quality further extended to the low phosphorous content of a substantial proportion of the supplies exported to Germany. These supplies increased during the war[119] and were deemed of crucial importance (*nicht ersetzbar*) to the production of high-grade steel. All in all, a loss of supplies from Sweden would have drastically added to the pressures the German war economy was increasingly faced with after 1941.

As could be expected, the Allies attempted to curtail Swedish supplies to Germany, partly through military means (for instance, through Russian submarine attacks against the ore shipments in the Baltic Sea), but largely through diplomatic and economic pressure. Until late 1942, Sweden was fortunate in that the British government accepted the importance of safeguarding the country's neutrality. Only modest pressure was used to force the Swedish government to take more far-reaching steps. When, in 1943, the US administration took a growing and hostile interest in Sweden's trade with Germany, the pressure on the Swedish authorities rapidly mounted. As in the case of other countries, the United States used Sweden's dependence on oil imports to seriously challenge the relations between the latter and the Third Reich.[120]

In Sweden's case, the foremost targets of the Roosevelt administration were supplies of iron ore as well as ball bearings. In November 1942, Secretary of State Cordell Hull emphasised 'that the traffic of iron-ore is the most important single contribution, in terms of raw material, made to Germany by any nation outside its pre-war borders'.[121] Hull's early, pronounced criticism set the tone for the subsequent attitude of the Allies towards Sweden. In simple terms, it was argued that, 'if Sweden dare not take part in the fight for democracy, she shall at least reduce the aid she furnishes to its enemies'.[122] For the Americans, it was, in fact, not simply a matter of reduction. The US government 'not only wanted Sweden to scale down its relationship with Germany, it wanted it completely ended – and quickly'.[123] During 1943 and 1944, the Allies made a concerted attempt to force the Swedish government into reducing the export of vital materials, most notably iron ore and ball bearings,[124] to the Third Reich.

On 10 May 1943, a Swedish delegation headed by Gunnar Hägglöf, the chief of the trade department of the Swedish Foreign Ministry, commenced a new round of trade negotiations in London. During the course of the talks, which lasted until 19 June, the British government demanded an end to all transit traffic by 1 October at the latest and a reduction in Swedish exports to German-occupied Europe in 1943 by SEK 130 million compared with 1942. For 1944, supplies of iron ore to Germany were to be cut to 7.5 million mt and supplies of ball bearings to SEK 30 million, respectively. In exchange for implementing these changes, the Allies offered an increase in Sweden's oil quota.

As shown above, the transit traffic was radically curtailed soon after. In addition, an agreement between Sweden and the Allies on the basis of the demands made in London was finally put into effect on 23 September 1943.[125] The agreement notwithstanding, the Third Reich continued to enjoy the benefits of discreet Swedish commercial compliance. With regard to ball bearings, a particular bone of contention for the US government,[126] the Swedish government tried to make out that the trade with Germany was not of major importance. Confronted about the export of ball bearings, the sole Swedish producer, Svenska Kullagerfabriken (SKF), told the British Foreign Office that they were not vital to the German armaments industry, making up at the most 8 per cent of the total production capacity of Axis Europe. SKF, in fact, held out until 12 October 1944 before it 'yielded to *force majeure* and ceased exporting ball-bearings to Germany'.[127]

Fears about Nazi economic or even military reprisals certainly influenced the Swedish government against satisfying Allied demands. Yet as Martin Fritz has acutely argued, ultimately 'Sweden had a fundamental economic interest in maintaining its commercial intercourse with Germany at the highest possible level. ... [In the case of ball bearings b]oth government and company [SKF] had a common interest in keeping relations with Germany as undisturbed as possible.'[128] This meant that, in

Table 3.10   *Swedish ball bearing exports to Germany, 1937–1943*

Year	Million SEK	% of total exports
1937	4.0	9.1
1938	6.9	13.3
1939	8.3	16.2
1940	14.7	26.1
1941	25.2	40.3
1942	34.2	52.0
1943	47.5	64.9

Source: Fritz, 'Swedish Ball-bearings', table 2, 17.

Table 3.11 *Production of ball bearings in Germany, 1938–44 (million RM)*

Year	Total	VKF[a]
1938	162	92
1939	185	104
1940	199	113
1941	218	128
1942	251	148
1943	?	149
1944	?	116

Note: [a] The main German producer of ball bearings, Vereinigte Kugellagerfabriken (VKF), was owned by SFK. Detailed information on SKF's business links in Germany can be found in Gerard Aalders and Cees Wiebes, *Die Kunst der Tarnung* (Frankfurt, 1994), 112–48.
Source: Fritz, 'Wirtschaftliche Neutralität', 68, table 14.

1944, Germany continued to receive satisfactory supplies over the ball-bearing sector as a whole. While exports of ball bearings decreased, supplies of ball-bearing steel and ball-bearing production machinery actually increased substantially compared with 1943.[129]

In view of continued Swedish supplies to the Third Reich it is not surprising that relations between Sweden and the Allies 'remained characterized for the rest of the war by suspicion and anger on the part of the Allies and nervousness over post-war trade prospects among the Swedes'.[130] Although, by 1944, Germany was evidently losing the war, Sweden continued to make a vital contribution to the German war effort. In September 1944 Churchill brought the attitude of the Swedes to a point when he accused them of 'calculated selfishness, which has distinguished them in both wars against Germany'.[131] Why did the Swedish government not respond more readily to the growing Allied pressure?

One important reason was that, even during the second half of the war, the Swedish government and an overwhelmingly pro-Allied Swedish public accepted trade with Germany as a national right under international law.[132] During the course of 1944, this line of argument rang increasingly hollow in the light of growing evidence about the horrifying nature of the atrocities committed by Nazi Germany. Leading members of the Swedish government continued to believe, however, in the need to retain normal relations with the Nazi regime. Historians have highlighted particularly the attitude of the leader of Sweden's government, Per Albin Hansson.

According to Alf Johansson, a leading Swedish authority on wartime Sweden, Hansson continued to believe in the threat of a German invasion long after it had ceased to be a realistic possibility. Moreover, Johansson argues, 'Hansson's role during the last years of the war was to act as a brake on all attempts towards an activism of Swedish policy in one direction or the other.'[133] Essentially, Hansson seems to have wanted to sit out the war without having to make any radical changes in the course of Sweden's policy of neutrality. In this undertaking Hansson was very willingly supported by his foreign minister, Günther. On the basis of observations made by various of Günther's fellow officials, Levine has concluded that Günther's policies were quite pro-German even in the later stages of the war.[134]

Ultimately, of course, the Swedish government always favoured a victory by the Western Allies.[135] It accepted the need to refocus its policies towards the Allies. It is just that Sweden's policies tended to lag behind Allied demands. When, for instance, a new German–Swedish trade agreement was concluded in January 1944 which incorporated the reductions in exports agreed upon in London in 1943, this was no longer enough for the Allies. On 17 March 1944, a memorandum from the Allies demanded a further reduction of iron ore and ball-bearing exports over and above the agreement of September 1943. This demand was reinforced by a further note in April which targeted ball-bearing supplies in particular. Faced by this ever-growing pressure, the Swedish government adopted a graduated approach. 'Informally and quite "unintentionally"' it reduced exports to Germany.[136]

While, in May 1944, ball bearings were still being supplied in accordance with the agreement of January, their export declined noticeably in June and July.[137] Despite this decline, the Swedish authorities by and large complied with the January economic agreement in July 1944.[138] Over the subsequent months 'Swedish–German relations worsened step by step, but without any incidents occurring, and not beyond the maintenance of normal diplomatic relations.'[139] By 19 November 1944, all ball-bearing supplies had stopped, while iron ore supplies were near cessation.[140] Less than two months later, the uncompromising attitude of the Allies finally forced the Swedes to refuse the conclusion of a trade agreement with the Third Reich for 1945.[141] Trade with Germany had effectively ended.

Notes

1 Kent Zetterberg, 'Neutralitet till varje pris? Till frågan om den svenska säkerhetspolitiken 1940–42 och eftergifterna till Tyskland', in Bo Hugemark (ed.), *I Orkanens Öga; 1941 – osäker neutralitet* (Stockholm, 1992), 13.

2 On the 'buffer function' see Thomas Munch-Petersen, *The Strategy of Phoney War: Britain, Sweden, and the Iron Ore Question 1939–40* (Stockholm, 1981), 14–15.

3 In plebiscites, Switzerland's population and cantons rejected the proposed entry into both organisations.

4 On the history of Swedish neutrality see, *inter alia*, John Logue, 'The Legacy of Swedish Neutrality', in Bengt Sundelius (ed.), *The Committed Neutral: Sweden's Foreign Policy* (Boulder CO, 1989), 35–66; Krister Wahlbäck, *The Roots of Swedish Neutrality* (Stockholm, 1986); Sverker Åström, *Sweden's Policy of Neutrality* (Stockholm, 1977), and in a more recent, revised version 'Swedish Neutrality: Credibility through Commitment and Consistency', in *The Committed Neutral*, 15–33.

5 Åström, *Sweden's Policy of Neutrality*, 6.

6 Bengt Sundelius, introduction to *The Committed Neutral*, 4.

7 Åström, *Sweden's Policy of Neutrality*, 11.

8 Sten Carlsson, 'Die schwedische Neutralität. Eine historische Übersicht', in Bindschedler *et al.* (eds), *Schwedische und schweizerische Neutralität*, 21 and 27.

9 On Sweden's military position in 1939 see Börje Furtenbach, 'Sweden during the Second World War: Armaments and Preparedness', *Revue internationale d'histoire militaire/International Review of Military History* 26 (1967), 74–8; see also Klaus-Richard Böhme, 'The Principal Features of Swedish Defence Policy 1925–1945', in Comité International des Sciences (ed.), *Neutrality and Defence: The Swedish Experience* (Stockholm, 1984), 119–34, and Arvid Cronenberg, '1936 års försvarsbeslut och upprustningen 1936–1939', in Carl-Axel Wangel (ed.), *Sveriges militära beredskap 1939–1945* (Stockholm, 1982), 25–53.

10 On 3 September 1939, Sweden's army consisted of 58,000 troops, its navy and coastal defences of 24,300 and its air force (180 serviceable aircraft) of 6,000. By 15 April 1940 the size of the army had increased to 225,000 men; see statistic for period 3 September 1939 to 31 May 1945 in Carl-Axel Wangel, 'Verteidigung gegen den Krieg', in Bindschedler *et al.* (eds), *Schwedische und schweizerische Neutralität*, 47. Data on the pre-war military preparations of Sweden's Scandinavian neighbours are given in Bengt Åhslund, 'Det militärpolitiska läget vid krigsutbrottet 1939', in Wangel (ed.), *Sveriges militära beredskap*, 24, table 1.

11 *Hitler's Table Talk 1941–1944*, intro. Hugh R. Trevor-Roper (London, 1953), 28.

12 Hans-Jürgen Lutzhöft, *Deutsche Militärpolitik und schwedische Neutralität 1939–1942* (Neumünster, 1981), 32. From SEK 258 million in the budget year 1938/39 Sweden's defence spending increased to around SEK 2 billion in 1941/42; Zetterberg, 'Neutralitet', 25.

13 Article 10 of Convention V; see Brown Scott (ed.), *The Hague Conventions*, 135.
14 Articles 2 and 5 of Convention V; see *ibid.*, 133–4.
15 A protest note by the British government to the Swedish government on 29 August 1942 explicitly refers to Article 2; see Rune Karlsson, *Så stoppades tysktågen; den tyska transiteringstrafiken i svensk politik 1942–1943* (Stockholm, 1974), 32.
16 See *ibid.*, 41–2.
17 Stig Hadenius, *Swedish Politics during the Twentieth Century* (Stockholm, 3rd edn, 1990), 45.
18 Gunnar Hägglöf, in charge of the trade department of the Swedish Foreign Ministry until January 1944 and a leading figure in war trade negotiations, later argued that, during the inter-war period, Britain had 'the greatest moral influence in Scandinavia'. During the war (in March 1943) the British government estimated that 80 per cent of the Swedish population favoured the Allies; Gunnar Hägglöf, 'A Test of Neutrality: Sweden in the Second World War', *International Affairs* 36, 1 (1960), 154; Alf Johansson, 'La neutralité suédoise et les puissances occidentales entre 1939 et 1945', *Revue d'histoire de la Deuxième Guerre Mondiale* 109 (1978), 21. On pre-war Swedish attitudes towards Nazi Germany see Lutzhöft, *Deutsche Militärpolitik*, 24–30.
19 The Swedish government adopted a stance of non-belligerence in favour of Finland rather than remaining neutral. This included providing its embattled Scandinavian neighbour with supplies of arms, food and even volunteers; see, in particular, Alf Johansson, *Finlands sak; Swensk politik och opinion under vinterkriget 1939–1940* (Stockholm, 1973).
20 Hadenius, *Swedish Politics*, 46–7. A summary of various views on Günther, largely by other members of the Swedish wartime government, can be found in Paul A. Levene, *From Indifference to Activism: Swedish Diplomacy and the Holocaust 1938–1944* (Uppsala, 1996), 84–5. Sandler's fall from power over the issue of Sweden's assistance to Finland is well summarised in Erik Lönnroth, 'Sweden's Ambiguous Neutrality', *Scandinavian Journal of History* 2 (1977) (special issue on 'The Great Powers and the Nordic Countries 1939–1940'), 97–100.
21 Levene, *From Indifference to Activism*, 81, calls it 'Hansson's *idée fixé* of keeping Sweden out of the war'.
22 Cited in Steven Koblik, 'Sweden's Attempts to Aid Jews 1939–1945', *Scandinavian Studies* 56 (1984), 89.
23 *Hitler's Secret Book*, intro. Telford Taylor (New York, 2nd edn 1962).
24 W. M. Carlgren, *Swedish Foreign Policy during the Second World War*, trans. Arthur Spencer (London, 1977), 85–6.
25 Martin, 'Deutschland und die neutralen Staaten Europas', 375 and 388 n. 66.
26 Carlgren, *Swedish Foreign Policy*, 86.
27 BA 25.01/6334, report by Curt Drews (Reichsbank), 'The Swedish mentality as a factor in the Continental European desire for unity', May 1943.
28 Hans-Jürgen Lutzhöft, 'Deutschland und Schweden während des Norwegen-feldzuges 9. April–10. Juni 1940', *Vierteljahreshefte für Zeitgeschichte* 22 (1974), 382, citing an OKH document of December 1938.
29 *Ibid.*, 386.

77

30 Henrik S. Nissen 'Adjusting to German Domination', in H. S. Nissen (ed.), *Scandinavia during the Second World War* (Minneapolis MN, 1983), 108. In all likelihood, German planning was also influenced by the possibility that an invasion of Sweden might lead to a Soviet advance into Finland.

31 On the reassurances see Carlgren, *Swedish Foreign Policy*, 62–3.

32 Lutzhöft, 'Deutschland und Schweden', 388–9.

33 Upon his retirement in February 1943, Wied was replaced by Hans Thomsen.

34 John M. West, 'The German–Swedish Transit Agreement of 1940', *Scandinavian Studies* 50, 1 (1978), 76.

35 Hansson's comment in a radio speech, 12 April 1940, *ibid.*, 77.

36 Ulf Brandell, 'Die Transitfrage in der schwedischen Außenpolitik während des Zweiten Weltkrieges', in Bindschedler *et al.* (eds), *Schwedische und schweizerische Neutralität*, 83.

37 Swedish Ministry of Foreign Affairs communiqué, 22 April 1940, in West, 'German–Swedish Transit Agreement', 77.

38 Munch-Petersen, *The Strategy of Phoney War*, 218.

39 On the same day, the Swedish authorities confiscated three German wagons at Trelleborg because, on inspection, arms and munitions were found hidden among horse fodder; Lutzhöft, 'Deutschland und Schweden', 403. On pp. 400 ff. (and in *Deutsche Militärpolitik*, 81–97) Lutzhöft provides detailed information on the transit question during the Norwegian campaign. On Göring and Dahlerus see Johann Wolfgang Brügel, 'Dahlerus als Zwischenträger nach Kriegsausbruch', *Historische Zeitschrift* 228 (1979), 70–97.

40 West, 'German–Swedish Transit Agreement', 80–1. See Krister Wahlbäck and Göran Boberg (eds), *Sveriges sak är vår: Svensk utrikespolitik 1939–45 i dokument* (Stockholm, 1967), 99–102, for Dahlerus's post-war recollection of the 6 May meeting, and 102–4 for Hägglöf's post-war recollection of the 11 May encounter.

41 See Lutzhöft, 'Deutschland und Schweden', 410–11. Richert believed that, in view of the Wehrmacht's advance in the west, a German victory was not impossible. Rejecting Germany's demands was therefore potentially 'suicidal'. Germany's demand was also supported by the commander-in-chief of the Swedish army, Olof Thörnell, for similar reasons to those of Richert; West, 'German–Swedish Transit Agreement', 83.

42 Hansson's diary entry in West, 91; and, translated slightly differently, in Nissen 'Adjusting to German Domination', 106. Similar comments by other leading Swedish politicians can be found in Maria-Pia Boëthius, *Heder och Samvete: Sverige och andra världskriget* (Stockholm, 1991), 30–1. Boëthius, a journalist, has come under much criticism for her attempt to indict severely the policies of Sweden's war-time government. Referring to Boëthius's book as a 'long "list of sins" of Sweden's *eftergiftspolitik* towards Germany', Zetterberg, a firm defender of Sweden's wartime policy, accuses it of being 'one-sided, tendentious and filled with strange views'; Zetterberg, 'Neutralitet', 36 n. 13.

43 Summarised in detail in Lutzhöft, *Deutsche Militärpolitik*, 97–104.

44 A further additional agreement was added on 5 December which again strengthened Germany's position; see Lutzhöft, *Deutsche Militärpolitik*, 118–21.

45 BA/MA RW5/v.396, translation of a Swedish *promemoria*, 18 November 1941.

46 In February 1941, the number of German troops travelling north exceeded those homebound by 15,920, in March by 20,966, by far the largest monthly imbalance in the history of the transit traffic; Leif Björkman, *Sverige inför Operation Barbarossa: Svensk neutralitetspolitik 1940–1941* (Stockholm, 1971), 475. On the *Marskrisen* see *ibid.*, 87–151. In response to Sweden mobilising 80,000 troops in mid-March, the German government stopped the Göteborg traffic (see below).

47 From February 1941, the Swedish government was aware that, under the codename *Barbarossa*, Germany was planning an attack on the Soviet Union; Lothar Gruchmann, 'Schweden im Zweiten Weltkrieg: Ergebnisse eines Stockholmer Forschungsprojektes', *Vierteljahreshefte für Zeitgeschichte* 25 (1977), 601.

48 The attitude and mood of the Swedish government at the time of Operation Barbarossa is summarised in Alf W. Johansson, 'I skuggan av operation Barbarossa: attityder och stämningar 1940/1941', in Hugemark (ed.) *I Orkanens Öga*, 75–104.

49 Even Åström mentions the 'Engelbrekt [*sic*] Division' in his very short pamphlet on *Sweden's Policy of Neutrality*, 14.

50 See Lutzhöft, *Deutsche Militärpolitik*, 104–5, on British and Norwegian protests at Sweden's 'flagrant breach of … neutrality' and 'direct assistance' of Germany.

51 In Directive 21 (Operation Barbarossa) of 18 December 1940 Hitler had foreseen the possibility of using Swedish railways and roads for the movement of German troops; Hugh R. Trevor-Roper (ed.), *Hitler's War Directives 1939–1945* (London 1966), 95. For detailed information on Sweden's intended and actual role in Germany's preparations for Operation Barbarossa see Horst Boog, Jürgen Förster, Joachim Hoffmann, Ernst Klink, Rolf-Dieter Müller and Gerd R. Ueberschär, *Der Angriff auf die Sowjetunion*, vol. IV of *Das Deutsche Reich und der Zweite Weltkrieg*, ed. Militärgeschichtliches Forschungsamt (Stuttgart, 1983), 407–12.

52 Carlgren, *Swedish Foreign Policy*, 115.

53 See Wahlbäck and Boberg, *Sveriges sak*, 149, for Communications Minister Gustaf Andersson i Rasjön's diary entry of the decisive meeting.

54 Hadenius, *Swedish Politics*, 51.

55 The transit was completed on 12 July; Lutzhöft, *Deutsche Militärpolitik*, 163.

56 By the end of the year the overall transport figure had grown to 100,000 mt, 60 per cent of which constituted war material. The number of injured soldiers in transit had increased to 15,500; BA/MA RW5/v.396, German translation of a confidential Swedish memo, 20 January 1942.

57 So-called courier flights continued until the end of May 1944 and involved a total of 3,157 flights; Brandell, 'Die Transitfrage', 93. Allied courier flights across Swedish air space totalled 3,333; Göran Andolf, 'Interneringen av britter och tyskar 1943–1944', in Bo Huldt and Klaus-Richard Böhme (eds), *Vårstormar: 1944 – Krigsslutet skönjes* (Stockholm, 1995), 229.

58 For more detail see Wolfgang Wilhelmus, 'Zu den Beziehungen zwischen dem faschistischen Deutschland und Schweden nach dem Überfall auf die

Sowjetunion (Juni bis Dezember 1941)', *Zeitschrift für Geschichtswissenschaft* 26 (1978), 690–1.

59 BA/MA RW5/v.396, German translation of a Swedish memo, 18 November 1941. BA R901/68583, Schnurre to AA, 23 October 1941 contains a report on the first contract for the purchase of 2,000 tents (in exchange for flax) and the lease of 300 lorries (in exchange for 5,000 t of Petsamo nickel and 50 t of Buna). See also Lutzhöft, *Deutsche Militärpolitik*, 197–8, and Klaus Wittmann, *Schwedens Wirtschaftsbeziehungen zum Dritten Reich 1933–1945* (Munich and Vienna, 1978), 261–2.

60 Although far cooler in its attitude towards Finland than during the Winter War, the Swedish government nonetheless permitted pro-Finnish activities which were *ipso facto* also to the advantage of the German war effort. Although very small in number (806 volunteers in the Hangö battalion until late autumn 1941; 548 in the Svir company between 1942 and 1944), Swedish army volunteers were permitted to join the Finnish forces on the eastern front; Furtenbach, 'Sweden during the Second World War', 90; see also Anders Grafström, 'Svenska frivilligförband 1939–1944', in Wangel (ed.), *Sveriges militära beredskap*, 142–9. At the beginning of September 1941, the Swedish government made it clear that, apart from the Finnish army, Swedes were not permitted to volunteer for a foreign force. Only a tiny number of Swedish volunteers joined the SS; Boog et al., *Der Angriff auf die Sowjetunion*, 926–8.

61 Kent Zetterberg, '1942 – Storkriget vänder, Sveriges utsatta läge består', in Bo Hugemark (ed.), *Vindkantring: 1942 – politisk kursändring* (Stockholm, 1993), 114. Zetterberg refers to Goebbels as a 'notorious critic of Sweden'.

62 Wangel, 'Verteidigung', 40.

63 Wilhelmus, 'Zu den Beziehungen', 692 and 694.

64 The alpine division in question, which the OKW was moving from Greece to the Finno-Soviet front, eventually arrived in the middle of October, two months later than planned; see Ohto Manninen, 'Operation Barbarossa and the Nordic Countries', in Nissen (ed.), *Scandinavia during the Second World War*, 160–1; also Lutzhöft, *Deutsche Militärpolitik*, 164–8.

65 See Lutzhöft, *Deutsche Militärpolitik*, 142–3.

66 Throughout the war, anti-German 'propaganda' in Sweden was widespread not only in the newspapers but also in the theatre and cinema; see BA/MA RW4/v.653, report on German–Swedish relations, 19 November 1944. On the policies of the Swedish government *vis-à-vis* the Swedish press see, *inter alia*, Göran Andolf, 'De grå lapparna: Regeringen och pressen under andra världskriget', in Bo Hugemark (ed.), *Nya Fronter? 1943 – spänd väntan* (Stockholm, 1994), 304–49. On Nazi Germany's propaganda efforts in Sweden see Thomas Roth, 'Schweden erwache! Tysk propaganda mot Sverige 1942', in Hugemark (ed.), *Vindkantring*, 153–69.

67 On 23 February, Sweden rejected Germany's request for the transfer of 6,000 troops to Finland. The Nazi regime did not adopt any counter-measures despite the tension that had built up in relations between the two countries (the so-called 'February Crisis'); see Gruchmann, 'Schweden im Zweiten Weltkrieg', 603–5.

68 Reference is again being made to the preferential treatment of German ships

in Swedish waters and German aircraft crossing Swedish territory.

69 Mallet, British ambassador in Stockholm, to Anthony Eden, 21 July 1941, quoted in Johansson, 'La neutralité suédoise', 17.

70 Lutzhöft, *Deutsche Militärpolitik*, 189. Schnurre's conclusion is confirmed in BA 09.01/68452, Wied to AA, 25 September 1941.

71 Detailed information on the British memo of 11 June can be found in Karlsson, *Så stoppades tysktågen*, 26–8.

72 Johansson, 'La neutralité suédoise', 19.

73 BA/MA RW5/v.396, copy of a report by AA, 10 August 1942.

74 Kent Zetterberg, 'Le transit allemand par la Suède de 1940 à 1943', *Revue d'histoire de la Deuxième Guerre Mondiale* 109 (1978), 76–7.

75 Covered in detail in Karlsson, *Så stoppades tysktågen*, 26–51.

76 Johansson, 'La neutralité suédoise', 19.

77 Gruchmann, 'Schweden im Zweiten Weltkrieg', 606.

78 Zetterberg, 'Le transit allemand', 76.

79 See appendix 3 in Karlsson, *Så stoppades tysktågen*, 475.

80 Aage Trommer, 'Scandinavia and the Turn of the Tide ', in Nissen (ed.), *Scandinavia during the Second World War*, 273.

81 Nissen, 'Adjusting to German Domination', 106–7.

82 'Policy of giving in'.

83 As the 'regular' transit traffic was not affected by the cessation of the agreement of 1940, Germany was able to continue with the movement of petroleum products through Sweden until 1 October 1943, and of coal and cement until June 1944. After that date only ambulance trains were allowed through by the Swedish authorities.

84 IWM Speer Collection Reel 25, FD3045/49, Sc. 396, undated draft of a Four Year Plan Planning Office order.

85 Alan Milward, 'Could Sweden have stopped the Second World War?', *Scandinavian Economic History Review* XV (1967), 127–38.

86 Rolf Karlbom, 'Sweden's Iron Ore Exports to Germany 1933–1944', *Scandinavian Economic History Review* XIII (1965), 71.

87 Jörg-Johannes Jäger, 'Sweden's Iron Ore Exports to Germany 1933–1944: a Reply to Rolf Karlbom's Article on the same Subject', *Scandinavian Economic History Review* XV (1967), 139–47.

88 Karlbom, 'Sweden's Iron Ore Exports', 65.

89 Milward, 'Could Sweden have stopped', 138.

90 See, in particular, Richard J. Overy, *War and Economy in the Third Reich*, Oxford, 1994. Karlbom himself, in a reply to Milward's criticism, objected to the economic *Blitzkrieg* theory.

91 Apart from also pointing out the importance of iron ore stocks in Germany, Jäger adds that Karlbom based his figures purely on those for the German Reich in its pre–1938 borders and not on those for the Greater German Reich, including Austria, the Protectorate of Bohemia and Moravia, and the annexed Polish territories.

92 Cf. Klaus Wittmann, 'Deutsch-schwedische Wirtschaftsbeziehungen im Zweiten Weltkrieg', in Friedrich Forstmeier and Hans-Erich Volkmann (eds), *Kriegswirtschaft und Rüstung 1939–1945* (Düsseldorf, 1977), 201–4.

93 BA 09.01/68452, Brinkmann (RWM) to Doehner (OKW), 2 April 1938.

94 Fritz, 'Wirtschaftliche Neutralität', 53, table 4.

95 Comment by Grundherr (AA) to Swedish naval attaché in Berlin at time of Munich Crisis, in Lönnroth, 'Sweden's Ambiguous Neutrality', 103.

96 Munch-Petersen, *The Strategy of Phoney War*, 21.

97 BA 09.01/68452, Brinkmann (RWM) to Doehner (OKW), 2 April 1938.

98 Klaus A. Maier, Horst Rohde, Bernd Stegemann and Hans Umbreit, *Die Errichtung der Hegemonie auf dem europäischen Kontinent*, vol. II of *Das Deutsche Reich und der Zweite Weltkrieg*, ed. Militärgeschichtliches Forschungsamt (Stuttgart, 1979), 193, 195.

99 Trevor-Roper (ed.), *Hitler's War Directives*, 61–2. To 'anticipate English action against Scandinavia and the Baltic' and to 'provide the navy and air force with expanded bases for operations against England' were the other two motives given by Hitler.

100 BA/MA RW19/441, No. 9, appendix 39, note for Head of OKW, 21 September 1939.

101 Cited in Patrick Salmon, 'British Plans for Economic Warfare against Germany 1937–1939: the Problem of Swedish Iron Ore', *Journal of Contemporary History* 16 (1981), 53–4.

102 See C. G. McKay, 'Iron Ore and Section D: the Oxelösund Operation', *Historical Journal* 29 (1986), 975–8.

103 Lutzhöft, *Deutsche Militärpolitik*, 68. The central importance of iron ore was again highlighted in the German–Swedish economic agreement of December 1940, in which the Swedish government acknowledged Nazi Germany's powerful position by further concessions; Boog *et al.*, *Der Angriff auf die Sowjetunion*, 407.

104 Fritz, 'Wirtschaftliche Neutralität', 51.

105 Robert Cole, *Britain and the War of Words in Neutral Europe 1939–1945: The Art of the Possible* (Basingstoke, 1990), 50. A similar interpretation was applied by Robert Hudson, the British Minister of Overseas Trade, in April 1939 (see Munch-Petersen, *The Strategy of Phoney War*, 24). Hudson told the Swedish financier Marcus Wallenberg that the continuation of ore supplies to Germany in wartime would lead to Sweden being treated as a hostile power. However, the British government never followed this extreme course of action.

106 The Skagerrak blockade consisted of a minefield from Skagen at the northern tip of Jutland to the southern tip of Norway.

107 Martin Fritz, 'Swedish Ball-bearings and the German War Economy', *Scandinavian Economic History Review* XXIII (1975), 17.

108 Fritz, 'Wirtschaftliche Neutralität', 57.

109 Boelcke, *Deutschland als Welthandelsmacht*, 130.

110 Fritz, 'Wirtschaftliche Neutralität', 76.

111 BA 09.01/68583, memo by Clodius (AA), 17 May 1943.

112 BA 09.01/68452, memo by Wiehl (AA), 12 December 1939.

113 BA 09.01/68583, memo by Wiehl (AA), 12 December 1942. German problems in complying with contractual obligations did not stop the Swedish military from showing an interest in German war material. Even as late as November 1944 the OKW received Swedish requests for armaments; see BA/MA RW19/3326, memo, 13 November 1944.

114 Trommer, 'Scandinavia and the Turn of the Tide', 269.

115 *Ibid.*, 271.

116 Fritz, 'Wirtschaftliche Neutralität', 77.

117 Introduction to Swedish report 'Sweden and the Nazi Gold' submitted to London conference, December 1997.

118 The following assessment is based on Fritz, 'Wirtschaftliche Neutralität', 63–5.

119 By October 1944, Sweden accounted for 35 per cent of Germany's consumption of low-phosporous iron ore; Wittmann, *Schwedens Wirtschaftsbeziehungen*, 243 n. 6.

120 For a brief overview of the economic warfare campaign of the Allies and Sweden see Anne Nilsson, *De Allierade och Sverige: Sveriges roll i de allierades ekonomiska krigföring under andra världskriget* (Stockholm, 1988).

121 Letter to J. Winant, in Levene, *From Indifference to Activism*, 193.

122 Fritz, 'Swedish Ball-bearings', 18.

123 Levine, *From Indifference to Activism*, 192.

124 In 1942 and 1943 Germany and Axis-controlled Europe took four-fifths of total Swedish exports of ball bearings. While Sweden supplied about RM 24 million worth of ball bearings in 1942, Germany's own output amounted to RM 251 million; Fritz, 'Swedish Ball-bearings', 17 and 32.

125 The Swedish declaration of 23 September can be found in W. N. Medlicott, *The Economic Blockade*, vol. II (London, 1959), 471–2.

126 The Roosevelt administration believed that imports of Swedish ball bearings constituted Germany's 'Achilles heel'. US officials even indicated that they might have to bomb the ball-bearing factories in Göteborg 'by accident'; Carlsson, 'Die schwedische Neutralität', 28.

127 Fritz, 'Swedish Ball-bearings', 20–2.

128 *Ibid.*, 23. In February 1943, Staffan Söderblom, head of the political department of the Swedish Foreign Ministry, argued along these lines in a conversation with a German diplomat. 'The mutual dependence and the interest of both countries in maintaining trade are undisputable. ... even if the Germans naturally had to anticipate a more restrictive attitude on the part of Sweden in some respects, it ought to be of great value to Germany to know that a change in Sweden's general policy toward Germany was unthinkable'; Trommer, 'Scandinavia and the Turn of the Tide', 271.

129 Fritz, 'Swedish Ball-bearings', 26. Switzerland also contributed to Germany's ball-bearing requirements with over 1.5 million units (SFr 7.1 million) in 1942 and just under 2.5 million units (SFr 9.2 million) in 1943. The Swiss ball-bearing manufacturer Arbon was owned by the German Automatische Gussstahl Kugelfabrik Fischer in Schweinfurt; Kamber, *Schüsse auf die Befreier*, 366.

130 Levine, *From Indifference to Activism*, 69.

131 *Ibid.*, 70. According to Levine, Sweden's humanitarian efforts during the war were one way in which the country could compensate for its feelings of guilt and reduce Allied pressure on it; see *ibid.*, 70–4, and 243–5 on the most famous case of the rescue of nearly 8,000 Danish Jews. See also Koblik, 'Sweden's Attempts to Aid Jews', *passim*.

132 Levine, *From Indifference to Activism*, 69. In contrast to the British, the US government never accepted this line of defence.

133 Levine, *From Indifference to Activism*, 82 (original quote in A. W. Johansson, 'Per Albin Hansson och utrikespolitiken under andra världskriget', in B. Huldt and K. Misgeld (eds), *Socialdemokratin och svensk utrikespolitik: Från Branting till Palme* (Stockholm, 1990), 50–9).

134 Levine, *From Indifference to Activism*, 84–5.

135 To most government members a Soviet victory was not desirable. In December 1942, for instance, Günther expressed his hope that Germany and the Soviet Union would exhaust each other in the war; Carlgren, *Swedish Foreign Policy*, 207.

136 Berit Nøkleby, 'Adjusting to Allied Victory', in *Scandinavia during the Second World War*, 289.

137 See BA/MA RW19/441, memo by OKW Economic Office, 8 August 1944.

138 BA/MA RW19/440, report on economic relations to neutrals, 14 July 1944.

139 Carlgren, *Swedish Foreign Policy*, 204.

140 BA/MA RW4/v.653, WFst/Ag. Ausland II A 2 memo *Germany – Sweden*, 19 November 1944.

141 Gruchmann, 'Schweden im Zweiten Weltkrieg', 611.

4

TURKEY

THE ACTIVE NEUTRAL

Turkey's hope is to take material from both sides and sell to both sides and to remain neutral throughout the war, and be rich and powerful at the end of the war.[1]

On 11 July 1939, Hitler advised General Wilhelm Keitel of his opposition to 'arms exports to hostile countries and to countries whose attitude in war was doubtful' and ordered the necessary steps to stop such exports to be taken.[2] By the time of Hitler's order, arms exports to Turkey had already fallen victim to concern about the 'political reliability' of the country. Just over five weeks before, Hitler had ordained that war material ordered by Turkey was to be withheld in Germany.

In previous years, Turkey had figured strongly in the order books of Germany's arms producers as one of the foremost purchasers of war material.[3] Prior to spring 1939, when Hitler had assessed relations with Turkey in a very positive light, he had even permitted contracts for fighter aircraft and submarines to be signed with the Turkish authorities. At precisely the time when Hitler's order was released, one German submarine was awaiting export to Turkey while engines and batteries for a second already delivered to the Turkish authorities were on their way to the eastern Mediterranean.[4] That Turkey was suddenly struck off the list of acceptable customers undoubtedly came as an unpleasant surprise to various companies which had signed business deals with the country.[5] Yet in the wider context of Hitler's preparations for war, the singling out of Turkey at that particular point in 1939 was highly understandable.

On 12 May 1939, an Anglo-Turkish declaration was announced in which both sides pledged to act against any acts of aggression in the

Mediterranean area. Faced with both this accord and the subsequent Franco-Turkish declaration of 23 June, Hitler anticipated that President Ismet Inönü's government would side with Germany's enemies in a future conflict. On 23 August he mentioned Turkey in one breath with France and the Soviet Union as countries which Britain was trying to recruit 'in her determination to annihilate Germany'.[6] Hitler's precautions were vindicated on 19 October 1939 when the Western democracies and Turkey signed a mutual assistance treaty to forestall Axis designs on the Balkans and in the Mediterranean.[7]

Yet despite Italy's entry into the war in June 1940 and the subsequent Axis campaign in the Balkans, which culminated in Germany's invasion and defeat of Yugoslavia and Greece in spring 1941, Turkey did not become a military partner of the Allies as Britain and France had expected in 1939. Germany's defeat of the latter in 1940 and its near-unstoppable military expansion had put a damper upon the commitment of the Turkish government to the Allies. When Germany invaded the Soviet Union in June 1941, the balance within the Turkish government took a more pronounced tilt towards the Nazi regime. By mid–1941, Turkey found itself in the curious situation of being bound to Germany in the Treaty of Friendship and Non-aggression of 18 June 1941 while, at the same time, still acknowledging its mutual assistance treaty with Britain.

The scene was thus set for Turkey's subsequent swings between both belligerent camps. As Edgar Bonjour put it, when contrasting Switzerland's neutrality with that of Turkey, the latter was 'geared towards specific occasions' and 'changeable'.[8] Turkey's neutrality was an acknowledgment of the country's desire to keep out of a conflict which others had caused and which it was very poorly prepared for. Yet the alliance and treaty policies of the Turkish government demonstrate that it responded to the potential effects of the war upon the country, not least because of its 'extremely sensitive geopolitical position'. Consequently, Turkey's attitude became one of 'active neutrality', which, as one official in the British Foreign Office lamented,

> enables the neutral power to preserve its preference for one belligerent or the other. There is something Ghandi-esque and positively immoral in this policy, but it is, I fear, typically Turkish and its astuteness and cleverness cannot be denied.[9]

Clever it may have been, but it also carried certain dangers. Owing to its vacillations, the Turkish government clearly risked antagonising both belligerents. The British government and the Nazi regime frequently voiced their annoyance with Turkey's attitude. Neither side, however, managed to entangle Turkey in the war at those points during the conflict when such a step might have made a difference to its course. As will be shown, the Turkish government turned decisively towards the Allies only during the course of 1944, a development which culminated in the country's declaration of war with Germany on 23 February 1945.[10]

German–Turkish relations prior to Operation Barbarossa

Of the five neutral countries under consideration, Turkey stands out as the only one which had been a military ally of Germany in the First World War. While the disastrous outcome of that experience had not done any long-term harm to German–Turkish relations, it contributed to making Turkey very apprehensive about German offers of an alliance in the late 1930s and during the Second World War.[11] During the 1920s relations between the two first-time republics, Weimar Germany (since November 1918) and Kemalist Turkey (since October 1923) developed in a stable manner, notably in the economic field, in which Turkey proved to be extremely dependent on German purchases of its agricultural products.

After 1933, relations between Germany and Turkey were not noticeably affected by Hitler's rise to power. While Kemal Atatürk, founding father and President of the Turkish Republic, expressed concern about the increasingly aggressive nature of the Nazi regime, Fascist Italy's foreign policy was a matter of much greater worry – particularly after Mussolini's speeches of 22 December 1933 and 19 March 1934. On these oocasions, the Duce pointed to Africa and Asia as Italy's historic mission. Mussolini's public rantings combined with the reality of Italy's occupation and remilitarisation of the Dodecanese islands off the western coast of Anatolia encouraged Atatürk to seek good relations with the sea power Britain to complement those with the land power Soviet Union, and to take an active role in the League of Nations. The mid–1930s saw Turkey even pitted against both fascist powers by its support of Ethiopia and the Republican side in the Spanish Civil War.[12]

Despite the anti-fascist thrust of Turkey's foreign policy, politically the country developed along lines more akin to the two dictatorships. This development reached a climax in 1935 when the ruling party, the Republican People's Party, inaugurated the unification of party and state, thus taking 'the final step towards formalising a party dictatorship in Turkey'.[13] Although, from an ideological perspective, Atatürk rejected Mussolini's

Fascism and Hitler's National Socialism, he observed developments in both countries with keen interest. Admiration was expressed for Hitler's achievements and relations with Nazi Germany remained fairly amicable. As Germany rapidly emerged from the economic depression of the early 1930s, it regained its role as a major exporter of manufactured products and importer of raw materials and agricultural products. Trade relations with Turkey experienced a fruitful upswing. In his infamous Reichstag speech of 30 January 1939, Hitler recognised this particular development: 'Our economic relations with [Yugoslavia] are undergoing constant development and expansion, just as is the case with the friendly countries of Bulgaria, Greece, Rumania, and Turkey.'[14]

From its trough in 1932, trade between the two countries had quadrupled by 1938.[15] As Turkey's leading trading partner, Germany took over 44 per cent of the country's total exports and accounted for half of Turkey's imports (47.5 per cent in 1938, 50.7 per cent in 1939). Although Turkish products played only a very minor role in Germany's foreign trade accounts (2–3 per cent), the nature of these products enhanced Turkey's position. Already in 1937, more than half of Germany's vital chromite imports originated from Turkey, producer of 16 per cent of the world's output. The reasons for the pronounced interest in the ferroalloy were similar to those for Germany's interest in Iberian wolfram. Chromium, of which chromite is the only source, 'possesses the property of imparting to iron and steel a high degree of hardness and tenacity …. Stainless steel contains as much as 18% of chromium.'[16]

During the late 1930s, Nazi Germany's strong interest in Turkish chromite attracted the attention of British officials. Seen in a wider context, British reactions to Germany's economic interests in Turkey, and vice versa, were an early indication of future economic warfare activities. Keenly aware of Turkey's attempt to modernise its economy and armed forces,[17] both sides tried to outbid each other. In May 1938, Britain signed a major credit agreement with Turkey amounting to £16 million (£6 million of it for purchases of British war material) which the Nazi regime promptly countered with the offer of a RM 150 million credit (RM 60 million for purchases of German war material) on 16 January 1939.[18] Although the credit agreement was never ratified,[19] Germany continued to woo Turkey in other ways, most notably by purchasing overpriced agricultural products (on average 30 per cent above world market prices) on a very much larger scale than other countries.[20]

While economic relations thus developed to the satisfaction of Germany and Turkey, political relations lagged behind. This was symbolised

Table 4.1   *Turkish chromite exports to Germany, 1936–39*

Year	mt
1936	64,500
1937	58,400
1938	68,500[a]
1939	114,500 (or 104,170)

Note: [a] Total imports 176,400.
Source: Boelcke, *Deutschland als Welthandelsmacht*, 141 and 200 n. 138; Alan S. Milward, 'The Reichsmark Bloc and the International Economy', in Gerhard Hirschfeld and Lothar Kettenacker (eds), *Der 'Führerstaat'. Mythos und Realität; Studien zur Struktur und Politik des Dritten Reiches* (Stuttgart, 1981), table 5, 405; Glasneck and Kircheisen, *Türkei und Afghanistan*, 154; BA/MA RW19/440, war diary 8 (appendix) for period 1 April–30 June 1944.

by the fact that, for five months between late November 1938 and late April 1939, the German government did not even bother to fill the vacant ambassadorial post in Ankara.[21] At precisely a time when Turkey was trying to reduce its economic and military dependence on Germany and to realign its foreign policy towards the Western powers, the Nazi regime remained inactive. This inactivity was subsequently followed by a show of annoyance when the Anglo-Turkish declaration was announced in May.[22]

Hitler's reaction to the British and French declarations led to a more pronounced deterioration of German–Turkish relations, not least in the economic sphere.[23] When, on 31 August 1939, the trade and clearing agreement between the two countries expired, Turkey refused to renew it. Whether the abrupt reaction of the Turkish government was due to Hitler's adverse attitude to arms exports or, as Deringil asserts, 'a form of protest against the Nazi–Soviet Pact',[24] a rapid decline in bilateral trade relations resulted and Britain took over from Germany as Turkey's most important trading partner. Yet economic necessity and military reality soon caught up with the Turks.

With Britain unable to replace fully Germany's purchasing power and French trading interests eliminated by military defeat, the Turkish government was forced to soften its approach towards the Third Reich. Within weeks of Germany's successful military campaign in the west – a shocking surprise to Inönü, who had expected the war in France to last four or five years[25] – a new German–Turkish commercial agreement was signed.[26] The decision to put a new agreement in place had, in fact, been taken on 12

June, when France's defeat was already a near certainty. Instead of joining the Allies – a step which Turkey should have been obliged to take after Italy's entry into the war[27] – Prime Minister Refik Saydam and his government drew closer to the Axis powers.

In the period between the attack on Poland in September 1939 and the invasion of the Soviet Union in June 1941 relations between Nazi Germany and Turkey improved gradually. This did not mean, however, that the two sides learnt to trust each other. For Turkey the improvement in relations was a clear, though often grudging, acknowledgement of Germany's military prowess, strengthened by disappointment and concern about Allied military setbacks. Politicians and journalists alike displayed widespread disenchantment and anger over France's inadequate defence effort. According to Deringil, 'Turks had always admired military success and the weakness and defection of France filled them with distaste.'[28] On the other hand, Britain was praised for its stubborn stand against Germany's onslaught. Yet Britain's failure to give adequate support to Greece in 1941 reinforced the belief that being a direct neighbour of Germany's sphere of influence required some accommodation with the Axis – hence the agreement of 18 June 1941.

In view of official and unofficial Turkish comments it seemed out of the question for the country to join the Allies, even after Italy's entry into the war on 10 June 1940. Turkey's declaration of non-belligerence, decided upon on 14 June and announced twelve days later,[29] clearly lacked the kind of commitment to the Allies that Spain's declaration had shown towards the Axis.

Despite Turkey's obvious lack of commitment to the Allies, the Nazis feared that an extremely disappointed British government might at least try to use the services of the Turkish government to woo the Soviet Union. It was therefore decided not to allow relations between Ankara and Moscow to regain the closeness they had enjoyed prior to the Nazi–Soviet Pact. By publishing the secret documents of the French general staff as a White Book this tactic was pursued further. In a deliberate falsification, the White Book referred to the possibility of an 'offensive war' by Turkey against the Soviet Union, rather than the 'defensive war' mentioned in the original documentation.

To Franz von Papen, Germany's ambassador at Ankara, who had urged an improvement in Soviet–Turkish relations to undermine Turkey's relations with Britain, Ribbentrop argued bluntly that all that was needed was to bring about the fall of Sükrü Saracoglu, the pro-British Minister of Foreign Affairs. Very conveniently, the White Book highlighted Saracoglu's support for the 'offensive war' option. While the Nazi publication was not able to shake Saracoglu's position, it created the desired effect in Moscow. Molotov expressed his anger to the Turkish government and İnönü complained to Papen that the White Book had disrupted his country's relations with the Soviets.[30]

Germany's policy was not simply confined to disrupting attempts at achieving a *rapprochement* between Turkey and the Soviet Union. At one point in 1940, Turkey itself was considered a possible target of German military operations. This option was suggested by Admiral Raeder in September 1940 as part of his plan to push the British out of the Mediterranean region. While Raeder advocated an advance from Libya towards the Suez Canal and then on to Syria and finally to Turkey, a second proposal foresaw a military push from Bulgaria via Turkey to the Suez Canal.[31] With the attack on the Soviet Union firmly on the cards for 1941, both options were, however, temporarily discarded.

Turkey's benevolence had instead to be assured – at least until the Soviet Union was defeated. Towards the end of 1940, Papen was therefore heavily engaged in discussions with the Turkish government. Although no official agreement was reached, both sides reassured each other about their desire for peaceful co-operation. Moreover, efforts were to be directed at getting the Turkish government to assist Germany's war effort. Ribbentrop, in his usual rash manner, was adamant that Turkey was to condone unlimited transit facilities for Wehrmacht troops, arms and equipment. Annoyed by İnönü's reluctance, he even fumed about wiping out Turkey within a week.[32] It was left to Papen to tone down Ribbentrop's tirades and conduct negotiations with the Turkish government in a more accommodating manner. He was assisted in his efforts by an exchange of notes between Hitler and İnönü in March 1941. In his first note the German dictator assured the Turkish President that the movement of German troops into Bulgaria was not directed against the political and territorial integrity of Turkey.[33]

To the relief of the Turkish government, Hitler's assurances were confirmed after German troops had marched into Bulgaria. As promised, the Wehrmacht remained outside a previously agreed security zone. When Germany attacked Yugoslavia and Greece in April, relations with Turkey remained surprisingly free of tension. To the annoyance of the Churchill administration, the Turkish government again evaded its alliance obligations and did not intervene in the conflict. As the Wehrmacht did not extend its operations against Turkey, İnönü saw no reason to endanger his country by some military 'adventure'. Instead, Germany's victories and the ensuing Axis dominance of the Balkans forced Turkey to respond positively to Nazi demands for political negotiations.

On 5 May Hitler did his own bit to pave the way to closer relations to Turkey. In a far cry from his anti-Turkish comments of summer 1939, Germany's dictator openly praised his country's friendship with Turkey. Hitler's commendation was seemingly well received in Turkey. In view of the imminent attack on the Soviet Union it is, of course, easy to guess that Hitler's show of friendliness was a coolly calculated move to ensure Turkey's benevolence, even to entice the country away from its alliance with Britain and towards a fully fledged commitment to the Axis. Just over a week later, Ribbentrop admitted as much in a meeting with Mussolini. Discussions with Turkish government officials followed.

The Turkish reaction was encouraging. On 13 May Saracoglu gave permission – though it was withdrawn two weeks later – for the transit of German war material to assist the anti-British uprising in Iraq, while Inönü showed himself eager to conclude a non-aggression pact with Germany. While intent on improving relations with the Axis, Turkey's President remained, however, strongly opposed to dissolving the country's alliance with Britain. In this objective Inönü proved successful. When it came to signing the agreement, Hitler had to settle for a ten-year Treaty of Friendship in which Turkey promised benevolent neutrality, but which did not force the country to cut its ties with Germany's enemy. Both sides made a commitment to respect each other's territory and to take no hostile measures against each other, either directly or indirectly.[34] With the treaty signed on 18 June 1941 Hitler was able to attack the Soviet Union with Turkey's neutrality assured.

While Germany's direct control over much of the Balkans had already left a noticeable imprint upon German–Turkish relations, the Wehrmacht's advance into the Soviet Union had an even more marked impact. Operation Barbarossa substantially enhanced Turkey's geostrategic position,[35] particularly when the anticipated early victory failed to materialise. With Turkey ideally located as a potential conduit for Anglo-American supplies to the Soviet Union, Hitler had to make sure that President Inönü and his government did not tilt towards the Allies. As it turned out, these efforts were successful until well into 1944. At times, in fact, Turkish officials even considered taking a more wholeheartedly pro-German stance. Apart from Germany's continued military achievements two factors in particular were to assist Germany: the temptations of Pan-Turanism[36] and growing concern about Soviet intentions.

It came as no surprise to Germany's political and military leadership that the Turkish government voiced its appreciation of the invasion of the Soviet Union. After close relations until the mid–1930s, when the Friendship and Neutrality Agreement of 1925 was extended for a further ten years, Turkey and the Soviet Union had started to move apart. By the time of Operation Barbarossa the two countries had come to be extremely distrustful of each other. Despite official pronouncements to the contrary, Turkish concern about the unreliability of the 'Russian bear' antedated the events of the late 1930s. In a significant statement in 1932, Kemal Atatürk had, in fact, prophesied that Germany would start a world war between 1940 and 1945 and that, instead of Germany winning it, Bolshevik expansion would result from it:

> The main winner of a war in Europe will be neither England and France nor Germany, but only Bolshevism. As a nation that is the most fighting one [*sic*] with Russia and a neighbour [*sic*] country that is the nearest one to it, we, Turks, have closely followed the events taking place in this country, and openly seen its dangers for centuries ... Bolsheviks are the most potential power that does not only threaten Europe, but also Asia.[37]

Ever since October 1939, when, to a baffled Turkish delegation, Stalin and Molotov had proposed major changes in the 1936 Montreux Convention on the Straits, the Turkish government had felt growing unease about the intentions of its northern neighbour.[38] The obvious expansionist zeal which Stalin demonstrated in the Balkans, as experienced for instance by Romania in 1940, only added to Turkey's woes. Such concern was deliberately stirred by the Nazi regime when, after the commencement of Operation Barbarossa, it revealed to the Turkish government the demands Molotov had put to the Germans in November 1940. First on the list was the establishment of Soviet bases on the Straits, followed by a pact with Bulgaria to create a Black Sea 'security zone', and finally the recognition of territories south of Batum and Baku down to the Persian Gulf as a Soviet sphere of interest. Put into practice, all these demands would have deeply affected Turkey. Molotov, in fact, anticipated the need to apply diplomatic and military pressure on the country.[39]

It is easy to see Hitler's rationale behind revealing this particular aspect of the November 1940 Soviet–German discussions to the Turkish authorities. Inönü and his government were to be made to believe in the advantageous nature of Germany's eventual victory over the Soviet

Union. Even though the Turkish administration had grounds to remain suspicious of Germany's own intentions, the message appeared to have fallen on fertile ground. Even a year after the anticipated rapid victory of the Wehrmacht had not materialised, Papen was able to report that Saracoglu, Turkey's Minister of Foreign Affairs, and soon-to-be Prime Minister,[40] had affirmed his sincere hope of the fall of the Soviet Union. In addition, he apparently made the extraordinary statement that such a collapse required killing half the Russian population, giving independence to the minorities and turning the latter into enemies of Slavism.[41]

Turkey's positive response to Operation Barbarossa was therefore not guided purely by notions of self-protection. Rather it appears that members of Turkey's elites, including high-ranking government officials, toyed with their own territorial aspirations. German officials were made aware of such intentions very soon after the attack had commenced. At the beginning of August 1941, Hüsrev Gerede, Ankara's pro-German ambassador in Berlin, suggested to Ernst von Weizsäcker, permanent secretary in the AA, that excellent propaganda use could be made of the Russian–Turkish peoples in the areas now occupied, or about to be occupied, by the Wehrmacht. According to Gerede's 'personal opinion' the Axis should arrange for the establishment of an independent 'Turanian' state in the territory between the Black and Caspian Seas.[42]

Such 'advances' coincided with ongoing considerations in Germany. On Hitler's and Ribbentrop's orders, Papen was 'to transform the relationship with Turkey, if possible, into a close alliance in step with [Germany's] military operations'.[43] Among Germany's military leaders, Turkey's future role was a frequent topic of discussion. As Ernst von Weizsäcker succinctly noted only days after his meeting with Gerede: 'Turkey is at the centre of interest. It seems, however, that marching through Turkey *contra voluntatem* is for the time being not seriously contemplated. Makes sense to me!'[44] While he concluded correctly that military action to embroil Turkey in the war was not intended 'for the time being', Weizsäcker appears to have misjudged the level of contemplation in the OKW. As a swift victory over the Soviet Union was still expected, Germany's military leadership was already planning ahead for an invasion of the Middle East and Egypt, with German troops advancing from the Caucasus and via Turkey. Although such plans were never implemented, preliminary approaches were made to the Turkish government. Would the Turkish government, however, have permitted the transit of German troops?

In the light of Gerede's comments to Weizsäcker it could be argued that the Turkish government was tempted by the potential advantages of drawing closer to the Third Reich. Only a few weeks later, however, Gerede backed away from the suggestions he had previously made.[45] It can be assumed that, in view of the Red Army's continued resistance, Inönü and his government had adopted a more cautious attitude – somewhat similar to General Franco's reaction to Britain's stubborn resistance in the previous summer. In Turkey's case, evidence of the continued ability of the Allies to implement pro-active steps added to the caution. Without a doubt, the near-immaculate execution of the Anglo-Soviet invasion of Iran at the end of August constituted just such a step. Yet, as in the case of the admittedly greedier Franco, the temptation did not vanish.

From his reading of British and German primary sources, Weber is convinced that Pan-Turanism was just such a temptation, an 'official program of the Turkish government, continuously though surreptitiously cultivated'.[46] Weisband, on the other hand, adamantly denies that the Pan-Turanian movement ever managed to gain any influence upon the Inönü administration, that the latter ever planned to extend political and cultural dominance over Turkish peoples outside Turkey.[47] Unfortunately, the final word on this debate will have to wait until the relevant Turkish files are opened to examination.

In one respect, scholars clearly agree with Weisband's assertion. Pan-Turanism does not seem to have had any impact upon Turkey's President. Without any doubt, Inönü was careful not to flaunt adventurist or irredentist views, thus keeping up Turkey's official veneer of neutrality. Yet the veneer was clearly thin. Other leading government officials proved to be more susceptible to Pan-Turanian ideas. On 2 June 1941, in a conversation with Knatchbull-Hugessen, a cautious Saracoglu mentioned certain 'injustices' committed in the past which Turkey wanted to rectify when the time was right.[48] Just over a year later, in early August 1942, a much more outspoken Saracoglu introduced his first government pro-gramme by emphasising that 'we are Turks and Turkists. We will remain forever as Turkists. For us, Turkism is a matter of conscience and culture as much as a matter of blood. ... And we will always work in this direction.'[49]

Although, when quoting this speech, Çalis admits that it may have been 'a one-off', Saracoglu's public statement was important in view of Inönü's aversion to such ideas. It was made even more important by the fact that other officials seemingly shared the Prime Minister's sentiments. Both Numen Menemencioglu, first as Secretary General of the Ministry of Foreign Affairs and then as Minister from 1942, and Fevzi Çakmak, Chief of General Staff, were attracted by the views propounded by Pan-Turanists – and ultimately lost their respective positions in consequence.

But Inönü's unceremonious dumping of Menemencioglu in June 1944[50] (and Çakmak's forced retirement in January the same year[51]) occurred, of course, at a time when the star of the one country that could have ensured Pan-Turanist ambitions was rapidly waning. It is therefore advisable to turn our attention to that period during the war when Nazi Germany was still very much on the offensive.

During the second half of 1941, Nazi officials followed Pan-Turanian activities with keen and active interest. In July and September 1941, respectively, two members of a recently formed committee of experts on Turanian affairs, Nuri Pasha[52] and Ahmed Zeki Velidi Togan,[53] travelled to Berlin to discuss their aspirations with the German Foreign Ministry. As outlined by Nuri these included the creation of independent Turk-populated states allied to Turkey and the inauguration of propaganda activity among these people at present under Soviet rule. Though sceptical about the influence of these 'experts' on the Turkish government, the Nazi regime continued its encouragement of Pan-Turanism.[54] As Ernst Woermann, director of the political department of the AA, explained, 'it is obvious that only in alliance with Germany will Turkey be able to implement Pan-Turanian ideas. A Pan-Turanian Turkey will therefore necessarily have to be pro-German.'[55]

One likely way to draw Turkey closer to Germany was by playing upon its perceived irredentist temptations. In July 1941, Papen suggested to Ribbentrop that Turkey's territorial ambitions in northern Syria should be answered. Papen's proposal resulted from a conversation the German ambassador had had with Saracoglu on 9 July. Two days before the British and Free French troops succeeded in their military campaign in Syria, the Turkish foreign minister had inquired whether Germany would agree to his country's occupation of northern Syria 'as a provisional solution until a peace agreement had been signed'.[56] While Saracoglu's appeal was obviously unsuccessful, it proved that the Turkish government was certainly not immune to the temptation of territorial gain. According to Hans Kroll, Papen's first secretary, Aleppo and Mosul were additional targets on Turkey's potential wish list.[57]

In October 1941, Ribbentrop reacted by appointing AA official Otto Erwin von Hentig to act as Germany's contact person to the Pan-Turanian movement. As a former spy in the Middle East and, since 28 June 1941, responsible for matters concerning the 'south-east Russian peoples' within the so-called 'Russia Committee' of the AA, Hentig was regarded as something of an expert. Moreover, in view of Hentig's open support for Pan-Turanism, Germany's foreign minister had clearly opted for somebody who would promote pro-active policies. According to Weber, Hentig intended a major propaganda operation which was to include indoctrination broadcasts to Muslim prisoners of war in German camps, increasing their food rations, and smuggling selected prisoners into 'Turanian' Russia for espionage and subversion. There the population was to be influenced by propaganda leaflets dropped by German planes. Such actions would prepare 'Turanian' Russia for independence after Germany's victory over the Soviet Union.[58] Taken to its ultimate stage, Hentig looked forward to the unification of all Turkic people between the Volga and the Great Wall under the political leadership of Turkey.[59]

Papen, as Weber asserts, may well have been enthusiastic about Hentig's immediate plans, yet the American historian keeps strangely quiet about the response higher up the Nazi hierarchy. Would Hitler really have abandoned hard-won territory in an effort to please Turkey and the Pan-Turanists? It seems a very unlikely assumption indeed, in view of Hitler's firm claim on areas dear to Pan-Turanists. In a July 1941 meeting with Hermann Göring, Karl Lammers and Alfred Rosenberg, Hitler called for the Crimea, the Baku oilfields and the Volga region to be turned into German military colonies. Consequently, Hitler argued against making Turkey any promises in these areas.[60]

Even if Hitler had been supportive of Hentig's plans, their implementation would not automatically have satisfied Turkish Pan-Turanist aspirations. For one, by early 1942, the Nazi regime had come to the realisation that not all Soviet Turanians shared Turkish Pan-Turanian sentiments. Supported by Gustav Hilger, Friedrich Werner von der Schulenburg, last German ambassador to the Soviet Union, warned that the 'broad masses of the Islamic population of the Soviet Union were not at all attracted by the Pan-Turanian idea'.[61] Those Armenians, Azerbaijanis, Georgians *et al.* who rejected Moscow did not necessarily want to have it replaced by Ankara. In January 1942, Ribbentrop concluded that steps to please Turkey's territorial aspirations should still be taken, but not to the extent that they would cause trouble with the Turanians at present under Soviet rule. Support for Turkish Pan-Turanism was notably toned down and even the planned four Turkic Wehrmacht legions were not to carry the Turanian label.[62]

In early 1942, the Nazi regime opted for more caution on Pan-Turanism, though it continued to woo Turkey towards making a more fully fledged commitment to the Axis. Comments by Turkish officials were encouraging (though Turkish officials also expressed promising views to the western Allies). On 23 February 1942, Papen was able to report that Asim Gündüz, second-in-command of Turkey's general staff, had shown

himself interested in some form of secret co-operation with the Wehrmacht general staff. Beyond that, Gündüz even indicated that, once
German troops had reached the Caucasus, Turkey would have to take
account of the situation. In a similarly semi-committed way, Inönü told
Papen that 'he hoped that the arrival of German troops in the Caucasus in
autumn would create a new situation in which it would then be necessary
to take new decisions'.[63] Inönü continued, however, to keep his distance
from the Turanist movement. While Turanists were not prevented from
conducting their activities, official encouragement was painstakingly
avoided. Yet behind the scenes, German agents concluded, Pan-Turanism
still acted as a powerful magnet.

In mid–1942, with the Wehrmacht again on the advance and nearing
the Caucasus,[64] Papen was confronted by Saracoglu and Menemencioglu
about the future of the Turkic peoples in the Soviet Union. Within weeks
of Saracoglu's outspoken inaugural speech (see above) both he and his
foreign minister were again demanding the creation of a series of Turkic
buffer states along the Turkish border. In addition, both desired a say in
the administration of these territories. In conjunction with plans to
educate local youth in German and Turkish universities (to cleanse them
of Communism and instil in them Turkish nationalism) the way was to be
cleared for Turkish hegemony over these areas – though, of course, neither
Saracoglu nor Menemencioglu admitted this openly.[65] Still, the new
foreign minister was audacious enough to suggest to Papen that a written
promise to transfer Syria to Turkey at the end of the war might help to
accelerate chromite deliveries.[66]

Again, however, Turkish expansionist aspirations clashed with Hitler's
objectives. Not surprisingly, the Führer was not at all inclined to make
territorial concessions to a country which had not even committed itself to
the German war effort. On 12 September 1942, he ordered Papen to sus-
pend all talks on such matters until the Turkish government was prepared
'to change its overall political attitude in our favour against the belligerent
powers'. While the Pan-Turanist movement continued to occupy Turkey
at a domestic level,[67] in German–Turkish relations it ceased to be an issue.

German–Turkish relations after Stalingrad

Ever since the Turkish government had entered into a Treaty of Friendship
with Germany in June 1941, it had found itself in the curious situation of
being 'ally' to one belligerent side, Britain, and 'friend' of the other, Nazi

Germany. As a result, services were rendered to both sides. From mid–1941 Germany benefited, for instance, from Turkey's generous interpretation of the Straits Convention. Ships which were subsequently used for military purposes were allowed through the Straits under the official guise of commercial vessels. Nor, until early summer 1944, did the Turkish authorities ever intervene against the passage of ships carrying German troops and war material. In fact, even before Germany's attack on the Soviet Union, Saracoglu had informed Papen of his government's willingness to tolerate such transports. While the Turkish authorities insisted on the strict application of the Montreux Convention against the Soviet Union, Germany's Kriegsmarine (and also the British navy) was able to benefit from Turkey's tolerance.[68]

Despite Hitler's high hopes, however, Germany's military advance into the Soviet Union did not induce the Turkish government to join the Axis powers. Steps such as the concentration of twenty-six Turkish divisions on the border with the Soviet Union (in mid–1942) did not satisfy Nazi expectations. Evidently, Turkey would provide more substantial assistance only when the Wehrmacht had dealt the Red Army a decisive blow. Yet, during the last months of 1942, such a scenario became increasingly unlikely. By the beginning of November – not surprisingly coinciding with the Allied landings in North Africa – German observers detected a noticeable change of atmosphere in Turkish government circles.[69]

While Nazi hopes of a more compliant Turkish government were fading, similar British expectations also remained unfulfilled. In general, the Turkish government remained suspicious of Britain's alliance with the Soviet Union. It was also highly concerned about the extent to which the Allies would materially support a Turkish entry into the war. This issue proved to be the sticking point of a number of high-level negotiations during 1943, commencing with the Churchill–Inönü meeting at Adana at the end of January and ending with the Churchill–Roosevelt–Inönü summit in Cairo in December.[70]

At a time when the German authorities were trying to satisfy Turkish requests for arms, British officials were likewise engaged in attempts to raise the equipment level of Turkey's armed forces. In doing so, both belligerent sides were influenced by markedly different objectives. While Hitler and his regime viewed the supply of arms as a bargaining tool in their quest for Turkish chrome (see below), Germany's enemies were aiming much higher. For Churchill, Turkey's entry into the war constituted the foremost target. To the relief of the Germans, who proved to be well informed about Anglo-Turkish negotiations,[71] the British failed in their objective. To a certain extent German actions helped to bring about this failure.

Despite the obvious military decline of the Axis in 1943, Inönü and his government frequently put off Allied demands by pointing at Germany's continued ability to strike back. Churchill came to believe that he needed to counter this perception to bring Turkey round to the side of the Allies. An ideal opportunity arose after Italy's surrender in September, which opened up the possibility of taking over the Italian-held islands in the Aegean sea. In Churchill's own words, capturing Rhodes 'might be decisive on Turkey'.[72] Yet the plan backfired miserably when German troops took control of Rhodes on 13 September and subsequently recaptured Leros, Kos, Samos and a few other islands from the British forces who had landed there in September.

If Inönü required any proof of Germany's continued military capabilities, the fate of the Aegean islands provided ample evidence. It strengthened his will to stick to a promise he had given Papen in May 1943 after the latter had returned from official talks in Germany. There, Hitler and Ribbentrop had told the German ambassador to seek reassurances that the Turkish government would not abandon its policy of neutrality. Inönü was happy to oblige, as 'he and the Turkish government were unshakably committed to staying out of the war. [According to Inönü] Turkey was rearming only in order to be able to cope with any possible developments in Europe.'[73] Yet in view of regular meetings between high-ranking Allied and Turkish officials, the Nazi regime continued to be concerned about the possibility of Turkey joining the Allied camp. During the second half of 1943, and into 1944, the Nazi regime was therefore engaged in a policy of carrot-and-stick towards Turkey.

Indirectly, Germany's occupation of the Aegean islands made up one aspect of the latter approach. More directly, the 'stick' was used by Papen. In early 1944, the German ambassador repeatedly threatened Turkish officials with a German–Bulgarian invasion of Turkey and air attacks against Istanbul and Izmir should Turkey adopt a more favourable attitude towards the Allies. On the other hand, Papen also tried to woo the Turkish government by promising Germany's utmost resistance on the eastern front. When Hitler insisted on holding the Wehrmacht's last positions in the Crimea, he emphasised the negative effect a withdrawal would have on Turkey.

Yet the Crimea was lost in April 1944 and, unbeknown to the Turkish government, the OKW had already abandoned the possibility of an invasion of Turkey in January. At the same time, Turkey's commitment to neutrality came under increasing fire from the Allies. In April 1944, the Turkish government finally yielded to the primary demand of the Allies. On the 20th of the month, Menemencioglu announced the cessation of chromite supplies to Germany. This trade had been the central component of Germany's economic relations with Turkey for the previous sixteen months. The impact of Turkish chromite on the country's relations with the Third Reich will therefore be analysed in the following section.

Turkish chromite

Although regular economic relations had been pursued by the German and Turkish governments since 1940, Turkey's importance to the rapacious German war economy was only truly enhanced in 1943. Prior to 1942, trade between the two countries had been a very low-key affair despite frequent economic talks and negotiations. In the Treaty of 18 June 1941 each side had made unspecified economic commitments to the other. Since the commercial agreement of 25 July 1940 had been of only very limited value, both regimes viewed economic negotiations as of the utmost necessity. Not at all satisfied with British arms supplies, Turkey was keen to ensure sizeable quantities of German war material. In this quest it benefited from the fact that the Nazi regime was desperate to secure Turkish chromite for Germany's war production.

The deterioration of German–Turkish economic relations in the second half of 1939, followed by their near collapse in 1940, had had a marked effect on German chromite imports. At a time when the Nazi regime was keen to ensure adequate supplies of strategic raw materials, it was faced with a massive decline in imports of chromite. In 1941, largely owing to the absence of ore supplies from Turkey, Germany's purchases of chromite abroad (25,400 mt) sank to 14.4 per cent of their 1938 level (176,400 mt).[74]

During the first half of the war, the German war economy was deprived of Turkish chromite not simply by the inclement nature of bilateral trade relations. In January 1940, Britain and France had taken advantage of Turkey's refusal to sell chromite to Germany by concluding a comprehensive purchasing agreement.[75] It gave the Western powers the exclusive right to purchase all of Turkey's chromite production and stocks for two years. Turkey was permitted to produce a maximum of 250,000 mt a year, with 200,00 mt destined for Britain and France and the remainder for the United States. Even when Germany's defeat of France disrupted the original arrangement, Britain and the United States continued to enjoy an

Table 4.2   *Total Turkish exports to Germany, 1940–43*

Year	Million RM
1940	51
1941	82
1942	100
1943	160

Source: Boelcke, *Deutschland als Welthandelsmacht*, 141.

Table 4.3   *Total German exports to Turkey, 1940–43*

Year	Million RM
1940	13
1941	26
1942	109
1943	250

Source: Boelcke, *Deutschland als Welthandelsmacht*, 141.

import monopoly.[76] From 1940 to the beginning of 1941 Britain imported 79,095 mt of chromite while a further 66,120 mt went to the US.[77] The main object of the British government, namely to deprive Nazi Germany of its Turkish chromite supplies, was achieved, though at a price. As a *quid pro quo* the Turkish government forced Britain to import some of the agricultural produce previously purchased by Germany.

Judging from comments by German officials, the Inönü administration kept to its side of the bargain. In fact, Anglo-Turkish negotiations in August 1941 resulted in an extension of the chromite agreement for a further year, to 8 January 1943. In anticipation of the exhaustion of chromite stocks in early 1942, the Nazi regime put considerable pressure on the Turkish government to release chromite in 1942.[78] For the time being, however, the Turkish government remained committed to its agreement with Britain. On 27 September 1941, Carl Clodius, then in charge of commercial negotiations with the Turkish government, confirmed 'that all attempts have failed to induce Turkey to supply chromite before January 1943'.[79] Yet despite strong objections by Clodius and the OKW, who were opposed to supplies of German arms to Turkey if chrome was not forthcoming,

Papen was able to sway government opinion in favour of a trade agreement. It was concluded on 9 October 1941. As far as chromite supplies were concerned, the German government had to settle for deliveries to recommence after the expiry of the British monopoly of exports of the raw material.

In October 1941 it was agreed that, from 15 January 1943, Germany would again be permitted to import Turkish chromite – to be precise, 180,000 mt until the end of 1944. Hence a Janus-faced Turkish government showed no reluctance to permit exports to Nazi Germany despite Britain's obvious interest in preventing precisely that scenario. Why else would the British government have pushed for a costly agreement in 1940 and its renewal in 1941? Why did the Turkish government not await a further request for a renewal of the agreement before signing away supplies to the Nazi regime? Again, Turkey's alliance with Britain did not pull sufficient weight to overcome a mixture of *realpolitisch* and opportunistic considerations.

One obvious political and military motive has been ascertained before. Already well placed on the Balkans, the Wehrmacht's military advance in the Soviet Union was also bringing it closer to other territories bordering upon Turkey. Yet the Turkish government was also swayed by economic considerations. Despite the chrome agreement with Britain the economy was suffering from the absence of the kind of trade the country had enjoyed with Germany before the war. Moreover, in view of the objectives Atatürk had set out in two successive four-year plans in 1934 and 1938, the Inönü administration hungered for products which would provide a thrust to modernising the country. Moving away from its more liberal economic policies of the 1920s, the Turkish regime had found itself attracted to the economic policies adopted by the Nazi, Fascist and Soviet regimes. In the 1930s and during the war,

> the main principles followed [by Turkey] were autarchy and tariff protection as well as state-sponsored industrialization particularly in such fields as metallurgy, textiles, and glass. These economic activities, undertaken through two major public holding companies (the Etibank for mining and electric power and the Sümerbank for manufacturing), added to the government's economic activities in public transport and utilities, in the state monopolies (tobacco, alcoholic beverages), and in the armaments industry.[80]

Turkish modernisation efforts included the country's armed forces. Until his death, Atatürk had pursued the acquisition of modern military technology in order to establish Turkey as a significant regional power.[81] On the eve of the Second World War, Turkey continued, however, to be inadequately prepared for the demands of modern warfare. According to the sober assessment of one Turkish army commander, 'a new era had dawned in the techniques and tactics of war. We were just learning the rules of the First World War. Our arms, tactics and technique dated from that time.'[82] After the outbreak of war in 1939, Inönü pursued the modernisation of Turkey's armed forces with great urgency – in particular by appealing to Turkey's alliance partners Britain and France. Yet despite British (and very limited French) supplies of war material, Turkey's military, dissatisfied with the quantities provided by Britain, desired renewed imports of German arms by mid–1941.[83]

The trade agreement of October 1941 certainly boosted the hopes of Turkey's economic and military elites. Both sides pledged to ensure an exchange of goods valued at a projected RM 200 million in each direction until 31 March 1943. Germany was to regain the position of Turkey's most important trading partner.[84] While Germany negotiated for supplies of cotton, copper, oil, tobacco, other agricultural products and, of course, future supplies of chromite, industrial machinery and railways figured heavily on the Turkish wish list, as did war material.[85]

Attention has been drawn to Hitler's mid-1939 pronouncement against the continuation of arms exports to Turkey. Hitler's opposition, however, was not total. At various times between late 1939 and 1941 Hitler considered releasing blocked German products to Turkey – always, however, on condition that chromite was forthcoming. In the October 1941 agreement the Nazi negotiators finally settled for the release of RM 36 million of war material before 31 March 1943[86] and of RM 10 million between 1 April 1943 and 31 December 1944 – all, of course, in exchange for chromite supplies.[87] For the period 15 January and 31 March 1943 Turkey guaranteed the delivery of 45,000 mt, the supply of which had been agreed upon in a contract between the Krupp company and Etibank on 24 August 1942.[88] A further 135,000 mt of chromite was to follow between 1 April 1943 and 31 December 1944.

Despite the agreement, Hitler continued to have concerns about Turkish requests for arms. In autumn 1942, for instance, he queried the negotiations about equipping Turkey with a tank division: 'Are they not one day going to attack us with these tank divisions?'[89] When war material was released, it was initially seldom of up-to-date quality. Finally, however, towards the end of 1942, the German dictator was forced to accept a more wholehearted return to his regime's earlier pro-export approach. Hitler's armaments minister, Albert Speer, played a central role in the Führer's change of mind.

Table 4.4 *German arms exports to Turkey, 1937–43 (contracts only)*

Year	Million RM
1937	14.6
1938	11.7
1940	0.08
1941	0.5
1942	136.0[a]
1943	8.4[b]

Notes: [a] Ten per cent of total German arms export contracts
[b] 0.6 per cent of German arms export contracts.
Source: Boelcke, *Deutschland als Welthandelsmacht*, 142.

While the OKW appeared to have encouraged Hitler in his scepticism, Speer made it abundantly clear that imports of Turkish chromite were of 'extraordinary importance to the war effort' and that supplies of German war material should therefore be speeded up.[90] Hitler seemed to have accepted his minister's position on the matter. In early 1943 more attention was paid to fulfilling the massive number of deals German exporters had signed with the Turkish authorities in 1942. In that year the total sum of contracts with Turkey by far exceeded that of all other war years combined. Not only that, but, in total terms for 1942, 10 per cent of Germany's total export deals were concluded with Turkey.

To allow the notoriously cash-strapped Turkish government to make such purchases, the Nazi regime consented to extend credit facilities to a total of RM 100 million. Forty per cent of the agreement was taken up by supplies from the aircraft producer Focke-Wulf while Krupp, Rheinmetall and Daimler-Benz products accounted for most of the remainder.[91] After the credit agreement had been signed on 31 December 1942,[92] Turkey was to receive the contracted RM 136 million of war material by the end of March 1943, while Germany was to take delivery of 45,000 mt of chromite by the end of 1943. As usual, however, in Nazi foreign trade relations, an insurmountable chasm opened up between plan and reality – despite Speer's earlier strong words. The gap between contracted and actual exports to Turkey, which Clodius already had to admit in September 1942,[93] continued to grow.

New negotiations were therefore arranged for April 1943. Clodius returned to the negotiating table in Ankara and quickly managed to conclude a new agreement with the Turkish government. On 18 April, the day the agreement was signed, a contented Menemencioglu was able to announce that Turkey continued to be keen to promote economic relations between his country and Germany in any way possible. In concrete terms, this meant that, until the expiry of the agreement on 31 May 1944, Germany could look forward to deliveries of RM 240 million worth of vital raw materials and food. Clodius proudly reported back to the AA that 'Germany is taking in over half of Turkey's total exports. Indeed, of the most important minerals, chromite and copper, it is to receive by far the greatest part of the country's total production.'[94]

Yet the first chromite consignment of 45,000 mt did not arrive as speedily as the German government had hoped. By 6 November 1943, the Turkish authorities had issued licences for only 30,500 mt – just under 100 per cent of Germany's total chromite supplies in 1943[95] – owing to the fact that the Nazis had not supplied the promised quantities of arms on time.[96] Instead of late March 1943, the Turkish military were, in fact, forced to wait until late April 1944 before the importation of all the German arms previously guaranteed was completed.[97] The delay also meant that the negotiations for the second chromite agreement took place later than originally planned. Finally, on 22 October 1943, Krupp and Etibank signed the contract for the supply of the outstanding 135,000 mt of ore.

Even though less than half the total amount contracted (83,000 mt) reached Germany before Menemencioglu announced the cessation of chromite exports to Germany on 20 April 1944, the stocks accumulated covered some 80 per cent of Germany's chrome consumption.[98] Papen (and hence the German government) had been well aware of the ever-growing pressure the Allies were exerting on the Turkish government to end its obvious support of Germany's war economy. For months the British government had been lobbying the Turkish government while restraining the more impatient efforts of the US administration. On 14 April 1944, finally, a joint note to the Turkish government demanded the total cessation of chrome exports to Germany.[99]

Yet when the announcement was made only a week later, it came as a complete surprise to both sides. Almost right to the last minute the German embassy had been bombarding the Turkish government with a mixture of appeals and threats. Yet in view of the rapid decline of Germany's military position – the loss of the Crimea preceded Menemencioglu's announcement – the Turkish government finally succumbed to the inevitable – though it secretly permitted further deliveries until 1 May.

After 20 April 1944, the economic relationship between Turkey and the Third Reich experienced a massive decline. In the first instance, this was, of course, due to the embargo itself as it annulled the vital component of Turkey's trade with Germany. The effect of the embargo was aggravated in its immediate aftermath by a German transport blockade on goods to Turkey.[100] Finally, at the end of May and beginning of June 1944, the Allies contributed to the severe disruption of Turkey's communication links with the rest of Europe by bombing twenty-one bridges along or near the border between Bulgaria and Turkey.[101]

Attempts to keep economic relations between Turkey and Germany afloat met with little success. Although the Turkish government endeavoured to interest the Nazi regime in other goods, including cotton,[102] none was of even remotely the same attraction as chromite. As Speer was to write to Hitler on 5 September 1944 – a comment which the latter apparently ignored – the armaments production battle would be decided not by the loss of Finland's nickel mines, but by the cessation of chromite supplies from Turkey – which had, of course, already ended.[103]

By then, in fact, all relations with Turkey had ceased. In mid-June, after the so-called *Kassel* affair,[104] the Turkish government announced a ban on German ships passing through the Straits. The signing of a confidential trade protocol on 18 July 1944, while ensuring the official continuation of economic relations between Germany and Turkey, ultimately served only a propaganda purpose – and only for a very brief period. On 31 July 1944, in a brief telegram to the AA, Papen reported that 'owing to the political situation' he had requested the German mission in Bulgaria to 'immediately order the cessation of all German supplies of goods to Turkey'.[105] Two days later, the Turkish government brought its diplomatic relations with the Third Reich to an end.[106]

Notes

1 British Foreign Office official (Chancery), 24 September 1941, in John Robertson, *Turkey and Allied Strategy 1941–1945* (New York and London, 1986), 75.

2 PA/AA R106418, Becker (OKW) to Wiehl (AA), 22 July 1939; see also Hans-Erich Volkmann, 'Außenhandel und Aufrüstung in Deutschland 1933 bis 1939', in Volkmann and Friedrich Forstmeier (eds), *Wirtschaft und Rüstung am Vorabend des Zweiten Weltkrieges* (Düsseldorf, 1975), 95.

3 See Christian Leitz, 'Arms Exports in the Third Reich 1933–1939: the Example of Krupp', *Economic History Review* LI (1998), 133–54. In 1937 Turkey ranked third (behind China and Hungary) on the list of Germany's customers, taking 8.3 per cent of its arms exports.

4 See various documents in BA 09.01/68459 AA Abt. W, Handel mit Kriegsgerät, Türkei, Bd. 1; see also Johannes Glasneck and Inge Kircheisen, *Türkei und Afghanistan. Brennpunkte der Orientpolitik im zweiten Weltkrieg* (East Berlin, 1968), 44–6. A contract for the supply of sixty Messerschmitt 109 fighters was signed in April 1939 but subsequently cancelled on Göring's orders; see BA 09.01/68460, Müller (RLM) to AA, 6 October 1939.

5 See the lengthy list of company representatives who discussed the *Türken-Verträge* (Turkey contracts) on 2 February 1940 in BA 09.01/68460.

6 Baynes (ed.), *The Speeches of Adolf Hitler*, vol. II, 1680.

7 Treaty reproduced in Selim Deringil, *Turkish Foreign Policy during the Second World War: an 'Active' Neutrality* (Cambridge, 1989), 189–92.

8 Edgar Bonjour, 'Türkische und schweizerische Neutralität während des zweiten Weltkrieges', in Saul Friedländer, Harish Kapur and André Reszler (eds), *L'historien et les relations internationales; recueil d'études en hommage à Jacques Freymond* (Geneva, 1981), 199.

9 Quotation in Selim Deringil, 'Turkish Reactions to European Crises 1943', in Roulet (ed.) *Les états neutres*, 167.

10 For having declared war on Germany before 1 March 1945, the deadline set by the Allies, Turkey was permitted to participate in the founding session of the United Nations in San Francisco.

11 Deringil, *Turkish Foreign Policy*, 55 and 63–4.

12 On Atatürk and Fascist Italy see Brock Millman, 'Turkish Foreign and Strategic Policy 1934–1942', *Middle Eastern Studies* 31 (1995), 485–7.

13 Feroz Ahmad, *The Making of Modern Turkey* (London, 1994), 64.

14 Baynes (ed.), *Speeches of Adolf Hitler*, 1577.

15 Boelcke, *Deutschland als Welthandelsmacht*, 92–3.

16 Although historians frequently refer to Turkish chromium or chrome, chromite, or chrome iron ore, is, in fact, the correct term; see *Rutley's Elements of Mineralogy* (London, 27th edn, 1988), rev. C. D. Gribble, 191.

17 In a major economic congress only months after the foundation of the Turkish Republic, Atatürk had set out to advance the industrialisation of his country. A slow process during his lifetime, the pursuit of modernising Turkey's economy continued after his death; see Bahri Yilmaz, 'Die wirtschaftliche Entwicklung der Türkei von 1923 bis 1980', *Südosteuropa Mitteilungen* 33 (1993), 351–5.

18 Intended as a large component of Turkey's second five-year plan, the credit agreement was to provide the country with mining installations, an agricultural development programme, power plants, rolling stock and merchant vessels; Deringil, *Turkish Foreign Policy*, 26–7.

19 See BA 09.01/68751, memo by Wiehl, 27 February 1942.

20 See Brock Millman, 'Credit and Supply in Turkish Foreign Policy and the Tripartite Alliance of October 1939: a Note', *International History Review* XVI (1994), for an account of the failure of Britain and France to counter Germany's trade policy.

21 The new ambassador, Franz von Papen, Hitler's first Vice-chancellor, arrived in Ankara on 27 April 1939.

22 Klaus Schönherr, 'Die türkische Außenpolitik vom Vorabend des Zweiten Weltkrieges bis 1941', *Österreichische Osthefte* 36 (1994), 302.

23 In *The Evasive Neutral; Germany, Britain and the Quest for a Turkish Alliance in the Second World War* (Columbia MO, 1979), 36, Frank G. Weber erroneously asserts that the declaration had little impact on Germany's relations with Turkey.

24 Deringil, *Turkish Foreign Policy*, 27.

25 *Ibid.*, 97.

26 The agreement covered the exchange of Turkish agricultural products (tobacco, oilseed, barley, olive oil, mohair, nuts, hides, raisins) against German industrial products (railway engines and wagons).

27 The Turkish government used the so-called 'Russia clause' to get itself out of its alliance obligations, i.e. it claimed that entering the war would result in a military conflict with the Soviet Union.

28 Deringil, *Turkish Foreign Policy*, 99.

29 Declaration abridged in *ibid.*, 105.

30 Zehra Önder, *Die türkische Außenpolitik im Zweiten Weltkrieg* (Munich, 1977), 61–3.

31 Glasneck and Kircheisen, *Türkei und Afghanistan*, 59.

32 Weber, *Evasive Neutral*, 96.

33 Schönherr, 'Die türkische Außenpolitik', 310.

34 Glasneck and Kircheisen, *Türkei und Afghanistan*, 71–5; Önder, *Die türkische Außenpolitik*, 121–4.

35 'Situated between Europe and Asia, bordering on Greece, Bulgaria, the USSR, Iran, Iraq and Syria, Turkey was and still is the link between the two continents. ... The important geostrategic position in the eastern Mediterranean and her control of the Straits made sure that the country was a sought-after partner'; Klaus Schönherr, 'Neutrality, "Non-belligerence", or War; Turkey and the European Powers' Conflict of Interests 1939–1941', in Bernd Wegner (ed.), *From Peace to War; Germany, Soviet Russia and the World 1939–1941* (Providence RI and Oxford, 1997), 481.

36 Although some scholars prefer to use the term Pan-Turkism over the broader concept of Pan-Turanism, I have decided to adopt the latter, owing to its much more frequent use by Nazi officials (and many Turkish Pan-Turkists). According to Charles Warren Hostler, cited in Edward Weisband, *Turkish Foreign Policy 1943–1945; Small State Diplomacy and Great Power Politics* (Princeton NJ, 1973), 237 n. 27, the difference between Pan-Turkism and Pan-Turanism is that the former 'was born under the reciprocal influence of the Eastern Turks threatened by "Russianization", and Western Turks exposed to Russian expansion. Pan-Turanism (seeking unity among Turkish, Mongol and Finnish-Ugrian peoples), in contrast to Pan-Turkism (seeking unity of Turkish peoples), followed in the wake of Russian expansion in the Balkans, and is correlated to Turkish and Hungarian experiments in anti-Slav collaboration.' See Jacob M. Landau, *Pan-Turkism; From Irredentism to Cooperation* (London, 2nd edn, 1995) for a comprehensive examination of the subject.

37 Şaban Çalis, 'Pan-Turkism and Europeanism: a note on Turkey's "pro-German neutrality" during the Second World War', *Central Asian Survey* 16 (1997), 108–9. Interpreting the same statement, Millman accords more importance to Atatürk's concern with Germany as the long-term threat. That Atatürk apparently predicted Germany's eventual defeat and the emergence of the

Soviet Union as one of the two remaining great powers (the United States being the other) lends, however, more credence to Çalis's anti-Bolshevik interpretation; Millman, 'Turkish Foreign and Strategic Policy', 487 and 505 n. 27.

38 In June 1936 the demilitarisation of the Straits and neighbouring territories was ended, while the Straits Commission and with it international control of the Straits was abolished. Turkish troops immediately occupied the demilitarised zone and the country was granted supervisory powers over all shipping through the Straits; see Ernst Tennstedt, *Die türkischen Meerengen unter der Konvention von Montreux im Zweiten Weltkrieg* (Hamburg, 1981), 5–6.

39 Önder, *Die türkische Außenpolitik*, 72–3; Çalis, 'Pan-Turkism and Europeanism', 104.

40 Saracoglu succeeded Refik Saydam in July 1942.

41 Deringil, *Turkish Foreign Policy*, 131–2. British officials frequently commented on Turkey's hostility towards Russia, or as Orme Sargent put it in August 1941, 'the Turkish disease (Russophobia)'; Robertson, *Turkey and Allied Strategy*, 63.

42 Weber, *Evasive Neutral*, 110.

43 BA 09.01/68461, memo by Papen (for Ribbentrop), 20 September 1941.

44 Leonidas E. Hill (ed.), *Die Weizsäcker-Papiere 1933–1950* (Frankfurt, Berlin and Vienna, 1974), 263, dated 13 August 1941.

45 Gerede apparently confided to German officials that, personally, he continued to sympathise with Pan-Turanism, but was not able to do so publicly; Glasneck and Kircheisen, *Türkei und Afghanistan*, 110.

46 Weber, *Evasive Neutral*, 113.

47 Weisband, *Turkish Foreign Policy 1943–1945*, 246 ff.

48 Olmert, 'Britain, Turkey and the Levant Question during the Second World War', *Middle Eastern Studies* 23 (1987), 447.

49 Çalis, 'Pan-Turkism and Europeanism', 107.

50 Menemencioglu was succeeded by Saracoglu, who again, as he had done briefly in 1942, held both the position of Prime Minister and that of foreign minister.

51 According to the official explanation for Çakmak's departure he had contributed to a worsening of Anglo-Turkish relations by making exaggerated demands for arms. In addition, it was stated that his conservative attitude had prevented the modernisation of the Turkish army; Önder, *Die türkische Außenpolitik*, 229.

52 Brother of Enver Pasha, who as Minister of War bore the major responsibility for bringing the Ottoman Empire into the war in 1914 on the side of Germany. During the first six months of the Russian campaign the Pan-Turanist generals Hüsnü E. Erkilet and Ali Fuad Erdem were also met by German officials. Erkilet was taken on a tour of the eastern front.

53 In the 1920s Togan conducted Turcological research in Germany to which he returned from 1932 until 1938. On Togan see Landau, *Pan-Turkism*, 95.

54 Deringil, *Turkish Foreign Policy*, 131. According to Weber, Nuri Pasha had been briefed by Saracoglu before his departure, while Gerede paid his expenses; Weber, *Evasive Neutral*, 114.

55 Glasneck and Kircheisen, *Türkei und Afghanistan*, 107.

56 Önder, *Die türkische Außenpolitik*, 120.

57 Deringil, *Turkish Foreign Policy*, 140. Kroll's view that Turkey would be keen to regain Aleppo and Mosul (the latter owing to its oil resources) was shared by the British Foreign Office; see Olmert, 'Britain, Turkey and the Levant Question', 438.

58 Weber, *Evasive Neutral*, 116–17.

59 Glasneck and Kircheisen, *Türkei und Afghanistan*, 101.

60 *Ibid.*, 102–3.

61 *Ibid.*, 103.

62 Weber, *Evasive Neutral*, 124–5. Around the same time the Pan-Turanian enthusiast Hentig was replaced as contact person by envoy von Tippelskirch, though Hentig continued to produce reports about meetings with leading Pan-Turanists.

63 Glasneck and Kircheisen, *Türkei und Afghanistan*, 83–4.

64 Sevastopol was taken in May, followed by the occupation of the Ukraine.

65 Glasneck and Kircheisen, *Türkei und Afghanistan*, 111.

66 Weber, *Evasive Neutral*, 151.

67 See Landau, *Pan-Turkism*, 116–17, for the actions taken by the Turkish government against Pan-Turanists in spring 1944.

68 Önder, *Die türkische Außenpolitik*, 117.

69 See Glasneck and Kircheisen, *Türkei und Afghanistan*, 88–9.

70 Detailed information on relations between Turkey and the Allies can be found in Deringil, *Turkish Foreign Policy*, Önder, *Die türkische Außenpolitik*, Robertson, *Turkey and Allied Strategy*, and Weisband, *Turkish Foreign Policy 1943–1945*.

71 From October 1943 to March 1944 Elyasa Bazna, valet to the British ambassador Knatchbull-Hugessen, supplied Germany with a regular flow of information on British plans and the state of Anglo-Turkish relations; see Ludwig C. Moyzisch, trans. Constantine Fitzgibbon and Heinrich Fraenkel, *Operation Cicero* (London and New York, 1950) and Glasneck and Kircheisen, *Türkei und Afghanistan*, 143.

72 Deringil, 'Turkish Reactions', 172.

73 Glasneck and Kircheisen, *Türkei und Afghanistan*, 138.

74 *Ibid.*, 141, 200 n. 138; Glasneck and Kircheisen, *Türkei und Afghanistan*, 154.

75 See Robertson, *Turkey and Allied Strategy*, 65–70.

76 After the defeat of France the Turkish government ceded all the rights and obligations of the French under the chromite agreement to the British government; BA 09.01/68461, Clodius and Kroll to AA, 17 September 1941.

77 Boelcke, *Deutschland als Welthandelsmacht*, 200 n. 138.

78 BA 09.01/68461, memo by Papen (for Ribbentrop), 20 September 1941.

79 Boelcke, *Deutschland als Welthandelsmacht*, 141. Misjudging the situation, the Nazis considered taking over the chromite set aside by the Turkish government for France; BA 09.01/68461, Maltzan (AA) to Heise (RWM), 3 September 1941. Despite Turkey's contractual obligation to Britain, Menemencioglu had apparently offered Papen the French share of the agreement on a previous occasion, yet, surprisingly enough, the German government refused with the comment that Germany's needs were covered, presumably by supplies from the Soviet Union; Önder, *Die türkische Außenpolitik*, 107.

80 Dankwart A. Rustow, 'Politics and Development Policy', in Frederic C. Shorter (ed.), *Four Studies on the Economic Development of Turkey* (London, 1967), 14–15.

81 Gary Leiser, 'The Turkish Air force 1939–45: the Rise of a Minor Power', *Middle Eastern Studies* 26 (1990), 383.

82 Deringil, *Turkish Foreign Policy*, 38. On the woeful state of Turkey's armed forces in the late 1930s see *ibid.*, 32–8.

83 After the Turkish government had signed the chrome agreement with the Allies in 1940, Saracoglu repeatedly promised a continuation of chromite supplies to Germany if all arms supply contracts were completely carried out (see, for instance, BA 09.01/68461, memo by Papen, 14 March 1940). Hitler was, however, willing to release only limited amounts of armaments; see various lists of war material (*bedingungslos lieferbar, teilweise lieferbar, nicht lieferbar*) in *ibid.*, Süßkind-Schwendi (RWM) to Ripken (AA), 17 April 1940.

84 In 1943 imports from Turkey jumped from RM 100 million to RM 160 million while exports to Turkey more than doubled from RM 109 million to RM 250 million; Boelcke, *Deutschland als Welthandelsmacht*, 141.

85 On 28 June 1942, a syndicate of German companies concluded a contract with the directors of Turkey's state railways. Turkey was to receive fifteen locomotives, 200–300 wagons, parts and machinery to a total value of RM 22 million. Other deliveries of industrial material also increased during the second half of 1942; Glasneck and Kircheisen, *Türkei und Afghanistan*, 95–6.

86 A detailed list of supplies can be found in BA 09.01/68765, Faik Hozar (in charge of Turkish delegation) to Clodius, 31 December 1942.

87 BA 09.01/68751, memo by Wiehl, 27 February 1942. On Hitler's attitude see, *inter alia*, BA 09.01/68460, OKW to Spindler (RWM), 24 February 1940.

88 BA 09.01/68765, Süßkind-Schwendi to Speer, 15 November 1943. Etibank set up and owned Eastern Chromite, the company responsible for the mining of Turkey's chromite reserves.

89 Önder, *Die türkische Außenpolitik*, 136–7.

90 BA 09.01/68765, Süßkind-Schwendi to Speer, 15 November 1943.

91 PA-AA R114171, 'Üç Halka' Türk Ltd to Lebrecht, 25 April 1944.

92 Copy of credit agreement in BA 09.01/68765.

93 BA 09.01/68751, memo by Clodius, 27 September 1942.

94 Glasneck and Kircheisen, *Türkei und Afghanistan*, 148.

95 Willi A. Boelcke, *Die deutsche Wirtschaft 1930–1945. Interna des Reichswirtschaftsministeriums* (Düsseldorf, 1983), 296.

96 BA 09.01/68765, Süßkind-Schwendi to Speer, 15 November 1943. Logistical problems also contributed to the slower pace of chromite supplies. In response, a chromite transport agreement was signed on 8 November 1943. To improve the transport situation, ten locomotives and 148 wagons were to be supplied by Krupp on a hire basis. Their dispatch was, however, stopped immediately after the Turkish chromite embargo; *ibid.*, memo of meeting of 11 November 1943, and PA-AA R114171, Schenker & Co. to von Bellersheim (Krupp), 26 April 1944.

97 PA-AA R114171, 'Üç Halka' Türk Ltd to Lebrecht, 25 April 1944. A small amount of war material (just over RM 500,000) had not yet reached Turkey.

98 BA/MA RW19/440, war diary 8 (appendix) for period 1 April–30 June 1944.

99 Önder, *Die türkische Außenpolitik*, 227–8.
100 The transport embargo was ordered verbally and secretly on 21 April 1944. It was not completely adhered to; PA-AA R114171, Dr Kirchfeld (RWM) to Michler (Frachtenleitstelle Südost), 25 May 1944.
101 The first successful target of the Allies was the vital transport link between Svilengrad in Bulgaria and Edirne in Turkey; Weber, *Evasive Neutral*, 207.
102 Turkish cotton made up 35 per cent of Germany's consumption during the first half of 1944; BA/MA RW/441, memo for Chief OKW, 7 August 1944.
103 Boelcke, *Deutschland als Welthandelsmacht*, 174.
104 Upon their first thorough search of a German commercial vessel, the *Kassel*, the Turkish authorities discovered arms and uniforms destined for the German troops in the Soviet Union. The incident provided Inönü with a convenient reason to sack Menemencioglu, who had given his permission for the passage of the vessel; see Weber, *Evasive Neutral*, 207.
105 PA-AA R114172, Papen to AA, 31 July 1944.
106 Switzerland took over the representation of Germany's interests in Turkey.

5

SPAIN

THE AXIS NEUTRAL

Spain is virtually an axis country, her foreign minister [Ramón Serrano Suñer] attacks us [Britain] openly and declares his confidence in a German victory, Germany – if she is not invited in – can walk in without serious opposition whenever it suits her.[1]

It is without doubt astonishing that Francoist Spain did not become drawn into the Second World War – or, to be more precise, that it did not make a fully fledged military commitment to the Axis. If we ignore the belated and meaningless Turkish entry into the war, none of the five neutral European states under consideration came as close to becoming a belligerent as Spain. Moreover, none of the other neutral governments, including the Turkish, seriously contemplated an entry into the war as early during the conflict as the Franco regime. Although still a possibility thereafter, Spain's entry into the war was most likely during the second half of 1940 when negotiations between the German and Spanish governments were dominated by this particular issue.

Ultimately, Franco only burnt his fingers in the fires of war, yet he avoided the much more dramatic fate of his quasi-partners, Hitler and Mussolini. Yet none of the other neutral governments would have been as deserving of a similar *exitus* to the Nazi and Fascist regimes as the Franco dictatorship. While all neutrals implemented unneutral policies at various points during the war, the near-consistently one-sided, pro-Axis attitude of the Franco regime stood out. In the Spanish case, neutrality was clearly *un mito*, a myth.[2] In fact, in 'defence' of Franco it can even be said that he admitted his total disregard for strict neutrality in numerous speeches and, most overtly, by switching to Axis-friendly non-belligerence in June 1940, a status which he did not revoke until late in 1943.

In addition to the attitude and actions of the Franco regime it was also Nazi views on Spain's neutrality/non-belligerence which made the country stand out from the other neutrals. At various points during the war, Hitler and his fellow leaders complained, sometimes bitterly, about the failure of the neutral European states to jump on the Axis bandwagon. Yet the level of vitriolic comments reserved for Franco's Spain was un-surpassed. The country that came closest to joining the Axis was also attacked the most virulently for not doing so. Why? A major reason for the grave annoyance of the Nazi regime can be found in the immediate prehistory of the Second World War.

While Spain had remained neutral in the First World War, the decision to do so again during the Second World War cannot be explained by some traditional commitment to neutrality – no similarity here to either Switzerland or Sweden. Instead Spain's neutrality and the attitude of the Nazi regime towards it need to be seen in the context of the Spanish Civil War, which unfolded between 1936 and 1939.

German–Spanish relations during the Spanish Civil War

Although denied or disputed for decades by the Franco regime and its supporters and apologists both in Spain and elsewhere, it is now a well established fact that General Francisco Franco Bahamonde owed his rise to power to substantial support from Nazi Germany and Fascist Italy. From just after the outset of the civil war in July 1936 to its end in March 1939, both regimes dispatched ample quantities of men and material to aid Franco's cause. Not only did Franco, with his war effort thus bolstered, eventually win the civil war, Hitler's and Mussolini's intervention also helped to ensure his rise to leadership of the insurgents early in the conflict.[3]

Spain's Caudillo consequently turned out to be a creation of his two fellow dictators and, as both Italy's Duce and Germany's Führer would have clearly had it, thus dependent upon them. Hitler's famous comment that without Mussolini and him there would have been no Franco reveals as much about the level of support Franco received as about the perceived need for Franco to be eternally grateful. Moreover, it unveils Hitler's barely hidden anger that Franco did not quite turn out to be the puppet both the Nazi leader and his Italian counterpart would have wished. By and large, Franco did all the 'right' things when he willingly allowed Spain to become a training ground for German troops and equipment, when he grudgingly permitted the economic exploitation of the country's resources, when he secretly became a member of the Anti-Comintern Pact on 27 March 1939 (made public on 6 April) and when he happily signed a Treaty of Friendship with Germany on 31 March 1939. Even Franco's declaration of neutrality in early September 1939 was viewed with understanding by the Nazis. Yet the fact that Franco did not take the final step of entering the war was never forgotten or forgiven by Hitler.

After all, Hitler had made a commitment on 25 July 1936 which was to bring a total of 16,800 German troops to Spain[4] together with a large amount of planes, tanks and other military equipment. In December 1940, the total cost of Germany's intervention was calculated at RM 579 million of which only RM 109 million, had been paid yet.[5] Not surprisingly, Franco's financial and moral debt to the Axis powers was cited as a major reason for him to follow Germany's lead.

The Nazi regime should have been warned, however, as early as September 1938 that Franco was not slavishly committed to his supporters in Germany and Italy. Then, in the midst of the Sudeten crisis, when a European war seemed imminent, Franco hastily assured Britain and France of his intention to remain neutral. But while the impresario of Germany's intervention in Spain, Hermann Göring, expressed his annoyance with the ungrateful Franco, even Hitler had to admit that, considering the ongoing conflict in Spain, Franco was left with little choice. Viewed rationally, Franco's attempt at achieving control of Spain would have foundered close to the finishing line if the hitherto non-interventionist France and Britain (as enemies of his 'sponsor' Nazi Germany) had thrown in their lot with the Spanish Republic.

Despite his seemingly ungrateful behaviour Franco was left unpunished. Although, for a few months, the Nazi regime held back on vital supplies, this deliberate delay had much more to do with Franco's opposition to Nazi economic policies in Spain than with his attitude during the Sudeten crisis. These economic policies, which, if fully instituted, would have ultimately turned Spain into an economic adjunct of Germany,[6] served as a warning to Franco. While it did not seriously affect Nationalist Spain's relations with Germany, it made Franco slightly more cautious about Nazi intentions. The Nazi regime, on the other hand, and specifically Göring, was clearly miffed about Franco's reluctance to condone Germany's economic expansion in Spain.[7] With Franco dependent upon German aid, and distinctly unable to pay for an overwhelming proportion of it, the Nazis expected him to agree to other options to reduce his debt. When, under increasing pressure, Franco ultimately agreed to Nazi demands, German aid started to flow again and Franco was able to 'wrap up' the war in a few months. Still,

Table 5.1 Share of Spanish (Republican and Nationalist) exports to major countries, 1935–38 (%)

Country	1935	1936	1937	1938
France	8.7	14.1	1.2	0.3
Germany	13.1	10.7	38.5	40.7
Great Britain	16.6	15.5	8.2	11.7
Italy	2.4	3.3	4.3	15.3
United States	19.9	17.9	22.1	13.5

Source: Rafael García Pérez, Franquismo y Tercer Reich: las relaciones económicas hispano-alemanas durante la Segunda Guerra Mundial (Madrid, 1994), 60.

Germany's economic policies in Civil War Spain left a recognisable imprint upon relations between the two countries during the Second World War.[8]

Although Germany's intervention in the Spanish Civil War evolved not entirely free of problems, the outcome was overwhelmingly positive. Hitler's and Mussolini's decision to intervene in the Spanish conflict had helped to transform Spain from a left-leaning democratic republic into a right-wing authoritarian dictatorship. This ideological transformation of Spain's political system was to the obvious advantage of both Nazi Germany and Fascist Italy (though it was to the latter that the Franco regime felt more closely related). In Berlin and Rome it was anticipated that ideological proximity to the regime in Madrid would automatically lead to continued close relations while Spain's relations with the other great powers would suffer owing to their ideological detachment.

That Nazi Germany's future enemies were negatively affected by the change of government in Spain was already apparent at the end of the Civil War.[9] Most troubled was France, which had lost a close friend and was now faced with a possibly hostile state on its southern flank and in Morocco.[10] Britain, though not nearly as badly shaken, nonetheless had reason to be concerned about the future behaviour of a regime which had openly voiced a demand for the return of Gibraltar.[11] The Soviet Union, finally, though strategically less concerned about Spain's future attitude, was confronted with a further strengthening of the circle of states which displayed open hostility to Communism in general and the Soviet Union in particular. Germany's armed forces, on the other hand, had gained a potential partner in future military endeavours while German industry, heavily engaged as it was in preparations for war, expected to reap benefits from Spain's wealth of raw materials.

In August 1939, the Reichsstelle für Wirtschaftsausbau (Reich Office of Economic Expansion) concluded that Spain's 'wealth of pyrites ..., iron ore ... zinc ... copper ... lead ... bismuth ... makes her an especially valuable partner. Spain forms a natural addition to south-eastern Europe, indispensable to the *Großraumwehrwirtschaft*.'[12] Not including the major reserves in Spanish Morocco, Spain's iron ore reserves were thought to be about 711 million mt. For the Huelva region alone it was estimated that its soil held over 200 million mt of pyrites.[13]

These positive assessments contrasted, however, with the harsh reality of Spain's circumstances in summer 1939. After three years of relentless fighting the country was utterly exhausted. With over a million dead, half a million in exile and nearly as great a number in the regime's prisons, the human cost had been atrocious.[14] Spain's economy had also suffered considerably, with industrial output down by 31 per cent from 1935 while agricultural output had decreased by 21 per cent.[15] Previously an exporter of food, Spain now became dependent on foreign supplies of grain. Its population was faced with the threat of starvation. Owing to the influence of the military within the regime, the armed forces were least affected by the shortage of food. They were, however, overwhelmed by the utter lack of adequate quantities of modern war material, an army of 'over half a million abysmally equipped men and 22,100 officers'.[16] Spain was clearly in no shape to fight another war in the immediate future.

Other factors also severely limited Spain's ability to make a positive contribution to Germany's forthcoming military campaigns. If, in summer 1939, Hitler's preparations for war had included Spain's involvement (which they did not), major logistical problems would have impeded his plans. In simple terms, after the British and French declarations of war on Germany, Spain found itself cut off from the latter. Obviously no German goods could obviously make their way to Spain via France, a route which the Nazi regime had in any case barely used since the outbreak of the Civil War. Yet the sea route via the Atlantic, Germany's preferred option during the Civil War, had also become a near impossibility. Until Germany's occupation of the entire French Atlantic coast, the Anglo-French blockade ensured that shipping between Germany and Spain was reduced to a trickle. With the more complicated route via Italy and the Mediterranean providing only minor relief,[17] Germany was clearly unable to supply the goods necessary to rebuild Spain's armed forces, let alone the country.

The Nazi regime was, in fact, partly unwilling, partly unable to supply sufficient essential goods. Sizeable quantities of German war material, as will be shown, started to make their way to Spain only after the likelihood of Spanish entry into the war had virtually disappeared. And even then those troops equipped with German hardware depended on oil supplied by the Allies, while grain and other foodstuffs were only ever supplied in sizeable amounts by the latter.[18]

Spain's dependence on imports from Germany's enemies was already evident during the second half of 1939. To a certain extent, Franco's declaration of neutrality was an admission of this situation. Moreover, of course, the military situation in September 1939 did not permit any adventurous commitment to the Axis. Threatened by France's armed forces across the Pyrenees and in Morocco and by the British and French navies in the Atlantic and the Mediterranean, Franco saw no reason to risk the existence of his newly established regime. Yet staying out of the war did not mean that the Caudillo observed 'the most strict neutrality' which he had announced on 4 September.

As was apparent to both Allies and Axis, Franco's sympathies lay with the latter (though not all members of the regime shared his feelings). Seemingly, Franco had taken to heart the particular section in Spain's Treaty of Friendship with Germany in which both sides had pledged to avoid 'anything in the political, military and economic fields that might be disadvantageous to its treaty partner or of advantage to its opponent'.[19] During an official visit to Rome in June 1939, Franco's brother-in-law and future minister of foreign affairs Ramón Serrano Suñer made it abundantly clear how little neutrality really meant to the regime. He told both Mussolini and Ciano that 'Spain will be at the side of the Axis because she will be guided by feeling and by reason. A neutral Spain would be destined to a future of poverty and humiliation,' though he did admit that Spain would require two, preferably three, years to prepare itself militarily.[20]

While time was not on Spain's side, the regime remained at least true to its disdain of neutrality, expressed by Serrano in June 1939 and, shortly afterwards, by Franco himself.[21] From the outbreak of the war, services were rendered to the Axis powers that were clearly in breach of Spain's neutral status. The most prominent case, the restocking and refuelling of German ships and submarines in Spanish coastal waters and ports, has been well documented by Charles Burdick.[22] Just two days after the attack on Poland, Germany's naval attaché in Spain informed the OKM and OKW that, with the help of Spanish officials, sufficient food and fuel supplies had been stocked in the Atlantic port of Vigo.[23] Clearly, Franco's earlier proposal to the head of Germany's Abwehr, Admiral Wilhelm Canaris, to establish logistical support stations at Cádiz, Vigo and Santander had yielded quick results. For most of the first half of the war, the

Kriegsmarine was able to make use of such facilities to replenish its U-boats and, for a time after December 1940, even its destroyers.[24]

The early days of the war also saw the commencement of other unneutral actions. Among the five neutral states the Spanish press proved to be exceptional in its almost utterly one-sided pro-Axis bias, a position strongly encouraged by the regime and maintained by a few papers until the end of the war. In contrast to its constant protests about Sweden's and Switzerland's press coverage of the war, the Nazi regime had little need to intervene in Spain, except, of course, by providing a constant stream of propaganda material and conferring bribes on 'deserving' papers and journalists.[25] The Spanish press had, in fact, the dubious honour of Hitler judging it 'the best in the world'! Without any doubt, the populations of the other four neutral states found it easier to gain a more balanced view of the war than the Spanish people.

Further actions in support of the Axis war effort were revealed in a UN Security Council investigation immediately after the war. According to the results of the investigation, Luftwaffe planes had attacked Allied shipping from Spanish airfields, reconnaissance aircraft had flown with Spanish markings, and radio stations within Spain had supplied the German air force with important information.[26] Spain became the most active area of engagement abroad for Canaris's Abwehr. It has been estimated that, in 1943/44, about 250 Abwehr agents and 2,000 V-men were active in the country.[27]

> Nazi observation posts on the Mediterranean coast were invaluable to Germany and were directly responsible, in the summer of 1943, for the damage inflicted on one British convoy amounting to 50,000 tons of shipping. Despite Franco's pledge, these observation posts were maintained, or new posts established, near Gibraltar and in Spanish Morocco, to monitor Allied shipping in the Mediterranean ...[28]

Not only did the Franco regime permit German intelligence gathering in Spain and Spanish Morocco, Spanish officials were also actively engaged in gathering a persistent, though not always reliable, stream of information for the Axis.[29]

In other areas, the collaboration between the two sides also proved 'fruitful'. An accord on police co-operation had been signed as early as November 1937; it led to an exchange of information between Franco's police and Himmler's Gestapo. In fact, three days before the only meeting of the German and the Spanish dictator in Hendaye, Heinrich Himmler visited Madrid on 20 October 1940. Although, during his brief stay, the Reichsführer-SS was largely concerned with recreational activities – he visited a bullfight and went on a hunting trip – it has been assumed that, apart from deliberating matters of security for the forthcoming Hitler–Franco meeting at Hendaye, the collaboration between the Gestapo and the Spanish police was discussed.[30]

It is clear that, from the beginning of the war, the Nazi regime enjoyed the active support of Spanish government agencies and officials in both their intelligence gathering and, to a lesser extent, their policing activities. As Carlos Collado Seidel has shown, this was not only due to greater ideological or personal affinity with the Axis or individual German officials (than to the Allies, whose agents experienced much harsher treatment), but also because the activities of the German agents proved to be of value to the Spanish military authorities.[31] Until the end of the war, and despite mounting protests and threats by the Allies, many German agents were able to continue their work.[32] In fact, as late as 30 March 1945, William J. Donovan, director of the Office of Strategic Services, reported to Roosevelt that the US Navy Moroccan Sea Frontier Command had 'noted that the considerable Allied shipping losses suffered in the Straits of Gibraltar in the last months were such as to indicate that German authorities were still receiving prompt data on convoy movements from clandestine observers in Tangier or Spanish Morocco.'[33]

From Phoney War to Operation Barbarossa: Spain's near entry into the war

> Hitler's startling conquest of France … drastically altered the foreign policy of the Spanish regime. … Germany's sudden ascendancy [opened] a new period of temptation combined with danger for both Spain and its government.[34]

During the Phoney War the Franco regime showed little respect for the demands of neutrality. Despite various actions in support of the Axis it did, however, refrain from moving towards open belligerency. The Caudillo gained the courage to consider seriously Spanish entry into the war only after the Wehrmacht had already done most of the hard work. When, in mid-June 1940, the French armed forces were on the verge of collapse and the British troops were pushed back across the Channel, Franco seized the opportunity to alter Spain's official status.

On 13 June 1940, the regime publicly announced it had switched to non-belligerence, a decision which had been made the day before and had already been relayed to Berlin and Rome. To the delight, though not the surprise, of the Nazi regime,[35] the Spanish government interpreted its new status to mean that it remained officially neutral, but 'that its sympathies and hopes for the outcome of the war were with the Axis powers' and that 'it had a vital interest in a German victory'.[36] In effect, Franco had made public his partiality towards the Axis. Both Axis and Allies assumed that a declaration of war would follow in the near future. Franco was seemingly ready to act out his role of 'a cowardly and rapacious vulture'.[37]

Evidently, however, Hitler did not get excited about the possibility of a Spanish entry into the war. In fact, when, on 19 June 1940, Franco had a message delivered to Berlin which contained an offer to enter the war, Hitler did not even bother replying for nearly a week. And even then Hitler's interest in Franco's offer could only be described as lukewarm. Clearly, at that particular point in the war Hitler saw no need for Spanish help, in fact he had not even been overly elated about Fascist Italy's belated entry into the war. France was about to fall while Britain was expected to either accept Germany's peace terms or be itself defeated. Why, with this scenario in mind, should Hitler allow Spain to be rewarded (which is what Franco had in mind) for what could amount only to a minute contribution to Germany's victory?

In hindsight, we know of course that Hitler was to see only half his expectations fulfilled. France fell, Britain did not. When, as became obvious during July and August 1940, Britain was not succumbing to direct aggression, Germany's political and military leadership was forced to develop indirect strategies by which it could force the country into submission. Suddenly, Franco's offer to enter the war, which he had publicly restated on 18 July 1940,[38] gained in attractiveness. With Spain in the war, joint military operations could be mounted against Gibraltar, Britain's lone outpost on the southern tip of the Iberian peninsula. With Gibraltar conquered, so the plan went, Britain would be dealt a vicious blow. It was anticipated that the loss of Gibraltar would deprive Britain of the Mediterranean route to the Middle East and its Eastern colonies while at the same time give the Axis control of the Mediterranean.[39] On 2 August 1940, Ribbentrop acknowledged the change of mind the Nazi regime had undergone when he told Germany's ambassador in Spain, Eberhard von Stohrer, that 'what we want to achieve now is Spain's early entry into the war'. With Franco still keen to oblige, the scene was set for negotiations on the issue.

During the second half of September, the first major round of talks on Spain's entry into the war got under way in Germany. Spain was represented by a large delegation led by Ramón Serrano Suñer, Franco's brother-in-law, interior minister, soon-to-be minister of foreign affairs and second most powerful man in Spain. In his first meeting, on 16 September 1940, significantly the day before the indefinite postponement of Operation Sealion, Serrano Suñer was treated to the rather unpleasant experience of having to exchange views with Ribbentrop. As on so many other occasions, the latter again proved that he lacked the diplomatic skills which were to be expected of the man in charge of Germany's foreign affairs.

Instead of cleverly wooing Franco's representative, Ribbentrop gave Suñer an early taste of his (and his regime's) arrogance. While Hitler's seemingly more amenable approach somewhat pacified Suñer, neither the Führer nor his underling at the helm of Germany's foreign ministry managed to get Franco's brother-in-law, or for that matter Franco, who followed the negotiations closely, to agree on an outright and immediate commitment to war. Yet while Franco, owing to Britain's continued resistance, may have become concerned about whether victory for the Axis would come quickly, believe in it he still did. Hence he still desired to get Spain involved, though at the right time and, even more important, at the right price.

Without any doubt, the latter issue lay at the heart of the disagreement between the two sides. Both Hitler and Franco had firm ideas of what they expected to get out of Spanish entry into the war. In a word, Franco's objective can be summed up as 'empire', or more precisely a share of France's colonial empire and possibly control over Portugal. In addition, the Franco regime produced ever longer lists of material requirements for its army and population.[40] At the other end, Hitler never envisaged Spain as a fully equal fighting partner. Instead, Spain's entry into the war was a means to an end – and, according to recent research, that end was not merely the defeat of Britain. In a radical departure from the common assumption that Hitler pursued only a 'peripheral strategy' against Britain, Norman Goda has argued that

> Hitler's interest in Spain might have had more to do with the fate of the French empire in north-west Africa and with the Spanish and Portuguese islands off the coast. The Germans hoped to obtain base sites in this general region for development and eventual use in a future war against the United States.[41]

Whether the global aim of a war with the United States or the more continental objective of the defeat of Britain was foremost in Hitler's mind – with the latter in any case always having to precede the former – the Nazi regime was clearly intent on securing bases in North-west Africa. On 20

June 1940, days before the armistice with France, Hitler and Grand Admiral Raeder referred to future German bases in Morocco, Senegal, and the Spanish and Portuguese islands.[42] In particular the openly expressed objective of taking over one of the Canary Islands set alarm bells ringing in the Spanish regime. So did Nazi demands in the economic sphere. The Nazi regime was clearly intent on replacing British and French with German commercial interests. For Hitler and Göring, the time had come to complete what had been started during the Civil War, namely to turn Spain into an economic colony of Germany. Not surprisingly, Franco was unimpressed by Germany's objectives. Yet negotiations continued and even produced a vague agreement on the future of British and French mining companies in Spain and Spanish Morocco – which Hitler was keen to see transferred into German hands.[43]

Yet at the end of September Spain was no nearer joining the Axis than it had been when the Spanish delegation arrived in Germany. To meet their respective objectives, both sides needed to break the deadlock. What better way to achieve this than to take the discussions to the highest level! On 23 October 1940, Hitler and Franco met, talked (or rather listened to each other's monologues) – and failed to reach a conclusive agreement on Spain's entry into the war.[44] The reasons for the failure are not difficult to discern – indeed, they are symbolised by the fact that Hitler had come to see Franco at Hendaye after he had been having talks in Vichy France (with Pierre Laval) and before he returned there to see Marshal Pétain.

Hitler had asked himself whether it would be wise to grant Franco his heartfelt wish and allow him to take control of most of French North-west Africa. He quickly arrived at a negative answer.[45] Hitler judged it inopportune to antagonise Vichy's leadership and decided that leaving these territories under Vichy French control would be less of a risk to Germany's plans than handing them over to Spain. For one, Franco's military forces in Africa were clearly in no shape to put up a determined resistance against a likely Anglo-Free French incursion.[46] Pétain's troops in North Africa, on the other hand, had just proved their worth by successfully beating off an Anglo-Free French landing attempt at Dakar.

The Wehrmacht's negative verdict on Franco's troops was not restricted to his detachments in North Africa, but extended to the bulk of the armed forces on the Spanish mainland. It was deemed impossible to capture Gibraltar without considerable German input. This input, and thus the whole operation, depended, however, on whether Franco would allow German troops and material to march through Spain. In view of the inconclusive Hendaye meeting between the two dictators it did not seem very likely. Franco had neither received comprehensive territorial promises nor been given any binding assurances about forthcoming German supplies of vital goods. Hitler, on the other hand, had come away without having gained a definite date for Spain's entry into the war. That Spain would eventually enter the war, was however still expected by both sides. In fact, just over a week after the meeting Hitler received a letter from Franco in which the latter 'promised faithfully that he would now carry out his verbal promises to enter the war and went on, at enormous and serpentine length, to repeat his territorial claims in French North Africa'.[47]

During November, and despite Franco's continued insistence on rewards, Hitler arrived at the firm conviction that Spain's entry into the war, and thus an attack on Gibraltar, was assured. Spurred on by the urgent need to deny British ships access to the Mediterranean, Hitler set in motion the necessary operational planning and preparations, including the training of crack troops, for the march through Spain and the assault on Gibraltar. Operation Felix, which had seen the light of day in August 1940 and was properly formulated in Hitler's Directive 18 of 12 November, foresaw the entry of Wehrmacht units into Spain on 10 January 1941, with the attack on Gibraltar scheduled for early February.[48]

Hitler was not prepared for the nasty surprise he was to receive in December. Canaris, who had been sent to Spain to work out final preparations for Felix, was instead confronted with bad news. On 7 December, Franco threw Hitler's plans into total disarray by rejecting Spain's immediate entry into the war.[49] Without Franco's assistance, Operation Felix could not commence on 10 January 1941. Only three days after the bad news had been conveyed to him, Hitler suspended the operation. Yet despite being severely put back, Hitler did not completely abandon his plans. Even while preparations for Operation Barbarossa, the invasion of the Soviet Union, were coming into full swing, Hitler was still pondering ways to activate Operation Felix.

As the direct approach to convince Franco, part of Hitler's 'Grand Deception', had clearly failed, Hitler decided to appeal to the Spanish leader via his Italian Axis partner Mussolini. Yet despite a friendly meeting between the Caudillo and the Duce on 12 February, the latter was no more successful than the Nazi leader. In fact, Italy's military setbacks almost certainly contributed to Franco's growing wariness.[50] Much later, in a letter to Mussolini in December 1944, Hitler admitted as much. According to the Führer, Italy's attack on Greece gave the English the courage to successfully start an offensive in Lybia, which made Franco for the first time hesitant. ... If, rather than attacking Greece, Italy had resolved the Spanish problem together with Germany, the development of the war could have taken a different course.[51]

Not surprisingly, Hitler conveniently ignored the effect that his own failure to implement Operation Sealion may have had on Franco. While Britain kept up its stubborn fight against the Axis, discussions on Spain's entry into the war continued to remain inconclusive. In fact, even though the Wehrmacht provided further powerful evidence of its military prowess by occupying Yugoslavia and Greece, Hitler significantly concluded that 'the spring of 1941 [had] provided the last opportunity to exercise pressure upon Spain'.[52]

Hitler's 'pressure' never included any wholehearted commitment to an invasion of Spain. First and foremost, in May 1941, to deal with Spain in an openly hostile manner would have had to wait until after the defeat of the Soviet Union – a victory the Wehrmacht, of course, never achieved. Yet it is also questionable whether Hitler ever really intended an attack against Franco's Spain. A British assessment of May 1941 summarised well some of the reasons which deterred Hitler from opting for open aggression:

> Hitler plainly does not relish the idea of an opposed occupation of Spain. He hesitates to attack Spain because –
> (a) he would have to admit that the Axis had lost a so-called partner.
> (b) the effect on Italy and France would be serious. They would see a Latin and Catholic state in conflict with the New Order in Europe.
> (c) South America would be touched through racial and cultural ties.
> (d) Hitler reads history and knows where Napoleon's power was first sapped.
> (e) The lack of supplies in Spain, especially oil, the dependence of the Peninsula on sea-borne imports, the shocking state of the railways, etc., would make a campaign costly and difficult.[53]

While the last two points in particular weighed heavily in Hitler's mind, the assessment is strangely incomplete in a further important aspect – even more so in view of the fact that it came from David Eccles. As a Ministry of Economic Warfare official Eccles should have been expected to emphasise not solely the negative repercussions of a German invasion of Spain, but also – as was well known to the British government – that the Iberian country's neutrality also offered advantages to the Axis. As has been shown, these were partly of a military, but increasingly of an economic nature. In his December 1944 letter to Mussolini, Hitler certainly highlighted this particular fact.

Finally, it should also be remembered that, while Hitler's ability to put pressure on Franco may have diminished by May 1941, the possibility of Spain's entry into the war did not completely vanish. Only a month after Eccles's letter, the execution of Operation Barbarossa helped to again strengthen Franco's commitment to the Axis – at least for a while.

From 'moral belligerence' to 'vigilant neutrality': German–Spanish relations from June 1941 to October 1943

It is well known that Franco Spain is stooging for Nazi Germany and has troops fighting our most effective ally, the Soviet Union ...[54]

In June 1941, Germany's invasion of the Soviet Union led to a marked change in German–Spanish relations. By encouraging the dispatch of Spanish troops to Germany's eastern front,[55] Franco overstepped the boundaries of neutrality even further than he had done already. In fact, by doing so he came again within a whisker of fully fledged belligerency. In the jargon of the Franco regime (or more precisely of Serrano), Spain, in fact, adopted a posture of 'moral belligerency' in summer 1941.[56]

Much has been written about the military role of Spain's División Azul (Blue Division). In view of its size, precisely 18,694 troops in July 1941 (and a small air squadron), the division clearly played only a minor role in Germany's campaign against the Soviet Union. Comments by Nazi political and military leaders reveal, however, a general appreciation of the commitment of the Spanish troops, who, for most of their service, were deployed in the environs of Leningrad. Hitler himself commented on the fearlessness of the Spanish soldiers and the fact that their German counterparts were 'always glad to have Spaniards as neighbours in their sectors'.[57]

How did Hitler perceive the dispatch of the Blue Division in more general terms? For Hitler, the division was not intended to be simply a minor military contribution to Germany's war effort, but rather the final transitional point towards Spain's full-blown entry into the war. Conquering Gibraltar was still very much on the agenda of German planning. Franco, however, pursued his own slightly different agenda. Like Hitler, Franco was driven by an ardent anti-Communism. In the Caudillo's *Weltanschauung*, the Spanish Civil War was interpreted as the first victorious battle over the contamination spread by the Soviet Union.[58] Again, like Hitler, Franco considered the dispatch of the Blue Division as a possible stepping-stone towards Spain's entry into the war.[59] Yet he did not see this as an automatic consequence. Instead, Franco 'strove to tie

Spain to the Axis via a pact that was binding enough to ensure the eventual achievement of his territorial desiderata in North Africa but loose enough to assure him the freedom of action to join, or abstain from, the fray, as might seem appropriate in the developing circumstances.'[60]

In July 1941, Franco felt hugely confident about the outcome of the war. In his most openly pro-Axis speech during the war, on the fifth anniversary of the Nationalist rising, Franco openly admitted Spain's involvement in the war against the Soviet Union by boasting that 'the blood of our youth is to mingle with that of our comrades of the Axis'.[61] Franco grandly announced that

> I do not harbour any doubt whatever ... about the result of the war. The die is cast, and the first battle was won here in Spain. The war is lost for the Allies. France and every people in the continent of Europe realize it. ... There is no mortal force that can change the destiny to come.[62]

As it turned out, Franco's inflated assessment proved to be much mistaken. The Soviet Union turned out to be a more resilient enemy than predicted. With every week and month that passed a German victory receded further and further into the distance. In fact, despite suffering huge casualities during the first months of the war, the Red Army went on the offensive in December 1941. The war in the east was clearly destined to continue for some time. Axis hopes were dealt a further blow when the United States entered the fray in the same month. According to Preston, American involvement in the war made even Franco realise that the war 'would be a long and titanic struggle' which forced him 'to postpone Spanish entry into the war indefinitely'.[63] While Hitler was still keen to see Gibraltar conquered, the possibility of an attack through Spain was very rapidly disappearing.

In open acknowledgement of the growing pressures exerted upon Germany by the war in the east, Operation Felix was finally abandoned in 1941.[64] That the execution of Hitler's plan was dependent on the 'whims' of the ungrateful Franco made the latter less and less endearing to the Nazi regime. Not surprising, then, that some German officials came to the conclusion that it might be wise to eliminate the Caudillo and replace him with a more malleable member of his regime.[68]

In their quest to take some kind of action against Franco, Nazi officials were able to count on support among those Civil War supporters of Franco who had become disenchanted with the policies of the regime. Plotting against Franco commenced even before the Nazi regime had reason to feel angered about Franco, that is, such planning antedated the inconclusive

German–Spanish negotiations of the second half of 1940. The futile machinations of dissident Falangists in early 1940 were followed by various other plots and plans in subsequent years.[66] Although German officials were not always involved in oppositional activities, success for the plotters would usually have meant closer relations with the Nazi regime.

Yet despite many critical voices, Franco did not really face a serious challenge until early 1942. Groups opposed to Franco were either too weak or did not gain German support.[67] Owing to Spain's contribution to the war against the Soviet Union, one group, the Blue Division, did, however, possess the necessary means to force a radical, germanophile transformation of the regime. This was recognised by a number of Nazis, most notably Stohrer's predecessor, Nazi Germany's first ambassador to Nationalist Spain, General Wilhelm Faupel. As director of the Ibero-American Institute in Berlin, Faupel, an ardent supporter of the 'old' Falange, acted as a go-between between camisas viejas in Spain and in the Blue Division.

To Franco and Serrano, who were acutely aware of these contacts, the object of such activities was obvious – as was shown by their reaction. From late 1941, attempts were made to convince the Nazi regime of the importance of having certain Blue Division members of the Falange sent back to Spain. In February 1942, Serrano even pleaded for a temporary complete withdrawal of the Blue Division, though ultimately all the OKW agreed to was a regular turnover of troops.[68]

Increasingly, General Agustín Muñoz Grandes, as commander of the Blue Division, advanced into a key position. This was clearly recognised by Franco, who, in mid-May 1942, recalled Muñoz Grandes from his post, albeit unsuccessfully. In talks with Admiral Canaris, Franco was persuaded to leave the general in his post, a decision which might have had serious consequences for his regime. Yet despite a secret meeting between Hitler and Muñoz Grandes on 12 July 1942, in which the general promised to 'bring about the necessary order in Spain',[69] this potential threat to Franco's regime ultimately produced no effect.

Surprisingly enough, it was Franco's removal of Serrano Suñer on 3 September which largely extinguished Hitler's interest in using Muñoz Grandes as a political weapon. Long gone were the days when the Nazi regime had regarded the cunadíssimo's presence in the Spanish government as of advantage to the Axis. In fact, on 1 August 1942, Hitler complained: 'The most evil spirit is undoubtedly S[errano] S[uñer]: he has the task of preparing the Latin Union; he is the gravedigger of the new Spain!'[70]

For the Nazi leadership in Berlin, the removal of Serrano meant hopes of improved German–Spanish relations. For Stohrer, who had developed a very good relationship with the foreign minister, it meant the beginning of the end of his ambassadorship. The success of Operation Torch, the Allied landings in Algeria and French Morocco on 8 November 1942, further undermined Stohrer's position. Finally, only hours after the signing of the German–Spanish economic agreement of 17 December, Ribbentrop withdrew Stohrer from his post. During the second half of 1942, Spain had regained a crucial role in German planning. In the efforts of the Nazi regime to make Spain move closer to the Axis, the hispanophile Stohrer, it appears, had become a potential liability.[71]

By spring 1943, German plans for a transformation of the Spanish government, including possibly Franco's overthrow, had been abandoned. Although the secret German–Spanish protocol of 10 February 1943 provided some reassurance of Spain's continued proximity to the Axis,[72] political relations were becoming slowly more detached. After Operation Torch in late 1942, the Axis defeat at Stalingrad in early 1943, and with the fall of Mussolini and the Allied invasion of Italy in mid–1943, Franco had reason to become more cautious about the outcome of the war. As a sign of this increased caution, in October 1943, Franco finally 'uttered publicly and solemnly, *for the first time*, the hitherto tabooed word of "neutrality" to define Spain's international position'.[73] Yet as Carlton Hayes, the US ambassador, correctly added, this was not meant to imply 'that we are entirely out of the woods in Spain'. The reason for Hayes's remaining concern about Spain's future attitude were, however, as he asserted, to be found not solely in increased German counter-efforts, but also in continued willingness by the Franco regime to accommodate German needs, most notably in the economic sphere.

Spanish wolfram

Wolfram is one of the commodities most needed by the German Government for the prosecution and prolongation of the war.[74]

In economic terms, 1943 proved to be the high point of German–Spanish relations during the war. Precisely at a time when Germany's military fortunes were taking a marked downward turn, Franco's Spain increased its contribution to Germany's war economy. Admittedly, Spanish exports never amounted to much in Nazi Germany's overall balance sheet (at most 2 per cent of Germany's total imports), yet this fact conceals the importance of individual products, notably wolfram (tungsten ore). In May 1944, one German official made the succinct comment that 'no other Spanish

Table 5.2 *Spain's foreign currency earnings and wolfram, 1940–44 (£ million)*

Year	Total	From wolfram exports
1940	19.785	0.073
1941	36.088	0.248
1942	51.641	3.965
1943	79.024	15.657
1944	59.740	16.261

Source: Leitz, *Economic Relations*, 172, table 5.1.

products even approach wolfram in importance'[75] while, in 1943, Hitler himself described wolfram in dramatic fashion as *kriegsentscheidend* (decisive to the outcome of the war).

Such conclusions find confirmation in both Spanish and Allied comments. Both the British and US ambassadors to Spain, Samuel Hoare and Carlton Hayes, expressed their views on wolfram in a theatrical way. While Hoare expected 'the word "wolfram"' to appear on his tombstone, Hayes warned that wolfram had made its way into the dreams of members of his embassy. That the Franco regime attached major significance to the sale of wolfram is easily discernible from the proportion of foreign currency Spain gained from exporting wolfram not just to Germany but also to the Allies, who tried to preempt Nazi purchases. From a negligible £73,000 in 1940, Spain's foreign currency earnings from wolfram exports grew to £15.7 million in 1943, a level which was even slightly exceeded in 1944.

Although, in purely financial terms, the Allies contributed far more to this increase than Germany – in 1943 the British and US governments purchased 3,000 mt of wolfram against Germany's 1,300 – it was the Nazi regime which had instigated the 'struggle for wolfram' and the German economy which was far more dependent on the raw material. For the Allies it was largely a question of 'depriving the Germans of every possible ton of wolfram'[76] as the United States produced sufficient quantities of molybdenum, a substitute product, for its own needs as well as those of Britain. Germany's industry, on the other hand, was not only much more geared to the use of wolfram, but also found itself deprived of most other sources of this particular ferro-alloy after the outbreak of war. Hitler's emphasis on the importance of wolfram was based on his awareness that, among other hardened steel products, most types of steel-armour penetrating projectiles were manufactured with wolfram while producers of aeroplane engines and propellors also made use of the ferro-alloy.

Table 5.3 *German wolfram imports from selected countries, 1936–40 (mt)*

Year	China	India	Portugal	Spain	Total
1936	5,100	900	300	136	8,700
1937	8,037	1,229	304	150	11,400
1938	8,962	1,295	658	119	14,200
1939	4,142	62	638	74	8,000
1940	800	—	61	394	n.a.

Source: Leitz, *Economic Relations,* 173, table 5.2. After September 1939, some supplies from the Far East continued to reach Germany via the Trans-Siberian railway (until June 1941) and on blockade runners.

Spain's economy also provided the German war effort with other services, including vital supplies of skins and hides, oranges, mercury, cork, fluorspar, ambligonite and iron ore. When, during the first winter in Russia, the Wehrmacht was faced with a catastrophic lack of adequate clothing, Spanish supplies of clothing hides were particularly appreciated. Subsequently, 35 per cent of the hides used by Germany's armed forces originated in Spain.[77] In 1943, the pre-emption of warm clothing from Spain was, in fact, the second most important target (after wolfram) of the Allied economic warfare campaign in the country.[78] Finally, by sending workers to Germany, Spain even contributed, albeit in a minor way, towards alleviating the Reich's labour shortage. At the highest point, in summer 1943, about 8,000 Spanish workers were employed in Germany.[79]

Yet despite Spain's other contributions to Germany's war economy, wolfram constituted by far the most important single item in the economic relationship between the two countries. The Nazi regime, in fact, not only relied on Spanish producers, it also controlled its own group of mines via the state-owned Rowak concern. Yet the output of these mines was comparatively small. In 1943, German mines produced only 97 mt of wolfram while Spain's total production amounted to over 3,600 mt. In any case, Germany depended on the goodwill of the Spanish government to permit the exportation of wolfram from either German or Spanish-owned mines.

'Goodwill' became essential as Hitler's ability to put pressure on the Franco regime diminished at the same time as Germany's requirements and imports of wolfram increased. During the period of German military decline, January 1943 to summer 1944, Germany managed to import a total of 1,670 mt of wolfram with 712 mt as the comparative figure for the years 1940 and 1941. In broad terms, Franco permitted the Third Reich

Table 5.4 *Germany, the Allies and Spanish wolfram, 1940–44 (mt)*

Year	Spanish output	German imports	Allied imports
1940	296.0	394	n.a.
1941	503.6	318	20
		(800)	(72)
1942	1,475.5	794	438
		(805)	(771)
1943	3,618.7	834.3	943
		(1,309)	(3,021)
1944[a]	n.a.	834.6	336[b]
		n.a.	(1,088)

Notes: [a] January to July. [b] To April. Total annual amounts of Spanish wolfram purchased by Germany and the Allies appear in parentheses below the import figures.
Source: Leitz, *Economic Relations*, 176, table 5.3.

continued – indeed, increased – access to a raw material vital to Germany's war effort just when the tide of war was turning very clearly in favour of the Allies. After the war, the regime was distinctly embarrassed about its obvious pro-Axis stance. While a major defensive argument consisted in reiterating the military threat Germany had apparently continued to pose, the Spanish authorities also employed economic data to downplay their contribution to Germany's war economy. For 1943, the Francoist figures give, in fact, the impression of a huge gap between wolfram exports to Germany, 560 mt, and the Allies, 2,100 mt, while the actual gap amounted to only just over 100 mt.[80]

Even during the war the Allies were largely aware of the extent of Spain's trading relationship with their enemy. The deception clearly did not work. Nor did Franco's argument hold much water that exports to Germany were a necessity to ensure counter-supplies. In value terms, Spain supplied consistently more products to Germany than vice versa. In fact, by mid–1943 Germany's total clearing deficit had reached nearly RM 250 million. Moreover, the bulk of Germany's supplies in 1943 and 1944 consisted of war material, that is, products which did not offer any benefit at all to Spain's economy or to its suffering population. In 1943 alone, the Spanish state accomplished the unenviable achievement of spending 63 per cent of its expenditure on the military sector. In direct correlation to this figure, arms imports from Germany increased markedly during the same year.

Table 5.5   *Spanish exports to Germany, 1935–43*

Year	Million RM
1935	118.3
1936	97.7
1937	123.4
1938	110.1
1939	118.9
1940	19.96
1941	146.1
1942	166.0
1943	210.0

Source: Leitz, *Economic Relations*, 93, table 3.1;
Boelcke, *Deutschland als Welthandelsmacht*, 102
and 216 n. 111.

In contrast to these 'achievements', the Nazi regime failed miserably when it was asked to supply products of vital importance. Ironically, in view of Franco's earlier temptation to enter the war, he came to rely on Spain's potential enemies to satisfy Spain's most urgent economic requirements. Vital supplies of grain, cotton and oil were either imported direct from the United States and Britain or by Allied arrangement. In view of their vital contribution to the survival of Spain's population and economy the Allies had undoubtedly reason to expect some gratitude from the Spanish government.

Yet the reaction of the Franco regime was, to put it mildly, disappointing. Instead of scaling down Spain's economic relations with Germany, the Franco regime came to the assistance of the Nazi regime when its acquisition of wolfram was threatened by lack of funds in late 1943. Germany's purchasing campaign, so successful at the beginning of 1943, was clearly faltering during the second half of the year. From a high point of 279 mt of wolfram in February 1943 purchasing activities reached rock-bottom in mid-year, when no wolfram at all was purchased during July, August and September. Little improvement had been achieved by the end of the year, with acquisitions amounting to a risible 5 mt in December 1943. German buyers were simply no longer able to pay for a product whose price had increased so dramatically over the year.

Although Allied buyers were also affected by higher prices (and state surcharges on production and transport permits), their overwhelming

Table 5.6   *German arms exports to Spain,*
1939–43 (contracts only)

Year	Million RM
1939	0.08
1940	0.90
1941	5.40
1942	76.00
1943	258.00

Source: Boelcke, *Deutschland als Welthandels-*
macht, 136.

financial advantage appears to have brought them closer to a successful conclusion of their pre-emptive purchasing campaign. Yet London and Washington had not reckoned with Franco. Strongly encouraged by Demetrio Carceller, his minister for industry and commerce, the Spanish dictator decided to help out German buyers before they were forced to abandon their purchasing campaign.

In November 1943, the Franco regime advanced Nazi Germany a purchasing credit of RM 100 million, of which the bulk (57 per cent) was to be used for the purchase of wolfram and the payment of related charges. Franco's act of support was not guided by feelings of friendship towards the Third Reich alone – even though he continued to hope for a German victory. Rather the dictator's actions were based on hard-headed economic and financial considerations. Franco was very much aware that the survival of the wolfram 'bubble' (as one British official referred to the huge interest in the raw material) depended on the continuation of purchasing activities by both belligerent camps. If Germany stopped acquiring the raw material, there would be no further need for the Allies to continue their campaign – which is precisely what happened during the second half of 1944. No wolfram sales meant a reduction in foreign trade and foreign currency earnings and an increase in unemployment in the affected mining areas of north-west Spain, while the Spanish state would lose a lucrative source of revenue. Franco also hoped that with the RM 100 million he would finally rid himself of the remaining Civil War debt to Germany.[81]

Franco was guided rather more by such concerns than by any strong feelings of germanophilia. This, of course, made no difference to the Allies, in this case particularly to the Roosevelt administration. From the point of view of the US government, Franco was giving vital assistance to Germany's

Table 5.7   *German exports to Spain, 1935–43*

Year	Million RM
1935	105.7
1936	69.3
1937	58.7
1938	94.1
1939	67.7
1940	23.2
1941	56.6
1942	119.0
1943	190.0

Source: Boelcke, *Deutschland als Welthandels-macht*, 102 and 216 n. 111; Leitz, *Economic Relations*, 94, table 3.3.

war effort and thus acting in an 'unneutral' fashion. In January 1944, the Allies received a growing number of reports that 'the Germans have been actively purchasing everything available and must have obtained a considerably larger tonnage [of wolfram] than for many months.'[82] In precise terms, German purchases amounted to 225 mt during the first month of 1944. Already fuming with anger, the US administration finally decided to act. On 28 January 1944, it imposed on Spain the harshest measure used against any of the five neutral countries under consideration: a total oil embargo.

Although further conditions were subsequently attached,[83] the main rationale for the oil embargo was simple. Spain was to be forced to stop all wolfram exports to Germany. In view of the immediate reaction of the Franco regime it is clear that this particular objective was not achieved. Despite the serious repercussions of the oil embargo, which, as one State Department negotiator put it, constituted 'very nearly a knockout blow' to the country,[84] Franco did not wish to see an end of wolfram exports to Germany. Even though German buyers were officially denied licences from as early as 2 February 1944, exports of wolfram were only partially impeded. In fact, even during April 1944, the third month of the oil embargo, the Nazis managed to get 198 mt of wolfram out of Spain.

In the end, the US government, faced with a stubborn Spanish administration, caved in to the suggestions of its more generous British ally and agreed to a compromise arrangement. In the agreement of 2 May 1944 Spain was permitted to export limited amounts of wolfram to Germany, 20 mt in both May and June and 40 mt a month for the remainder of 1944. As it turned out, the agreement had little bearing upon the actual behaviour of Spanish officials and German buyers. As on so many previous occasions the Nazi regime could count on the deliberate 'non-neutrality' of the regime up to and including Franco. In June 1944, according to General Juan Vigón Suerodíaz, Franco's air force minister, the Caudillo wanted Germany to 'receive as much wolfram from Spain as possible ... [Franco] was convinced that the German officials in Spain would be able to smuggle sufficient amounts of wolfram across the border.'[85]

Franco's consent to the continuation of German wolfram smuggling activities in the face of the unrelenting Allied pressure can be viewed as further evidence of the Caudillo's senseless attempt to profit to the last possible moment from the rapidly cooling 'wolfram fever'. Moreover, Franco's attitude should be regarded as evidence of his continued hope (against the better judgement of many of his generals) for a reversal of the fortunes of war. As Paul Preston has so vividly described, this hope continued, in fact, to the end:

> In the final days of the Second World War, Franco was still nurturing secret hopes of Hitler's wonder weapons turning the tide in favour of the Third Reich, believing that Nazi scientists had harnessed the power of cosmic rays. Indeed, as Allied forces stumbled across the horrendous sights of the extermination camps ... the Francoist press played down the horrors of the Holocaust as the entirely unavoidable and comprehensible consequence of wartime disorganisation. When Berlin fell, the press printed tributes to the inspirational presence of Hitler in the city's defence and to the epoch-making fighting qualities of the Wehrmacht. ... Franco did not break off diplomatic relations with the Third Reich until 8 May, VE Day. Only at that time were the swastikas removed from the embassy building, which was duly sealed.[86]

Notes

1 PRO FO837/735, MEW memo, 9 May 1941.
2 A useful historiographical overview of the opposing views of a minority of historians defending Spain's attitude during the war as neutral and of the majority seeing it as 'undoubtedly belligerent' is provided by Rafael García Pérez, 'España en el Eje: la beligerencia y la opinión de los historiadores', in Stanley G. Payne and Delia Contreras (eds), *España y la Segunda Guerra Mundial* (Madrid, 1996), 11–36.
3 Franco's rise to the position of *generalisimo* is neatly traced in Paul Preston, *Franco: a Biography* (London, 1995).

4   Germany's military force in Spain, the Condor Legion, never numbered more than about 5,600 at any given time, though there was a frequent exchange of military personnel – hence the higher total figure.

5   Christian Leitz, *Economic Relations between Nazi Germany and Franco's Spain 1936–1945* (Oxford, 1996), 96.

6   See Christian Leitz, 'Hermann Göring and Nazi Germany's Economic Exploitation of Nationalist Spain 1936–1939', *German History* 14 (1996).

7   Göring's displeasure with Franco was heightened in May 1939 when his attempt to arrange a visit to Spain – presumably for an official show of gratitude – was thwarted by the Spanish dictator. Maybe not surprising then that, in September 1940, Göring coolly told Serrano Suñer that, if he was the Führer, he would have already invaded Spain. Serrano's recollections of his meetings with the Axis leaders have appeared in various autobiographical accounts. I refer here to his most recent essay, 'Política de España: amistad y resistencia con Alemania durante la Segunda Guerra Mundial', in Payne and Contreras (eds), *España y la Segunda Guerra Mundial*, 45.

8   As Angel Viñas has noted, in the early 1950s Franco justified his dislike of foreign direct investment by referring to Nazi economic penetration during the Spanish Civil War; Angel Viñas, 'Franco's Dreams of Autarky Shattered; Foreign Policy Aspects in the Run-up to the 1959 Change in Spanish Economic Strategy', in C. Leitz and D. J. Dunthorn (eds), *Spain in an International Context; Civil War, Cold War, Early Cold War* (New York and Oxford, 1999), 318 n. 31.

9   See Glyn Stone, 'Britain, France and Franco's Spain in the Aftermath of the Spanish Civil War', *Diplomacy and Statecraft* 6 (1995), 373–407.

10 See Peter Jackson, 'French Strategy and the Spanish Civil War', and Martin Thomas, 'French Morocco – Spanish Morocco: Vichy French Strategic Planning against the "Threat from the North" 1940–1942', in Leitz and Dunthorn (eds), *Spain in an International Context.*

11 Shortly after the Civil War, as if to confirm French and British concern, Franco substantially increased troop contingents on the border with France and near Gibraltar.

12 BA R25/53, memo 'Möglichkeiten einer Großraumwehrwirtschaft unter deutscher Führung', August 1939.

13 BA/MA Wi/IB 2.3 (copy b), overview of economic situation in Spain, November 1940.

14 Truman Library, President's Secretary Files, supplement to Situation Report (II) Spain, 15 November 1948, 36.

15 Stanley G. Payne, *The Franco Regime 1939–1975* (Madison WI, 1987), 246. An index of Spain's agricultural production put together by the Spanish economic historian Albert Carreras shows a decline from 96.0 in 1935 to 74.7 in 1940 and, after a slight improvement between 1941 and 1944, a further decline to 62.8 in 1945. Industrial production declined from 97.8 in 1935 to its lowest war-time level of 78.5 in 1940 (86.9 in 1945); Albert Carreras, 'Depresión económica y cambio estructural durante el decenio bélico 1936–1945', in J. L. García Delgado, *El primer Franquismo; España durante la Segunda Guerra Mundial* (Madrid, 1989), 28.

16 Preston, *Franco*, 327.

17 See Leitz, *Economic Relations*, 122–3.

18 On Spain's dependence on supplies from the Allies see Denis Smyth, *Diplomacy and Strategy of Survival: British Policy and Franco's Spain 1940–1941* (Cambridge, 1986); see also Christian Leitz, '"More Carrot than Stick": British Economic Warfare and Spain', *Twentieth Century British History* 9 (1998).

19 Cited in Preston, *Franco*, 326.

20 *Ibid.*, 331. In July 1939 Franco told Ciano that he needed five years of peace to prepare Spain economically and militarily.

21 In the July conversation with Ciano, Franco argued that, although he would declare neutrality in a future war, he would be on the side of the Axis; Paul Preston, 'Franco's Foreign Policy 1939–1953', in Leitz and Dunthorn (eds), *Spain in an International Context*, 4.

22 See Charles B. Burdick, '"Moro": the Resupply of German Submarines in Spain 1939–1942', *Central European History* 3 (1970), 256–84.

23 BA/MA RW19/226, Menzell to OKM and OKW, 3 September 1939.

24 As late as October 1942 the United States was still accusing Spanish ships of 'supplying submarines and using their wireless to reveal other ships' positions'; PRO FO 837/767, Hoare to FO, 28 October 1942.

25 According to one estimate, the German press attaché Hans Lazar had no fewer than 432 Spaniards on his payroll; Payne, *The Franco Regime*, 299.

26 UN Security Council report, in Preston, *Franco*, 361.

27 Carlos Collado Seidel, 'Zufluchtsstätte für Nationalsozialisten? Spanien, die Alliierten und die Behandlung deutscher Agenten 1944–1947', *Vierteljahreshefte für Zeitgeschichte* 43 (1995), 134.

28 David Wingeate Pike, 'Franco and the Axis Stigma', *Journal of Contemporary History* 17 (1982), 387. On the monitoring of Allied shipping into and around the Straits of Gibraltar see also Denis Smyth, 'Screening 'Torch': Allied Counter-intelligence and the Spanish Threat to the Secrecy of the Allied Invasion of French North Africa in November 1942', *Intelligence and National Security* 4 (1989), 335–56.

29 On the Spanish-run 'TO' spy ring see Smyth, 'Screening "Torch"', 336 and 348–50.

30 Manuel Espadas Burgos, *Franquismo y política exterior* (Madrid, 1988), 111. Payne plays down the professional side of the visit and emphasises that, while 'the Spanish police did receive some technical assistance from the Gestapo during this period, … the extent is not known and direct documentation has not been found'; Payne, *The Franco Regime*, 272 n. 21.

31 Collado Seidel, 'Zufluchtsstätte für Nationalsozialisten?', 143–5.

32 At the end of the war, the US administration identified nearly fifty Spanish firms as having undertaken espionage work for the Third Reich. The same assessment also identified about 3,000 German agents in Spain; Eizenstat Report, 42.

33 Roosevelt Library, President's Secretary Files (PSF), Box 152, Donovan to Roosevelt, 30 March 1945.

34 Payne, *The Franco Regime*, 266.

35 Hitler also expressed his delight at Franco's occupation of Tangier on 14 June, particularly as on this occasion Franco 'had acted without talking'.

36 PRO/AA 89/102800–1, Dieckhoff to AA, 3 October 1943. To the Italian

chargé d'affaires in Madrid, Franco announced that 'the present state of the Spanish armed forces prevented the adoption of a more resolute stance but that he was nonetheless proceeding to accelerate as much as possible the preparation of the army for any eventuality'; Preston, 'Franco's Foreign Policy', 6.

37 *Ibid.*

38 On the fourth anniversary of the Nationalist insurgency, Franco boasted that 2 million warriors were ready to fight to revive Spain's past imperial glories and to pursue the task of reconquering Gibraltar and expanding Spanish Africa.

39 On 15 August, General Jodl made it clear that Germany needed to seize the nerve centres of the British Empire, Gibraltar and Suez.

40 See Leitz, *Economic Relations*, 132 and 137. In September 1940, Serrano told Ribbentrop that 'geographically speaking Portugal really had no right to exist'; Paul Preston, 'Franco and Hitler: The Myth of Hendaye 1940', *Contemporary European History* 1 (1992), 5 (original comment in Ramón Serrano Suñer, *Entre Hendaya y Gibraltar*, Madrid, 1947).

41 Norman J. W. Goda, 'Germany's Conception of Spain's Strategic Importance 1940–1941', in Leitz and Dunthorn (eds), *Spain in an International Context*, 130. For a detailed examination see Goda, *Tomorrow the World; Hitler, Northwest Africa, and the Path toward America* (College Station TX, 1998).

42 Goda, 'Germany's Conception', 132.

43 See Leitz, *Economic Relations*, 133, 135.

44 The famous Secret Protocol, which was agreed upon at Hendaye and signed by Ribbentrop and Ciano on 6 November and Serrano five days later, made Spain basically a member of the Axis. Yet it left the date of Spanish entry into the war open, subject to a joint agreement by all three sides (i.e. including the Italians) and, even more important, subject to a process of economic and military preparation by Spain. For a very useful discussion of the Secret Protocol see Rafael García Pérez, 'España en el Eje: la beligerencia y la opinión de los historiadores', in Payne and Conteras (eds), *España y la Segunda Guerra Mundial*, 24–5 and 31–5.

45 To Franco, Hitler argued that a promise to hand over French Morocco would result in the defection of North-west Africa to the enemy.

46 To convince Hitler of the advantages of granting him French colonial territory, Franco had claimed that Spanish control of the whole of Morocco would prevent the danger of Gaullist rebellions in Algeria and Tunisia; US Department of State (ed.), *The Spanish Government and the Axis; Documents* (Washington DC, 1946), 15, Franco to Hitler, 22 September 1940.

47 Preston, *Franco*, 403. Two days prior to Franco's letter, on 28 October, Mussolini's troops had started their attack on Greece.

48 Felix was divided into six successive phases. Before Gibraltar was attacked – within twenty-five days after German troops had crossed the Pyrenees – the Luftwaffe was to destroy the Rock's port and the naval units anchored there. Portugal was to be invaded and the Spanish coastline reinforced. After the conquest of Gibraltar the Straits were to be closed, while German troops would be moved into Spanish Morocco.

49 Economic problems were given as the official reason, with an ever-growing

gap opening up between Spain's economic and military demands and Germany's offers. On Germany's failure to supply Spain with food, see Leitz, *Economic Relations*, 127.

50 On Italo-Spanish relations during the Second World War see Javier Tusell and Genoveva García Queipo de Llano, *Franco y Mussolini: la política española durante la Segunda Guerra Mundial* (Barcelona, 1985).

51 Templewood Papers, Box XIII/7, letter by Hitler to Mussolini, 27 December 1944.

52 *Ibid.*

53 PRO FO 837/735, Eccles to Norman Davis (Chairman of US Red Cross), 19 May 1941.

54 US National Maritime Union resolution, 12 March 1943, in PRO FO 837/774, Associated Press report, 13 March 1943.

55 Immediately after the attack Serrano Suñer told Stohrer that Franco favoured the dispatch of Falangist volunteer units to fight 'independently of the full and complete entry of Spain into the war beside the Axis, which would take place at the appropriate moment'; Preston, 'Franco's Foreign Policy', 10.

56 Serrano Suñer's comment to a correspondent of the *Deutsche Allgemeine Zeitung*, early July 1941.

57 On the Blue Division see Gerald Kleinfeld and Lewis Tambs, *Hitler's Spanish Legion: The Blue Division in Russia* (Carbondale IL and Edwardsville IL, 1979); Raymond L. Proctor, *Agonía de un neutral* (Madrid, 1972) and 'La División Azul', *Guerres mondiales et conflits contemporaines* 162 (1991). *In toto*, 47,000 Spaniards fought on the eastern front between October 1941 and January 1944.

58 On Franco's obsessive anti-Communism see Preston, *Franco*, 61.

59 While other factors also influenced Franco, including the pressure exerted by Falangists critical of the course of his regime, the attraction of contributing to and benefiting from Germany's victory was, I believe, still the overriding factor. A summary of influencing factors is provided by Rafael Ibáñez Hernández, 'Españoles en las trincheras: la División Azul', in Payne and Contreras (eds), *España y la Segunda Guerra Mundial*, 59–60.

60 Denis Smyth, 'The Dispatch of the Spanish Blue Division to the Russian Front: Reasons and Repercussions', *European History Quarterly* 24 (1994), 543. Preston, 'Franco and the Axis Temptation', in Paul Preston, *The Politics of Revenge; Fascism and the Military in Twentieth-century Spain* (London and New York, 1995), 76, arrives at the same conclusion. In financial terms, the Blue Division acted as a kind of reciprocation for the Condor Legion. In spring 1944 both sides decided to cancel the expenses of the Condor Legion (RM 115 million) against those of the Blue Division (RM 81.5 million + RM 20 million for indemnification of Spanish dead and wounded); Leitz, *Economic Relations*, 134.

61 Preston, 'Franco's Foreign Policy', 11.

62 Pike, 'Franco and the Axis Stigma', 381. In response to Franco's speech, the British government firmed up its commitment to a pre-emptive strike against the Canary Islands. On 23 July 1941 Churchill argued in favour of implementing Operation Puma (soon renamed Operation Pilgrim). September 1941 was set as the date of attack. In the meantime, however,

Churchill reconsidered the tone of Franco's speech and came to agree with the verdict of the British embassy in Madrid, which had judged it as very superficial, flowery and, most important, non-committal. Pilgrim was not carried out; PRO PREM4, 21/1, Alan Hillgarth to Churchill, 12 August 1941; Smyth, 'Dispatch of the Spanish Blue Division', 548–50.

63 Preston, 'Franco and the Axis Temptation', 78.

64 At the beginning of May 1941, Felix's replacement, Operation Isabella, was mainly concerned with repelling a possible British invasion of the Iberian peninsula. Isabella, in turn, was replaced by the less ambitious Operation Ilona one year later. See Chapter 6.

65 As early as 28 September 1940, when Hitler was still hopeful of Spanish entry into the war, he had, in fact, complained to Ciano about Franco and his regime. Hitler took exception to the fact that his demands for payment of the Nationalist civil war debt were 'often interpreted by the Spanish as a tactless confusing of economic and idealistic considerations, and as a German, one feels towards the Spanish almost like a Jew, who wants to make business out of the holiest possessions of mankind'; US Department of State (ed.), *The Spanish Government*, 19.

66 See Paul Preston, 'Franco and his Generals 1939–1945', in Preston, *The Politics of Revenge*, 85–108, and Klaus-Jörg Ruhl, *Spanien im Zweiten Weltkrieg. Franco, die Falange und das 'Dritte Reich'* (Hamburg, 1975), 63–4.

67 On German contacts with opponents of Franco, including the exiled royal family, see Ruhl, *Spanien*, 65–71.

68 *Ibid.*, 100–2.

69 *Ibid.*, 114.

70 Werner Jochmann (ed.), *Adolf Hitler. Monologe im Führerhauptquartier 1941–1944* (Bindlach, 1988), 323 and also 389.

71 In early September Hitler had already intimated to Ribbentrop that it was about time to recall the ambassador as quickly as possible; Ruhl, *Spanien*, 175 and also 191. Stohrer was replaced by Hans Adolf von Moltke. When the latter died within less than three months he was succeeded by Ribbentrop's brother-in-law, Hans Heinrich Dieckhoff.

72 US Department of State (ed.), *The Spanish Government*, 35, secret protocol between the German and Spanish governments, 10 February 1943.

73 PSF, Box 50, Carlton J. H. Hayes to F. D. Roosevelt, 4 October 1943.

74 Templewood Papers, Box XIII/24, *aide-mémoire* of a meeting between Hoare and Franco, 28 January 1944.

75 PRO AA 89/103414–6, Becker to AA, 9 May 1944. I have kept footnotes in the last section of this chapter to a minimum. For detailed references, readers are advised to consult Leitz, *Economic Relations*, chapters 4 and 5, and C. Leitz, 'Nazi Germany's Struggle for Spanish Wolfram during the Second World War', *European History Quarterly* 25 (1995), 71–92.

76 PRO FO 837/743, Dolphin (UKCC) to Nicholls (MEW), 4 November 1941.

77 BA/MA RW19/435, appendix 25 of *War Diary No. 4* of OKW WiAmt, Wi Ausl IVa to OKM/M Rü IIb, 30 January 1943.

78 PRO FO 837/769, report on meeting on Economic Policy towards Spain, 3 February 1943.

79 Rafael García Pérez, 'El envío de trabajadores españoles a Alemania durante la

Segunda Guerra Mundial', *Hispania* 170 (1988), 1031–65. In addition, the Nazi regime forced Spanish exiles in France to work in Germany and for the German occupation forces.

80 *Ibid.*, 176, table 5.3b.

81 The Nazi regime successfully insisted, however, that even after the autumn 1943 payment Spain continued to owe Germany money. The RM 100 million outstanding at the end of the war was finally cancelled in May 1948 as part of the agreement between the Allied Control Council and the Spanish government. This decision was officially accepted by the West German government in an agreement with Spain in 1958.

82 PRO FO 837/786, UKCC (Madrid) to UKCC (London), 7 February 1944.

83 These included the closure of the German consulate in Spanish-occupied Tangier, the handing over of Italian ships interned in Spanish ports, the withdrawal of the last remnants of the Blue Division and the expulsion of German spies from Spanish soil.

84 National Archives II RG59, Box 2192, 711.52/4–1144, memo by W. Perry George, 12 May 1944.

85 BA/MA RW19/440, memo by OKW Fwi Amt (Ausl.) 2./IIIb, 12 June 1944.

86 Preston, 'Franco and Hitler', 1–2.

6

PORTUGAL

THE ALLIED NEUTRAL

[Portugal's] security … has always depended on its ability to maneuver, to play one force off against the other, to 'sell' itself to both belligerents in the capacity of a neutral.[1]

On 23 March 1933, the German parliament passed the notorious Enabling Act which gave Adolf Hitler and his recently established government virtual free rein over the political decision-making process. Only days before, another European politician had gained almost complete dictatorial control over the future of his country. On 19 March 1933, Dr António de Oliveira Salazar, Portugal's Prime Minister since 5 July 1932, had his Corporative Constitution approved in a national referendum. In contrast to Hitler (after Hindenburg's death in August 1934), Salazar (like Mussolini) remained subordinated to his country's head of state.[2] Nonetheless, Salazar was, as a German official appropriately put it, 'ultimately the only power factor [in Portugal]'.[3]

Despite the coincidental origins of Salazar's and Hitler's regimes, neither dictator had much time for the other. The German dictator was not known to have referred to Salazar's rise while the Portuguese dictator, though 'deeply impressed by Mussolini's organizing genius … disliked and distrusted Hitler from the start'.[4] In the first half of the 1930s, relations between the two countries reflected this distance between the two leaders. Salazar's self-proclaimed *Estado Novo* was of very little consequence to Hitler's self-proclaimed *Drittes Reich*, either economically, owing to the very limited volume of trade between the two countries, or strategically, owing to Portugal's 'old alliance' with Britain.[5] In mid-1936, however, Nazi Germany's interest in Portugal was abruptly awakened by the dramatic events in neighbouring Spain. Hitler's decision in July to intervene in the Spanish Civil War very rapidly enveloped Portugal in Germany's supply operations for the Nationalist forces.

By mid-August Lisbon had become a loading station for German war material destined for the Spanish insurgents.[6] The Portuguese authorities even assisted the camouflaging of such supplies by signing orders for German arms destined for Franco's troops.[7] Salazar's initial assurances of Portugal's neutrality towards the Spanish conflict deceived nobody, particularly as he repeatedly made it clear that his hopes were of a successful outcome for the Nationalists.[8] Salazar was obsessed with the perceived threat of a Communist take-over in Spain and its potential repercussions for Portugal. In March 1937, the German minister in Lisbon, Baron von Hoyningen-Huene, reported as much to the AA:

> In the fight against Communism Portugal stands in full agreement with us. Thanks to the policy of the Führer and the support given to Spain, we have gained much ground in the country, not least among the government. Scarcely any other country is at present as strongly opposed to Bolshevism as Portugal.[9]

Salazar's openly anti-Communist stance was clearly appreciated in Berlin, as were his candidly expressed misgivings about the reluctance of the British government to recognise General Franco's government.

Aware of the frictions in the relationship between Portugal and Britain, Nazi officials tried to exploit them. Not only did they emphasise the shared hostility towards the Soviet Union, but the Nazis also tried to woo Salazar and the Portuguese military through arms deals. Representative was a comment by Dr Schwendemann, an official of the AA, in May 1938. With reference to a possible co-operative project between Portuguese and German shipbuilders, Schwendemann concluded that 'from a political point of view' the deal would be 'opportune'. He added that 'we have an interest in not letting the English take such positions of economic and potentially military importance in Portugal. Conversely, we should use this kind of co-operation as a foundation for our economic and political relationship [with Portugal].'[10]

Closer economic relations alone, however, did not automatically translate into closer political relations. Even Portuguese support for Nazi Germany's anti-Communist campaign could not conceal the fact that the Salazar regime, Portugal's media and the population at large were watching with growing unease the domestic and foreign policies of the Nazi regime. Only a month after Schwendemann's optimistic memorandum,

Hans Eltze, permanent deputy chairman of the AGK, and a frequent visitor to Portugal, sounded a note of alarm when he reported on his latest visit to the country:

> The attitude of the population and the leading figures of the country, which had previously been generally friendly towards Germany, has almost reversed. Particularly because of the press, but also because of those Portuguese who have recently visited Germany, Germany is being judged quite harshly. The *Anschluss* of Austria is seen as a warning sign with regard to Portugal's position *vis-à-vis* Spain, in particular because Germany exercises, at least at present, a strong influence in Spain, and because those Germans residing in Spain frequently propagate the idea of a United States of the Iberian peninsula. ... The horror stories about the persecution of the Jews are generally believed. News to the contrary are rarely circulated, owing to the lack of German influence on the Portuguese press. Germany is regarded as the trouble-maker of Europe.

In view of his rather gloomy conclusions, Eltze's only comfort was the fact that Britain did not fare any better in its relations with Portugal. Not at all happy about Britain's reluctance to endorse Franco, Salazar was even more annoyed about apparent attempts to expand Britain's influence in his country. According to Eltze, the Portuguese leader made it known that he would never allow Portugal to be turned into 'an expanded Gibraltar'. On an additional, more optimistic, note, Eltze anticipated a positive development of Germany's economic relations with Portugal.[11]

Mutual economic interests helped, in fact, to keep relations between the two countries on an even keel. According to German assessments, Portugal's economy desperately needed buyers for a surplus of goods produced. The Nazi regime expressed an interest in increasing its purchases in Portugal, especially as the Portuguese government continued to be keenly interested in the acquisition of German arms. Towards the end of the Spanish Civil War, negotiations were therefore under way to satisfy the requirements of both regimes.[12] At the same time, Portugal's relations with Britain also experienced an improvement, not least because the British government finally granted official recognition to Franco's government in late February 1939.

Within a month of Britain's act of recognition, the Spanish Civil War ended with Franco's victory. Yet Salazar's satisfaction at the destruction of the 'Communist' Spanish Republic did not lead him to lose sight of the uncertainties created by Franco's triumph. To win the conflict the Spanish Caudillo had permitted both Nazi Germany and Fascist Italy to gain a foothold in the Iberian peninsula. With the likelihood of a future Europe-wide conflict growing, Salazar wanted to make sure that Spain's pro-Axis stance would not have serious repercussions on Portugal. Even if Portugal remained neutral in a future war, the country's position would be greatly threatened should its neighbour become drawn in; hence the strenuous efforts of the Portuguese government to pin Franco down to a commitment to neutrality.

It was, however, the Franco regime which approached the Portuguese government about the neutralisation of the Iberian peninsula. In September 1938, hugely concerned about the potential repercussions of the Sudeten crisis, Francoist officials communicated their interest in a treaty between the two countries. Without hesitation, the Salazar regime responded to this opportunity to ensure the safety of Portugal. According to the Portuguese historian César Oliveira, 'Portugal's neutrality, and that of the entire peninsula, as the strategic objective of the foreign policy of the *Estado Novo*, was born during the Sudeten crisis, one year prior to the outbreak of the Second World War.'[13]

Despite the peaceful resolution of the crisis, the Portuguese government continued in its efforts to conclude an agreement with the Franco administration. Two days after Hitler had greatly increased the likelihood of war by marching his troops into Prague, Salazar's efforts were crowned with success. On 17 March 1939, the Hispano-Portuguese Treaty of Friendship and Non-aggression was signed.[14] From a Portuguese point of view, the so-called *Pacto Iberico* was to provide Portugal with a major safeguard against being drawn into any future military conflict in Europe. To ensure this, the pact was to prevent Franco's Spain from committing itself to the Axis.[15] Yet the precarious nature of the pact was demonstrated in its immediate aftermath. By signing a Treaty of Friendship with Germany and acceding to the Anti-Comintern Pact, the Franco regime demonstrated that it was neither wooed away from the Axis nor weaned off potentially hostile intentions against Portugal.[16] Salazar's only comfort was that the British government was forced to reassess its alliance with Portugal precisely because Spain had become an unknown quantity.

After the lacklustre state of Anglo-Portuguese relations prior to and during the Spanish Civil War, Salazar's attempts to keep the Iberian peninsula neutral gained him supportive attention from London. In an effort to protect Gibraltar, and thus Britain's passage to the Mediterranean, and to deny Germany access to the Azores, the British government actively encouraged Salazar to act as the 'pivot of the neutralisation of the peninsula'.[17] The Nazi regime was also keen to ensure Portugal's neutrality, though it pursued this objective for quite different reasons and with far less vigour.

In late August 1939, the Nazi regime assured Salazar that Portugal's integrity would not be violated if Portugal promised to remain neutral. In simple terms, the German government wanted to avoid the 'old' alliance from becoming a fully fledged one. Portugal was not to allow Britain to gain a military foothold in Portugal, nor was the country to stop supplies of important goods to Germany. In the event, both Britain and Germany obtained Salazar's commitment to neutrality on 1 September. The Portuguese dictator announced that Portugal would maintain an 'attitude of neutrality as long as this was possible and agreeable with our interests, duties, and dignity'.[18] The Nazis interpreted Portugal's status, as pronounced by Salazar and pursued over the following years, as

> neither in the objective nor in the theoretical sense as neutral. The government and the upper echelons of society accept quite openly the special position of England. Britain's naval power, the Anglo-Portuguese trading relationship, and the position of the Portuguese colonies are being emphasised and taken into account. On the other hand, this attitude does not involve any anti-German machinations. Instead, Portugal manoeuvres its neutrality as well as it realistically can among the belligerents.[19]

In September 1939, Salazar was reassured by Franco's almost simultaneous declaration of neutrality. For the next six years neutrality remained the foundation stone of Portugal's foreign policy. It was a policy which was never seriously challenged by either the Axis or the Allies. In fact, the only time Salazar considered entering the conflict was when the war in Europe was over. At that belated point, however, the Allies reacted to Salazar's offer to join the war against Japan with 'a wall of reservation and reticence'.[20]

Portuguese–German relations, 1939–41

> That ... Portugal retained a strictly neutral attitude during the first three and a half years of the war ... can be explained primarily by the tremendous successes of the German armed forces in all theatres of war. Germany's troops achieved huge victories against the Bolshevists, who are feared by Portugal, they were victorious in Africa and they advanced ... to the Franco-Spanish border and thus into considerable proximity of Portugal.[21]

In 1939, the initial development of the war meant that Portugal was almost totally cut off from Nazi Germany. Even more than in the case of Spain, the Allies managed to disrupt Portugal's communications, including its trade links, with Germany. Very limited exports, notably of wolfram and tin, continued via Spain and Italy.[22] In general, however, Salazar was not eager to assist Nazi efforts to run the Allied blockade. Instead, he deliberately maintained a much greater degree of detachment from Hitler (and Mussolini) than Franco. While, for instance, both Iberian regimes had been equally shocked at Hitler's pact with Stalin, Salazar, in contrast to Franco, was far less inclined to seek some rational explanation for it. In addition, Hitler's invasion and defeat of Catholic Poland, achieved in co-operation with the 'evil' Soviets, encouraged Salazar's lingering distrust of the Nazi regime while Franco was not nearly as much influenced by the event.[23]

Most important, of course, Salazar and Franco differed in their attitude to war. Salazar desired peace, as he had nothing to gain from war – indeed, he had much to lose. After the defeat of France, entering the war on the side of the Allies could have resulted in a German invasion of Portugal, while joining the Axis would have almost certainly led to the loss of the sizeable Portuguese colonial empire to the maritime powers, Britain and the United States.[24] Franco, on the other hand, though in need of a period of respite in order to rebuild Spain, had much to gain from a military conflict, as only a war, won of course by the Axis, would give him the chance to realise his dreams of empire.

Militarily, both sides were badly prepared for war. Despite the adverse effects of the Civil War on Spain's military position, Portugal's state of preparedness was, in fact, worse. An assessment undertaken by the general staff of the army in 1939 revealed major material and personnel deficiencies. Many soldiers were very young and inexperienced, with training made difficult by a high illiteracy rate (from 33 per cent among artillerymen to at least 40 per cent among infantrymen).[25] The country was also completely unprepared for the air warfare of the Second World War.[26] For Salazar, it was therefore essential to keep Portugal well away from the widening conflict in Europe yet, at the same time, to actively encourage improvements in the state of his country's armed forces. The pursuit of strict neutrality seemed best suited to this purpose.

While Salazar regularly reiterated the need to treat both sides in the conflict impartially, his initial stance clearly favoured the Allies. As a result of the Nazi–Soviet Pact and the invasion of Poland, Nazi Germany's relations with Portugal deteriorated. Despite the government's official espousal of Portugal's neutral status, it adopted a more openly anglophile attitude. Although some members of Portugal's leading circles retained their fondness for the Axis, relations with the Nazi regime became more detached. Yet Salazar did not totally embrace the British government either, as he was very concerned about the 'corrupting' influence British democracy might have upon his dictatorial regime. Illustrative of Salazar's attitude was a comment he made in 1940 to the British ambassador to Lisbon, Sir Ronald Campbell. The Portuguese dictator advised Britain's representative of the simple difference between the two countries. While Britain was `democratic, liberal and parliamentary, the Portuguese regime was anti-democratic, anti-liberal and anti-parliamentary'.[27]

In late 1939, Germany's propaganda apparatus, which continued to be active in Portugal during the Phoney War, attempted to exploit Salazar's views by emphasising that London was planning his overthrow. In view of the damage the Nazi–Soviet Pact had done, this, and other propaganda campaigns, were, however, blessed with little success. Nazi Germany's best propaganda weapon proved to be its military success. In March 1940, for instance, the British embassy concluded that Portugal's chief censor, 'hypnotised' by Hitler's success, showed extreme reluctance to permit any reference to Portugal's alliance with Britain and the obligations that it entailed.[28]

During the following months, the Portuguese government became even more cautious about emphasising the country's traditionally close links with Britain. The Wehrmacht's victories in Scandinavia and western Europe had propelled Hitler's talk about a new order in Europe from the realm of wishful thinking to that of near reality. With German troops on the border of the Iberian peninsula and Franco set to enter the war, Salazar was determined not to antagonise the Nazi regime. He was clearly worried that Spanish entry into the war would eventually lead to a joint Hispano-German attack on Portugal.

Despite the Hispano-Portuguese Treaty of Friendship and its Additional Protocol of 29 July 1940,[29] such a development remained a latent threat. As Samuel Hoare correctly concluded, 'the terms of the Agreement were not precise and … according as they were applied, they might mean little or much'.[30] Leading Francoist officials certainly voiced their disdain for Portugal's independence. While Germany's rise appeared unstoppable, they frequently made it known that they longed for Spain's hegemony over the entire Iberian peninsula.[31] Even Franco was attracted by the rallying cry 'Portugal belongs to Spain', though it was also clear to him that taking control of Portugal would not be possible without Germany's help.

Consequently, Salazar had reason to be concerned about Spanish and German intentions. His concern was heightened by Britain's obvious inability to provide Portugal with adequate military protection. All that Anthony Eden, the Foreign Secretary, could suggest in the event of a German advance across the Pyrenees was for Salazar to relocate his government to the Azores and offer only token resistance in Portugal.[32] In the meantime, however, while Spain remained on the sidelines of the war, Salazar opted for a two-pronged approach. His government tried to persuade the Franco regime to retain its neutrality (now non-belligerency), while, at the same time, it tried to reduce as far as possible any likely reasons for a German attack.

As a result, in the summer of 1940, an ironic situation emerged. After the fall of France, the Portuguese regime tried – unsuccessfully, of course – to persuade its British ally to sign a peace treaty with Germany.[33] While overwhelmingly anglophile, the Portuguese population was forced to downplay its support for Britain in favour of a 'strictly neutral' attitude. The government, in fact, censored all news to which the Nazi and Fascist regimes had objected.[34] Finally, Salazar even instructed Armindo Monteiro, his ambassador in London, to warn the British government that Portugal would defend the Azores against any British attack.

Yet these efforts did not stop Hitler from including Portugal in his operational plans. As the third stage of Operation Felix, which he revealed to his officers on 12 November 1940, an invasion of Portugal was likely. Troops were to be moved into Portugal should the British use the country as a point of entry for a counter-attack on the Wehrmacht and its Spanish ally. In the end, a German attack did not eventuate. Although Salazar continued to be concerned about the intentions of the Nazi regime, Portuguese–German relations evolved normally until Germany's attack on the Soviet Union.

Portuguese–German relations from Operation Barbarossa to the Azores accord

In December 1939, the British naval attaché predicted that 'Germany's only chance of gaining a substantial level of support among Portugal's influential circles was to declare a crusade against Russia.'[35] In the light of the regime's reaction to Germany's invasion of the Soviet Union in June 1941, the attaché's prediction proved only too right. While the regime as a whole was undoubtedly more anglophile than germanophile, it felt a very obvious affinity with the anti-Bolshevik 'crusade' of the Nazis. As in his dealings with Franco, Hitler was able to make use of Operation Barbarossa in his relations with Salazar.

Even before Germany's attack on the Soviet Union, the Portuguese Legion[36] had issued an order on 11 June 1941 in which it announced its solidarity with Hitler's crusade. This, according to Leitão de Barros, the 'only openly anti-neutral official act', appeared to signal that Salazar's Portugal was about to move closer to Nazi Germany and become more detached from Britain. To the delight of the Nazi regime, Salazar reacted strongly to Churchill's extolling of the entry of the Soviet Union into the war and his expressions of solidarity with the Russians. While Salazar showed understanding of Britain's appreciation of the substantial military help provided by the Russian troops, he also reminded Churchill that Stalin's policies, as demonstrated in Poland, Finland, the Baltic States and Bessarabia, stood in direct opposition to those of the British government.[37]

During the year following the invasion of the Soviet Union, disquieting reports reached Britain about a change of heart among many committed Portuguese anglophiles. Even in staunchly Catholic circles, who disliked the policies of the Nazi regime, germanophilia was registered to be on the increase. How did the Nazi regime make use of the more favourable response created by its attack on the Soviet Union?

In propaganda terms, Germany benefited from the new situation. During the first year of the war in the east, Germany's news service, the DNB, enhanced its profile in Portugal. British information providers, on the other hand, were negatively affected by the collaboration between the British government and the Soviet Union.[38] Salazar was clearly very worried about the growing level of co-operation between his country's ally and his arch-enemy, not least because it gave a boost to left-wing opponents of his regime. Just over a year after Operation Barbarossa had commenced, on 25 June 1942, Salazar delivered an address to the Portuguese nation in which he severely criticised the alliance between Britain and the Soviet Union. While this 'left a very good impression with the leadership in Berlin',[39] Campbell, the British ambassador, voiced concern that, using the war against Russia as a pretext, the Germans had achieved a considerable propaganda victory.

In general, however, the Nazi regime handled the seemingly advantageous situation far less convincingly. Instead of building upon the improved climate, it appears that in their attempts 'to cajole the Portuguese into supporting the Axis, the Germans set out to frighten them into it'.[40] The chance of a Portuguese entry into the war was, in any case, extremely remote. According to Leitão de Barros not a single member of Salazar's regime ever dared to suggest 'anything resembling entry into the war on Germany's side'.[41] In view of Salazar's worries about the effects of a German victory upon Portugal's independence – expressed, for instance, very openly to Franco in their meeting of February 1942[42] – it was indeed highly unlikely that others in the regime would advocate joining Germany in the war.

Instead, the threat of becoming embroiled in a war against Germany lingered on. After the failure to complete Operation Felix, Hitler switched to Operation Isabella in May 1941. To prevent a British expeditionary force from landing on the Iberian peninsula, Hitler decided, the final objective of the operation had to be the occupation of the most important Spanish and Portuguese ports. At this point, the Salazar regime still had reason to be concerned about Hitler's intentions. Yet Isabella was eventually abandoned on 29 May 1942. While a new operational plan, Ilona, continued to highlight the potential significance of the Iberian peninsula, it was of a purely defensive nature. The plan did not envisage an attack on Portugal, only the occupation of the Pyrenean passes and possibly the occupation of northern Spanish ports in order to protect the French Atlantic coast. The complete exclusion of Portugal from the plan was, however, unknown to the Portuguese government, which, instead, drew worrying conclusions about the sudden increase in the number of German troops in the south of France in mid–1942.

The situation in mid–1942 was symptomatic of the ambivalent attitude of the Portuguese government towards the Nazi regime for most of the period between June 1941 and June 1944. On the one hand, the possibility of an eruption of hostilities with the Third Reich was never completely discounted; on the other, the Salazar regime at times showed its appreciation of Germany's military efforts against the Soviet Union. Vocal support did not, however, translate into even the kind of minimal military assistance that Franco rendered with the Blue Division.[43] While germanophilia existed among officials in the army officer corps, the Portuguese Legion, the secret police, the international police and the youth movement, their activities in support of the German war effort were confined to Portugal itself. Most of these activities were, in fact, related to ensuring Germany's access to Portugal's vital wolfram production.[44]

In mid–1942, Hitler's temporary increase in the number of German troops near the Pyrenees had briefly alarmed the Portuguese government. A few months later, in November 1942, Salazar had considerably more reason to be anxious about the possibility of war. In the first instance, however, Allied, not Axis, activities heightened his concern. Operation Torch not only brought the fighting very close to the Iberian peninsula, it also increased the likelihood of both Portugal's and Spain's involvement. To allay Salazar's anxiety, Campbell, Britain's ambassador, passed on a message from Churchill that the actions of the Allies would not affect the neutrality of either Portugal or Spain. President Roosevelt had a similar message sent to President Carmona.[45] Until the Allied invasion of Sicily in June 1943, however, Salazar could not be sure that the Iberian peninsula would not become the target of either Allied landings or preventative measures by the Axis powers. As I have shown for Spain, German officials, in fact, considered the possibility of having to take control of the peninsula.[46] Portugal's main objective was therefore that Spain defended its neutrality 'like its most precious treasure, [as] war in Spain mean[t] war in Portugal'.[47]

In the end, the Portuguese government was relieved to discover that the Iberian peninsula did not become drawn into the conflict either through hostile acts by the belligerents or, in the case of Spain, on its own volition. Yet Salazar had no reason to relax. While Torch had not resulted in any adverse effects for Portugal, the threat of being drawn into the conflict was kept alive by repeated attempts on the part of the British government to gain military facilities on the Azores islands. These requests, which Salazar had always brusquely rejected, culminated on 18 June 1943 in a British note invoking Portugal's duties as set out in the alliance. This demand could therefore not be so easily brushed aside.

Notwithstanding the urgency of the matter, Salazar initially tried to delay a decision by referring to all kinds of potential dangers. In effect, he hypothesised about a possible peace between Germany and the Soviet Union which would allow Hitler to dispatch millions of soldiers to the Iberian peninsula.[48] This time, however, he was not able to avoid making this crucial concession to the British. A few days after the British note, Salazar finally acceded to Britain's demands and talks commenced in earnest.

After lengthy and often difficult negotiations,[49] the Azores bases accord was finally signed on 17 August 1943. The transfer date for the bases was set for 8 October 1943. Salazar's continued concern about ceding the bases to Britain had been allayed by three concessions. First, Britain promised to render Portugal all necessary military assistance in the event of an attack by German forces. Second, a joint plan of co-operation for the defence of Portugal was to be worked out, and, third, Britain was to supply war material and technical assistance.[50]

In hindsight, Salazar need not have been so apprehensive about Germany's reaction. The most worrying scenario, an invasion of the Iberian peninsula, did not eventuate. In view of Germany's military position it was in any case always impracticable. The Luftwaffe did not commence air attacks on Lisbon, nor did the Kriegsmarine attack Portuguese shipping.[51] The response of the Nazi regime was, in fact, negligible. When, on 12

October 1943, the Secretary-general of the Ministry of Foreign Affairs, Luís Teixeira de Sampaio, officially informed Huene of the accord with Britain, the German minister's reaction was rational and involved 'neither recriminations, nor insults, nor threats'.[52] Instead of the expected complaints, Huene simply demanded the clarification of several issues: what kind of facilities had been granted, would the British occupy the islands, would Portugal remain neutral, would the United States also be part of the accord? Sampaio replied to the apparent satisfaction of the German minister. Despite the concession granted to Portugal's ally, the country's neutrality was to be maintained.

Huene and other German officials in Portugal seemingly accepted the assurances of the Portuguese government.[53] When the minister subsequently reported back to Berlin, the reaction was one of disapproval, though with no apparent hostile intent. A strong protest was lodged with the Portuguese government, but beyond that repercussions did not follow. While rumours abounded in Lisbon about a substantial concentration of Germany's troops in Bayonne,[54] nothing actually happened. Not only was it clear to Hitler that he lacked the means to stage any aggressive response, but he was also aware that he had more to lose than to gain by reacting harshly. The Nazi regime was, in fact, able to use Salazar's obvious unease about his 'unneutral' concessions to the British. Salazar was, for instance, easily swayed to guarantee not to offer similar facilities to the United States. Germany's second major demand, not to impose an export embargo on wolfram, was even more agreeable to Salazar.[55] While the Azores accord was undoubtedly of military significance to the Allies,[56] Portugal continued to provide Nazi Germany with vital economic services.

Portuguese wolfram

In early 1944, Duke Domingos Palmela, as Monteiro's successor Portuguese ambassador in London since 30 September 1943, explained to John Winant, the US ambassador, that the Nazi regime had not reacted strongly to the Azores accord because Portugal kept up its wolfram supplies to Germany. Only if these supplies ceased, Palmela continued, would the Nazis take retaliatory action.[57] Probably deliberately, the ambassador clung to an exaggerated notion of the Reich's scope for retaliation. Moreover, Palmela's interpretation was also influenced by Salazar's keen interest in the continuation of the lucrative wolfram trade – though Palmela did not, of course, admit this openly. In essence, however, Palmela's conclusion held true. In late 1943 and 1944, the Nazi regime was, indeed, much more concerned about the most important product it received from Portugal than about the Azores accord.

For most of the Second World War, Nazi Germany's relations with Portugal were dominated by economic considerations. It has been shown that, despite many sympathetic comments about its military campaign against the Soviet Union, the Third Reich could never expect a military commitment by the Salazar regime. In contrast to his fellow Iberian dictator, Salazar never seriously pondered throwing in his lot with the Axis, nor did he provide the Third Reich with any military services comparable to those of the Franco regime.

Throughout the war, Salazar also repeatedly expressed misgivings about the Western Allies, most notably the United States. Characteristic was a comment the dictator made at the beginning of 1943. Salazar argued that 'an American victory … signifie[d] the triumph of the materialism of Wall Street and the immorality of Hollywood, not to mention the threat [it posed] to the Atlantic islands'.[58] Even Salazar's 'personal "war" against the US',[59] however, never amounted to a serious threat to Portugal's relationship with Britain and the United States. Ultimately, he preferred a victory of the Western Allies to the war being won by the Axis powers. Nonetheless, Salazar's attitude did not stop him from permitting the provision of services of immense value to the German war economy.

Of central significance among these services was, without any doubt, the supply of wolfram. In February 1942, the Economic and Armaments Office of the OKW made this very clear when it urgently requested Paul Pleiger, the Reich commissioner for coal, to release 100,000 mt of coal for export to Portugal. The office argued that

> Portuguese wolfram supplies are of *decisive* [emphasis added] importance to cover the *urgent* [emphasis added] needs of the armaments industry in the area of high-quality machine tools and in the manufacturing of contacts for the production of high-grade fuels. The significance [of Portuguese wolfram] can further be understood by the express order of the Führer to stop the use of wolfram in the production of extremely effective special munitions in favour of the requirements mentioned above.[60]

Portugal, like Spain, clearly benefited from the urgent need of the Nazi regime to secure sufficient quantities of wolfram, a benefit which was enhanced by the pre-emptive counter-measures taken by the Allies. Portugal, in fact, played an even more important role in the production and export of wolfram to Germany than its Iberian neighbour.

Table 6.1 *Portuguese wolfram production, 1938–44*

Year	mt
1938	2,300
1940	4,100
1942	4,100
1944	3,100

Note: Unless stated otherwise figures refer to wolfram ore with about 65% wolfram content.
Source: Telo, *Portugal na Segunda Guerra,* vol. II, 22.

The official Portuguese mining figures indicate how the importance of wolfram increased during the war (Table 6.1). Although in the Spanish case production went up much more dramatically, from below 300 mt annually up to and including 1940 to its highest level of just over 3,600 mt in 1943,[61] the importance of Portuguese wolfram antedated and exceeded that of Spanish wolfram. When, in July 1941, the British Ministry of Economic Warfare reported that 'the wolfram bubble ha[d] now spread from Portugal to Spain',[62] it acknowledged that Germany had initially shown more interest in the Portuguese than the Spanish output of the material. Apart from 1940, when only 61 mt of wolfram reached Germany, Portugal had consistently been the most important European source of wolfram even though its overall importance remained meagre until 1941. In 1939, for instance, it made up only 8 per cent of all Germany's wolfram imports (8,000 mt), only slightly up from less than 5 per cent in 1938 (total imports: 14,200 mt).[63]

During the second half of 1940, and particularly in 1941, Germany's interest in Portuguese wolfram grew rapidly. With safe transport routes available again soon after the defeat of France, German buyers made an all-out effort to increase imports of Portuguese products by rail via Spain and France. The bulk of the wolfram purchased originated from Portuguese producers, but, as in the case of Spain, Germany also benefited from the output of German-owned mines. Owned by Rowak, the organisation which had originally been founded in Berlin in October 1936 to control Germany's economic relations with Nationalist Spain,[64] the Minero Silvícola bought mining concessions and ran various mines for Germany's benefit. In 1943, Silvícola became the administrative centre of Nazi Germany's wolfram operations in Portugal,[65] which included the activities of two

Table 6.2   *German wolfram imports from Portugal, 1940–44*

Year	mt
1940	61
1941	1,968
1942	1,306[a]
1943	1,755[b]
1944	315 (possibly nearly 500)

Notes: Figures refer to wolfram ore with about 65% wolfram content.
[a] 62.5% of Germany's total importation of pure wolfram.
[b] 61% of Germany's total importation of pure wolfram.
Sources: Leitz, *Economic Relations*, 171 n. 3; IWM BA R13 XII/30 (previously Speer documents), Board of Trade German Division, statistics on steel-improvers, 10 July 1946.

other organisations, the Gesellschaft für Elektrometallurgie (GfE) and the Sonimi group.

German efforts paid off very quickly. In 1941, the Third Reich imported its largest annual amount of Portuguese wolfram ever, a total of 1,968 mt.[66] Yet just when matters were evolving to Germany's satisfaction, two developments threatened to thwart Nazi plans. In the first instance, German buyers were adversely affected by financial pressures. To disrupt the concerted Nazi acquisition campaign, the British government had decided to expand its own purchasing activities. As a result of the ensuing economic warfare over Portuguese wolfram, the price of the material rose dramatically, a development which Spain was to experience shortly afterwards. From about RM 2,800 in May 1941, the price per ton of Portuguese wolfram increased to RM 60,000–65,000 in the first two months of 1942.[67] At this point, Nazi wolfram purchasing operations were to be affected by a second development.

By the end of 1941, German buyers had become aware that the Portuguese regime was considering interventionist steps to control the rampant production of and trade in wolfram. Using methods of both intimidation and temptation, the Nazi regime tried to ensure that wolfram supplies from Portugal would not be reduced. On the one hand, Salazar and his government were confronted with the possibility of German attacks on Portuguese shipping – with the *Corte Real* incident as a clear reminder of the might of Germany's submarine fleet.[68] On the other hand, German negotiators, led by Eltze, tempted their Portuguese counterparts with the prospect of an economic agreement which included, among other sought-after products,[69] the offer of supplies of German war material.

By and large, the methods applied by the Nazi regime succeeded. In fact, even though it was not able to prevent the Portuguese government from taking control of the wolfram trade, the new arrangement introduced by Salazar was intended to work to the advantage of both economies. For Portuguese wolfram producers, however, February 1942 saw the end of a particularly lucrative period – though by smuggling to Spain, where the 'wolfram rush'[70] had not yet reached its climax, a considerable number of producers and middlemen continued to keep their profits at an extremely high level.[71]

What had happened? In contrast to Franco, Salazar had become so concerned that both the extent of wolfram mining concessions and the price of the raw material were running out of control that he imposed a system of restraints. Under the new regulations, which came into force on 1 March 1942, the state set strict limits on the production of wolfram and forcibly reduced its price to Esc 150 (about RM 15) per kilogram (including a government tax of Esc 70).[72] All wolfram produced, including that of mines owned by foreigners, was to be bought by a government commission at a set price and then sold on to the foreign customers. Severe penalties for the illegal mining and export of wolfram were introduced, with a state organisation, the CRCM (Comissão Reguladora do Comércio de Metais, Metals Regulatory Commission), as the only officially recognised buyer.

In introducing the new regulations, the Portuguese government tried to tackle two important issues. On the one hand, it was reacting to the growing disquiet of Portuguese agriculture about the loss of labour to the much more lucrative mining of wolfram.[73] On the other hand, it wanted to make sure that it was able to comply with German demands for wolfram.[74] Having received a contractual promise of up to 2,800 mt for 1942, the Nazi regime showed its satisfaction by relaxing its control over shipping to and from Portugal.

In the immediate aftermath of the agreement, German–Portuguese economic relations flourished. From 19 per cent in 1941, the Third Reich's share of Portugal's exports increased to nearly 25 per cent in 1942. In 1942, Germany also became the primary importer of Portuguese products.[75] As a whole, the trading relationship developed a clear imbalance in favour of Portugal. The gap between Portugal's imports from and exports to Germany, which in 1941 had only been just under RM 3 million in favour of the former, increased to nearly RM 71 million in 1942, and fell only slightly to RM 67 million in 1943. These official statistics conceal, however, the

Table 6.3   *Total Portuguese exports to Germany, 1938–44*

Year	Million RM
1938	24.7
1940	2.7
1941	33.7
1942	119.4[a]
1943	119.5
1944	36.1

Note: [a] 30% of total exports.
Sources: BA 31.02/6040, Reich Statistical Office, 'Ein- und Ausfuhr nach Ländern'. Slightly different figures are given in Boelcke, *Deutschland als Welthandelsmacht*, 140; BA 31.02/3352, table 5, 'Der deutsche Außenhandel mit wichtigen Ländern'.

Table 6.4   *Total German exports to Portugal, 1938–44*

Year	Million RM
1938	42.7
1940	3.7
1941	31.0
1942	48.7
1943	52.5
1944	41.7

Sources: BA 31.02/6040, Reich Statistical Office, 'Ein- und Ausfuhr nach Ländern'; Telo, *Portugal na Segunda Guerra*, vol. I, 240. Slightly different figures are given in Boelcke, *Deutschland als Welthandelsmacht*, 140; BA 31.02/3352, table 5, 'Der deutsche Außenhandel mit wichtigen Ländern'.

true level of expenditure the Third Reich was forced to apply in Portugal. In 1941 alone, RM 151 million went on the purchase of Portuguese goods, RM 97 million of it paid in hard currency.[76] As in Spain, wolfram was the main 'black hole', and, again as in the case of Spain, the Nazi regime resorted to a variety of ways and means to keep up with its growing financial commitments. In mid–1942, for instance, bank loans of RM 20 million were arranged in Portugal[77] while, in 1943, the Third Reich sold various ships to the Portuguese authorities which had been detained in Mozambique and Angolan ports since the outbreak of war.[78]

Most important, however, Portugal became the recipient of payments in gold. Switzerland's banks again played a pivotal role in these gold and currency dealings. In his indictment of the role of the Basel-based Bank for International Settlements (BIS) during the Second World War, the Swiss author Gian Trepp summarises the way in which the transfer system was initially conducted:

> The lucrative escudo deals with the Reichsbank ... were a perfect symbiosis of the BIS with the Swiss National Bank and the large commercial banks. Only the co-operation of the three parties made the turntable go round. In the words of National Bank president Ernst Weber [in a conversation with BIS president Thomas H. McKittrick in September 1941] ... 'The Banco de Portugal hands over escudos in exchange for gold which the Swiss National Bank in Berne, as a trustee, has ready for consignment to Lisbon. Paying in gold, the Reichsbank has also accumulated large quantities of escudos through Switzerland's commercial banks. By selling the gold, the banks have made Swiss francs available to the Banco de Portugal, which it, in turn, has used to buy gold from the National Bank. The National Bank will not have to sent to Lisbon the gold thus acquired by the Banco de Portugal.'[79]

Instead, the BIS, expert in the movement of gold, arranged the delivery of the gold from Switzerland to Portugal. Trepp's research reveals that, from the first 'test run' at the beginning of October 1941 to 5 January 1942, about 20 mt of gold (about SFr 100 million) were moved from Berne to Lisbon.[80] Very quickly, the Allies became aware of the consignments and eventually forced the Swiss National Bank to reduce the escudo deals to Swiss requirements only.[81] Portugal, however, continued to receive 'German' gold.[81] Allied post-war investigations revealed that, in total, the Bank of Portugal had been the recipient of between 38.45 mt and 46.76 mt of gold with a value of between US $43 and $53 million (about RM 109 million to RM 135 million).[83]

Germany's gold-for-escudos deals with Portugal proved to be vital in the acquisition of various services and products, most notably of course wolfram. In a significant way, the Nazis also resorted to a payment method it frequently used in its trade with other countries, exports of war material. Ever since 1936, the Portuguese armed forces had looked to Nazi Germany to supply part of their perceived requirements. Despite the greater willingness of the British government to provide war material to Portugal than, for instance, to its Iberian neighbour, and Portugal's comparatively low expenditure, Nazi Germany was able to win a very useful share of Portugal's increased purchases of armaments.

During the war years, the regime's expenditure on military equipment grew strongly. Under 30 per cent of the Portuguese state's total budget in 1938, military expenditure was to exceed 40 per cent in 1941, 1942 and 1943.[84] For the period from the mid–1930s, when Portugal embarked on its rearmament programme, to late 1943, Portuguese data show that German supplies of war material made up nearly two-thirds of Portugal's total military expenditure of about Esc 3.6 billion (about RM 370 million).[85] Even while the Axis was being defeated in both Stalingrad and North Africa, negotiations were under way for the supply of substantial quantities of German arms and arms-related material. In January 1943, Hitler agreed to all the demands for armaments the Portuguese military had raised in December 1942. Estimated to total RM 30 million, these arms included field cannons, anti-tank and anti-aircraft guns and ammunition, and track-laying vehicles.[86]

While arms supplies to Spain were deemed to have at least a partly military purpose (to help the Franco regime defend itself against an Allied invasion), German arms exports to Portugal served a purely economic end. In January 1943, Hitler acknowledged that supplies of war material to Portugal were intended to satisfy Germany's requirements of wolfram and, to a lesser extent, tinned sardines. After protracted negotiations, which led to various changes in the original list of offerings, a contract was finally signed in August 1943. It guaranteed the Portuguese military war material of a total value of Esc 267 million (RM 27.2 million). According to British sources, Esc 168 million of the contract was to be used to improve Germany's clearing imbalance while a further Esc 99 million was paid in gold via Switzerland direct to Germany.[87] The contract involved the supply in instalments of 129 field cannon, and 200 anti-aircraft guns with ammunition and 600 machine guns.[88]

Despite continued Portuguese interest in German war material, the August contract constituted the most important single deal of the remainder of the war. For the whole of 1943, war material contracts to a total value of RM 36.3 million were signed. Compared with Germany's total contractual arms export obligations in 1943 the quantities purchased by Portugal were fairly insignificant (about 2.8 per cent of the total). Still, it seems hard to understand why the Nazi regime should have released any war material to a government which had not the slightest intention of using it in support of the Axis. In fact, as the signing of the August 1943 contract and the dispatch of the first equipment both coincided with the signing and execution of the Azores accord, a fully fledged Portuguese attachment to the Allies seemed likely. Yet Hitler never expected Portugal

Table 6.5 *German arms exports to Portugal, 1937–43 (contracts only)*

Year	Million RM
1937	19.80
1938	7.20
1939	0.01
1940	0.06
1941	28.70
1942	1.00
1943	36.30

Note: In 1941 the value of actual arms exports to Portugal amounted to RM 14.6 million, in 1942 to nearly RM 10 million.
Sources: BA/MA RW19/3195, AGK statistics on war material contracts and exports, 6 and 7 September 1944; Boelcke, *Deutschland als Welthandelsmacht*, 136.

to commit itself to the Axis, while Salazar never intended to let the Azores accord become a major stepping stone to joining the Allied camp.

All the Nazi regime could hope for was a satisfactory continuation of wolfram supplies. The OKW official in charge of Portuguese affairs epitomised the German attitude in his report on the last quarter of 1943: 'To ensure the continuation of wolfram supplies, both the current negotiations and the consignments [of war material] have been continued despite the change which the enemy occupation of the Azores has brought about.'[89] Nazi officials, in fact, had little reason for concern. To the Portuguese dictator and the general staff of the country's armed forces, the arms deal with the Nazis was both a kind of compensation for the Azores accord and a recognition of the continued power of the Axis. All along, Salazar intended to keep the wolfram trade with Germany going.

At the beginning of 1944, both regimes had reason to be satisfied with their bilateral relations. Portuguese wolfram continued to arrive in Germany while German arms were dispatched to Portugal on schedule. Subsequently, however, shipments in both directions failed to meet the expectations of either side. Portugal never received all the armaments agreed in August 1943 (and in subsequent agreements) – even though the German authorities maintained supplies to the last possible moment. Of the major contract of August 1943, seventy-six field cannon were still outstanding in July 1944, just before land communications between the Third Reich and the Iberian peninsula were cut for good.[90]

The exportation of Portuguese wolfram to Germany had, in fact, ended slightly earlier. In June 1944, the German government failed to induce Salazar to withdraw an embargo on wolfram exports. The economic and financial advantages of the wolfram trade were not sufficient to change Salazar's mind. Germany simply could not match the huge pressure the Allies put upon the Portuguese government. In contrast to previous occasions, the Nazi regime did not even attempt to threaten Portugal.

Back in the second half of 1942, when Nazi officials had been strongly concerned about whether Salazar would renew the wolfram accord, threats were repeatedly made about shipping from and to Portugal. Even then, however, Salazar was not easily intimidated. Towards the end of July 1942, he angrily told his ambassador in Berlin: 'Germany cannot count on our goodwill for ever if, for reasons unacceptable to us, it wants to continue a policy of not recognising our interests and objectives by pursuing and attacking Portuguese shipping.'[91]

Subsequently, Nazi officials continued to put pressure on Salazar and he continued to refuse to negotiate a new wolfram agreement. In November 1942, the successful implementation of Operation Torch strengthened his growing belief that the power of the Axis was declining. He again resisted German demands for new negotiations. Talks with the Allies over supplies to Portugal failed, however, to develop to the regime's satisfaction, either. At the same time, Germany was intensifying its pressure. In early 1943, Ernst Eisenlohr, the Reich's envoy, threatened to have Portugal's fishing fleet and its shipping lanes to Britain, both vital to the country, attacked. In the end, against Britain's strongly voiced opposition, Salazar gave in. A new accord was signed for the period 1 March 1943 to 29 February 1944 during which Germany was to receive 2,100 mt of wolfram at steady prices of Esc 150 per kilogram. For the time being, and despite its military setbacks, Nazi Germany's intimidatory tactics combined with promises of various supplies continued to possess sufficient 'convincing' power.[92]

In 1943, Portugal had continued to be Germany's most important source of wolfram, followed by the only other source of significance, Spain. In fact, after a decline to 1,300 mt in 1942, well below the promised quantity, wolfram imports picked up again at a time when the likelihood of Axis victory became ever more remote. In 1943, Portugal, though again not supplying the guaranteed amount, exported 1,755 mt to Germany, a vital contribution to the country's war economy.[93] Measured in pure wolfram yield, Portugal accounted for about 62.5 per cent of the Reich's total imports in 1942 and about 61 per cent in 1943.[94]

As in the case of Spain, the Allies, particularly the US government, responded by pressing the Portuguese government to reduce or even completely stop wolfram supplies to the Third Reich.[95] From the figures quoted above, it is obvious that these efforts were only partly successful. Until well into 1944, British and US efforts, while reducing Germany's access to wolfram, did not have a marked impact. Even under pressure, Salazar was obstinately insistent on continuing exports to the Third Reich.

Salazar had various reasons to be concerned about a cessation of wolfram supplies. In many ways, his motives resembled those of Franco in neighbouring Spain. Salazar very clearly recognised the economic and financial benefits of selling wolfram to both the Allies and Germany, a point he repeatedly made to British government officials. To Campbell, Salazar explained that wolfram mining contributed £9 million to £10 million annually to the Portuguese economy, a contribution which translated into about £2 million for the coffers of the Portuguese Treasury.[96] During the period January to September 1942 alone, Portugal exported wolfram worth over Esc 1 billion (about £10 million), the equivalent of about 38 per cent of the country's total income from exports.[97] In employment terms, wolfram mining became a mainstay of the economy, employing at least 80,000 people at the height of the boom.[98] When, in early May 1944, General Carmona tried to persuade his Prime Minister to rethink his inflexible attitude on wolfram exports to Germany, Salazar made precisely this point to fend off the President's urging.[99]

Other factors helped to make the Portuguese dictator very reluctant to comply with Allied demands. Salazar, like Franco, was not at all happy about foreign governments, in this case particularly that of the United States,[100] interfering in his policy-making. Moreover, Salazar regarded his attitude to wolfram exports as proof of his country's neutral status. Denying one belligerent side supplies to which the other had continued access did not conform to his perception of neutrality. Finally, his anti-Communist zeal also induced him to give at least some support to the Third Reich and its fight against the Soviet Union.

Even Salazar, however, ultimately had to acknowledge the overwhelming power of the Allies, not only in military terms, but, more directly in the Portuguese context, in terms of supplies vital to the country. The embargo on petroleum supplies to Spain over a three-month period in the first half of 1944 reminded Salazar of the vulnerability of his position. At the beginning of March he received an official reminder that Portugal might soon be at the receiving end of the same treatment. At this point, however, he remained steadfastly opposed to accepting the demands of the Allies.[101]

Although Salazar did not emphasise his usual anxiety about Nazi retaliatory action, including an invasion of the Iberian peninsula,[102] various comments in a message to Churchill largely reflected concerns repeatedly expressed in the past. These included, first and foremost, Germany's campaign against the Soviet Union, the enemy of 'Christian civilisation', Germany's continued supplies of valuable goods, and finally Germany's right to make use of the mines it owned in Portugal.[103] It was clear that Salazar's concerns were of more relevance to the continuation of wolfram supplies than any visible action taken by the Nazi regime. Nazi counter-pressure could no longer match the intensity of Allied efforts to stop the wolfram trade with Germany.

In the light of what the Third Reich continued to receive from Portugal, there was, in fact, little need to react harshly. Until mid–1944, German–Portuguese trade relations remained on a steady, mutually beneficial course. During the period January to July 1944, Germany exported more to Portugal than during the same period in the previous year (RM 41.7 versus RM 31 million). Owing to a reduction in wolfram supplies, the value of imports from Portugal decreased (RM 36.1 million).[104] Generally, however, it appears that Salazar continued to apply his interpretation of neutrality, to the advantage of Germany. While negotiations over a renewal of the wolfram accord, which had run out in February 1944, did not produce a result, Germany nonetheless managed to import satisfactory quantities of wolfram.[105]

Yet the pressure of the Allies proved relentless and was finally crowned with success. On 24 May 1944, the British ambassador, Campbell, again approached Salazar about a total embargo on wolfram exports to Germany. This request was followed up by an offical note on 29 May in which the British government invoked the alliance between the two countries and demanded the cessation of all wolfram exports to Germany. Finally, after many fruitless approaches by the Allies in the past, the Portuguese government finally saw fit to conform with the demand. On 5 June 1944, Salazar agreed to implement an embargo on wolfram exports to all countries. Its official commencement date was set for 7 June.[106]

Shortly after wolfram supplies had ceased, communications between Germany and Portugal became radically restricted owing to the Allied advance in France. A major deal for supplies of tinned sardines, for instance, was fulfilled only to a very limited extent. Alongside wolfram and tin, tinned sardines had been a mainstay of Portugal's trade with Germany, indeed a mainstay of the country's trade as a whole.[107] As early as 1941, Germany had been Portugal's main customer for tinned sardines.

Table 6.6   *Exports of tinned sardines, 1938–44 (000 mt)*

Year	Germany	UK	Total
1938	10.0	4.6	30.4
1939	9.9	14.6	40.7
1940	—	17.2	36.2
1941	11.4	23.6	49.9
1942	19.0	7.1	32.9
1943	18.4	17.2	37.5
1944	17.2	20.7	33.5

Source: Telo, *Portugal na Segunda Guerra*, vol. II, 24.

Even then, however, such imports had been possible only if adequate quantities of German war material were furnished to the Portuguese authorities to counterbalance the value of the sardines supplied.[108] The Nazi regime appears to have been sufficiently successful in satisfying Portuguese demands. Throughout 1942 and 1943 Germany remained Portugal's main customer and even in 1944 the country still managed to import nearly a quarter of Portugal's production.

With the departure of the last German troops from the Pyrenees, however, the already reduced economic contact with Portugal virtually ended. Some products found their way to Germany via other neutral countries, primarily Switzerland and Sweden. Largely, however, relations between the Third Reich and Portugal after August 1944 were entirely dependent on the few remaining aircraft which continued to fly between the two countries. Apart from negligible quantities of products, these aircraft ensured the limited continuation of certain other services which the Nazis had enjoyed during the war. One indication of these services can be found in the number of German officials active in Portugal. Commenting on the fact that, in 1944, the number of personnel in the German embassy in Lisbon reached its highest level during the period of the Third Reich (one minister, six counsellors, two secretaries, thirteen attachés or assistants), Telo has sarcastically observed: 'This increase was certainly not justified by the economic relations with Lisbon.'[109]

It was instead clear evidence of the importance of Lisbon as a centre of the 'secret war' between the Axis and the Allies.[110] Throughout the war, Lisbon remained one of the few places in Europe where officials from both belligerent sides could spy directly upon each other or even conduct secret meetings. As one SS officer concluded in late 1941, Lisbon constituted the 'most interesting place for espionage, as England and Americans [*sic*] were in direct contact there'.[111] The importance of the city was further enhanced because it boasted the only major Continental port which continued to offer a regular transatlantic service.

Intelligence gathering was made easier by the fact that large numbers of refugees from Axis Europe had chosen Lisbon as their major point of confluence. Many hoped to acquire a place on one of the ships sailing to the Americas, yet not all succeeded. Along with those, usually wealthy, Europeans who had chosen Lisbon as their haven in which to sit the war out, many others found themselves detained in the city owing to a lack of funds or tickets. This varied colony offered both a fertile recruiting ground for the intelligence-gathering organisations of the Nazi regime and an effective way of camouflaging the activities of their own officials. Many a Nazi official was dispatched overseas via Lisbon, many found their way back into Europe again via the city.[112] At the end of the war, the files of X–2, the counter-intelligence branch of the Office of Strategic Services, listed 1,900 enemy agents in Portugal.[113]

Lisbon even offered the Third Reich the opportunity to circumvent the British blockade and continue limited trade relations, particularly with Latin America. In exceptional cases, such trade was even conducted with the reluctant agreement of the British government. The Brazilian government, for instance, managed to persuade the British to allow the passage of German war material which Brazil had ordered before the war but which the Nazi regime had managed to transport only as far as Lisbon when war broke out. By November 1940, over 100 field cannon and about the same amount of 8.8 cm anti-aircraft guns (with ammunition) had been transported to Lisbon though it took another year and lengthy Anglo-American–Brazilian negotiations before they finally arrived in Rio de Janeiro.[114]

Most trade was, of course, conducted against the wishes of the Allies. German smuggling activity via Lisbon was rife, in particular the secret carriage of small, valuable goods such as industrial diamonds and platinum. In view of these various opportunities offered by Portugal's neutrality it was clearly in the interest of the Nazi regime to encourage the Salazar regime to persist with its independent status.

Not only did Salazar sustain Portugal's neutrality until the end of the war in Europe, he also tried to continue 'correct' relations with the Third Reich. At the end of March 1945, Portugal still adhered to the Navigation accord with the Nazi regime, even though the Kriegsmarine was no longer able to enforce it.[115] On the news of the death of Hitler, Salazar even went so far as to order three days of official mourning which included the lowering of flags on official buildings. A few days later, he did, however, finally respond with 'unusual speed' to the demand of the Allies that he should sever diplomatic relations with the Third Reich and close down and seal its buildings in Portugal. Two days before Germany's total capitulation relations between the two countries finally ended.[116]

Notes

1 George F. Kennan to US Department of State, 4 February 1943, in Douglas L. Wheeler, 'The Price of Neutrality: Portugal, the Wolfram Question, and World War II', part I, *Luso-Brazilian Review* XXIII (1986), 110.
2 Until his death in 1951, Salazar's superior as President of Portugal was General Carmona.
3 PA-AA R106444, Huene to AA, 23 June 1937.
4 Hugh Kay, *Salazar and Modern Portugal* (London, 1970), 67.
5 On Portugal's alliance with Britain, see Glyn Stone, *The Oldest Ally: Britain and the Portuguese Connection 1936–1941* (Woodbridge, 1994).
6 According to a British intelligence report roughly 320,000 German rifles and 555,000 revolvers were transported via Portugal to Spain between January 1937 and August 1938; Stone, *The Oldest Ally*, 10.
7 See IWM Krupp, file 15a, Vaillant (Krupp Berlin), to Krawa (Krupp Essen), 8 September 1936.
8 See Kay, *Salazar*, 86–121.
9 PA-AA R106444, Huene to AA, 9 March 1937.
10 PA-AA R106445, memo by Dr Schwendemann, 7 May 1938.
11 PA-AA R106445, Reichsgruppe Industrie to Sabath (AA), 13 July 1938. On the crisis in the Anglo-Portuguese relationship, see Paolo Brundu Olla, 'La neutralité du Portugal pendant la seconde guerre mondiale', in Jukka Nevakivi (ed.), *Neutrality in History/La neutralité dans l'histoire* (Helsinki, 1993), 202–4.
12 See PA-AA R106446, Reichsgruppe Industrie to Sabath (AA), 16 March 1939.
13 César Oliveira, 'A sobrevivência das ditaduras e a neutralidade peninsular na Segunda Guerra Mundial', in *O Estado Novo; das origens ao fim da autarcia*, vol. I (Lisbon, 1987), 359.
14 On the history of the Spanish–Portuguese negotiations leading to the treaty, see Fernando Rosas, 'O Pacto Ibérico e a neutralização da península', in Fernando Rosas, *O salazarismo e a alliança luso-britânica; estudos sobre a política externa do Estado Novo nos anos 30 e 40* (Lisbon, 1988), 107–13.
15 Both countries pledged not only to respect each other's territories and frontiers, but also to deny help to any aggressor against either country, including to reject any pact or alliance which might involve aggression against either country.
16 While some authors emphasise that expansionist intentions were harboured only by sections of the Falange (see, for instance, Kay, *Salazar*, 156), the

future of Portugal was considered by the leadership of the Franco regime itself. In his first meeting with Ribbentrop, in September 1940, Serrano Suñer argued that 'geographically speaking, Portugal really had no right to exist; she had only a moral and political justification for independence ... Spain recognized this, but had to require that Portugal align herself with the Spanish group.' It is more than likely that Suñer's comments reflected Franco's own ideas; Preston, *Franco*, 377 and 359.

17 Júlia Leitão de Barros, 'Anglofilia e germanofilia em Portugal durante a Segunda Guerra Mundial', in Mario Carrilho *et al.*, *Portugal na Segunda Guerra Mundial; contributos para uma reavaliação* (Lisbon, 1989), 94.
18 Cited in Mário Neves, 'A diplomacia portuguesa nas duas guerras do século', in Carrilho *et al.*, *Portugal na Segunda Guerra Mundial*, 153.
19 BA/MA RW5/v. 643, Portugal report no. 40, 20 October 1943.
20 António José Telo, *Portugal na Segunda Guerra 1941–1945*, vol. II (Lisbon, 1991), 250.
21 BA/MA RW5/v.430, report by Hashagen (Lisbon) on the evolution of Portugal's position, 11 January 1944.
22 PA-AA R106446, memo by Wiehl, 7 February 1940. Portuguese goods were transported by rail to Spain. From Spain, the transport to Italy took place either by sea to Genoa or on transport planes to Italian airports; PA-AA R106446, Sabath (AA) to German mission in Lisbon, 24 February 1940.
23 In the aftermath of Poland's defeat Salazar publicly praised 'the heroic sacrifice of Poland'; Kay, *Salazar*, 153.
24 J. Freire Antunes, '1939–1945: a guerra de que nos livraram', *Semanário*, 6 May 1989, quoted in Maria Carrilho, 'Política de defesa e de rearmamento', in Carrilho *et al.*, *Portugal na Segunda Guerra Mundial*, 20.
25 Carrilho, 'Política de defesa', 23–4.
26 BA/MA RW5/v.430, report by Hashagen (Lisbon) on the evolution of Portugal's position, 11 January 1944.
27 Neves, 'A diplomacia portuguesa', 172–3.
28 Leitão de Barros, 'Anglofilia e germanofilia', 102.
29 See Rosas, 'O Pacto Ibérico', 114–7.
30 Templewood Papers, Box XIII/22, A Year and a half of Spanish Non-belligerency, report by Hoare, 5 January 1942.
31 The Falange (*FET y de la JONS*) demonstrated its intentions by producing maps of the Iberian peninsula which did not show Portugal; Oliveira, 'A sobrevivência das ditaduras', 366 n. 4. On similar views expressed by Spanish army officers see the report by the German air attaché in Madrid, Eckard Kramer, 7 May 1941, in Rosas, 'O Pacto Ibérico', appendix II, 126–8.
32 Franco Nogueira, *Salazar*, vol. III, *As grandes crises 1936–1945* (Coimbra, 1978), 324.
33 Telo, *Portugal na Segunda Guerra*, vol. II, 251.
34 Cole, *Britain and the War of Words in Neutral Europe*, 53.
35 Leitão de Barros, 'Anglofilia e germanofilia', 98.
36 The Legião Portuguesa, founded in September 1936, was a kind of voluntary Home Guard dedicated to the ideals of the national movement.
37 Nogueira, *Salazar*, 327.
38 Leitão de Barros, 'Anglofilia e germanofilia', 115. On Nazi propaganda

activities in Portugal (with examples of material used) see António José Telo, *Propaganda e guerra secreta em Portugal 1939–45* (Lisbon, 1990), 30–40.

39 Comment by Tovar, Portugal's ambassador in Berlin, in António José Telo, *Portugal na Segunda Guerra 1941–1945*, vol. I (Lisbon, 1991), 89.

40 Cole, *Britain and the War of Words*, 70–1.

41 Leitão de Barros, 'Anglofilia e germanofilia', 120.

42 Salazar argued that an Allied victory was less to be feared than an Axis success. A Nazi victory, he concluded, would lead to the Germanisation of Europe.

43 In contrast to the Franco regime, the Portuguese authorities never allowed German submarines into Portuguese territorial waters and ports; Kay, *Salazar*, 152.

44 See Douglas L. Wheeler, 'In the Service of Order: The Portuguese Political Police and the British, German and Spanish Intelligence Services 1932–1945', *Journal of Contemporary History* 18 (1983); Leitão de Barros, 'Anglofilia e germanofilia', 121.

45 Neves, 'A diplomacia portuguesa', 166.

46 See Christian Leitz, 'Nazi Germany and the Threat of an Allied Invasion of Spain 1942–1943', in Peter Monteath and Frederic S. Zuckerman (eds), *Modern Europe: Histories and Identities* (Adelaide, 1998), 133–43.

47 Monteiro to Portuguese Ministry of Foreign Affairs, in Neves, 'A diplomacia portuguesa', 178.

48 *Ibid.*, 180.

49 Detailed information on the negotiations can be found in Telo, *Portugal na Segunda Guerra*, vol. I, 151–63.

50 Neves, 'A diplomacia portuguesa', 187. Among other additional promises, Britain also guaranteed to protect Portuguese shipping.

51 The threat of German submarine attacks against Portuguese ships had been a real concern of the Portuguese authorities ever since December 1941, when the merchant ship *Corte Real* was sunk. It had been on its way to the United States and the Germans later insisted, probably correctly, that it had been carrying contraband, including wolfram; Telo, *Portugal na Segunda Guerra*, vol. I, 189. At least three other ships were also sunk by 'unidentified', i.e. presumably German, submarines.

52 Nogueira, *Salazar*, 471.

53 See, for instance, BA/MA RW5/v. 643, Portugal report no. 40, 20 October 1943.

54 Nogueira, *Salazar*, 474.

55 The Portuguese government also accepted German demands that Portuguese ships sailing to the Azores should not carry supplies for the Allied troops and that their cargo would not exceed pre-accord levels; Telo, *Portugal na Segunda Guerra*, vol. II, 181.

56 In view of the services rendered to the Allies in 1943, Carlos Bessa has argued that his country's neutrality was 'collaborative'. In Bessa's words, 'without these [services] the war would have developed differently, certainly less favourably'; Carlos Bessa, `La neutralité Portuguaise dans la Seconde Guerre Mondiale', in Roulet (ed.), *Les états neutres*, 151. In his article, Bessa also provides a useful summary of the Azores accord (pp. 144–6 and 148–50).

57 Nogueira, *Salazar*, 505.

58 Telo, *Portugal na Segunda Guerra*, vol. II, 112. On Salazar's disapproving attitude towards the United States see António Telo, 'Relações Portugal–EUA 1940–1941', in *O Estado Novo*, 371–93.

59 Telo, 'Relações Portugal–EUA', 387.

60 BA/MA RW19/433, draft of a letter, OKW to Pleiger, February 1942.

61 Portuguese figures in Telo, *Portugal na Segunda Guerra*, vol. II, 22. Spanish figures in Leitz, 'Nazi Germany's Struggle for Spanish Wolfram', 76.

62 PRO FO837/721, D. Davidson (MEW) to John Penton (Treasury), 3 July 1941.

63 Leitz, *Economic Relations*, 173, table 5.2. Spanish wolfram accounted for less than 1 per cent of Germany's total imports in both 1938 and 1939.

64 On the foundation, ownership and role of Rowak and Hisma, its counterpart in Spain, see Christian Leitz, 'Nazi Germany's Intervention in the Spanish Civil War and the Foundation of Hisma/Rowak', in Paul Preston and Ann L. Mackenzie (eds), *The Republic Besieged; Civil War in Spain 1936–1939* (Edinburgh, 1996), 53–86.

65 BA/MA RW19/435, memo of a meeting of German officials in Lisbon, 6 March 1943.

66 Leitz, *Economic Relations*, 171 n. 3.

67 PA-AA R109462, memo by Sabath on German–Portuguese economic relations, 8 June 1942.

68 See above.

69 Eltze's delegation also offered 60,000 mt of steel, ammonium sulphate, iron ore and paper; Telo, *Portugal na Segunda Guerra*, vol. I, 189.

70 Contemporary reports frequently drew a comparison with the California gold rush and referred to the 'wolfram fever'. See, *inter alia*, a Portuguese article in *Secolo* (11 January 1942) quoted in the *Dürener Tageszeitung*; IWM Speer Docs. FD2620/45, memo, 17 January 1942. Wheeler highlights a contemporary short story in which a German writer in Portugal compared wolfram's impact on the frontier mining area of Beira Alta with `the frenzy of a California gold rush'; Wheeler, `Price of Neutrality', part I, 115.

71 In 1942 the British authorities estimated that an additional one-third to half of the official wolfram supplies granted found their way to Germany via Spain. As in Spain, various Portuguese businessmen and public officials, including police officers, were involved in Nazi (and Allied) smuggling schemes. Even the Portuguese government was seemingly not averse to making use of the smuggling routes; Telo, *Portugal na Segunda Guerra*, vol. I, 214–16. See also Wheeler, 'Price of Neutrality', part II, 97.

72 On the decree, which also included Portugal's tin production, and its effects, see PA-AA R109462, memo by Sabath on German–Portuguese economic relations, 8 June 1942. On 10 July 1942 the official price of wolfram stood at Esc 120 per kilogram (about RM 12.5), four times the price paid for the raw material before the war. The price had risen to Esc 600 (about RM 61) by the end of 1942, before the government stabilised it again at Esc 120 in March 1943; see BA 25.01/4913, p. 219, and BA R7/962, report by Dr. Stahl, 26 October 1943.

73 On the dramatic effect of the *febre do volfrâmio* (wolfram fever) upon Portugal's society, see Wheeler, 'Price of Neutrality', part I, 114–16.

74 Telo, *Portugal na Segunda Guerra*, vol. II, 22–3.

75 BA/MA RW19/438, statistics on Portugal's imports and exports, February 1944.
76 PA-AA R109462, memo by Sabath on German–Portuguese economic relations, 8 June 1942.
77 Ibid.
78 Boelcke, Deutschland als Welthandelsmacht, 176.
79 Trepp, Bankgeschäfte mit dem Feind, 61.
80 Ibid., 62–3.
81 Only three days after the 5 January transport, McKittrick received a first warning from Montagu Norman, the governor of the Bank of England, about the gold movements to Portugal; ibid., 63–4.
82 Wheeler describes a foreign currency laundering scheme which the Nazis applied in Lisbon with the help of the Banco Espírito Santo e Comercial. The bank arranged the exchange of Reichsmark and Swiss francs into escudos, which were then employed to acquire wolfram; Wheeler, 'Price of Neutrality', part I, 113.
83 Eizenstat Report, xxx and 4. Despite a 'tentative' accord in February 1947, Portugal did not return any of the gold to its original owners.
84 See table 'Military expenditure', 1927–49, in Carrilho, 'Política de defesa', 32.
85 Telo, Portugal na Segunda Guerra, vol. II, 239–40.
86 BA O9.01/68449, Schüller (AA) to Koppelmann (RWM), 7 January 1943.
87 MEW memo, 6 October 1943, in Telo, Portugal na Segunda Guerra, vol. II, 238–9.
88 BA/MA RW19/445, p. 14, 'Portugal'; see also BA 09.01/68449, OKW to Sabath (AA), 7 September 1943.
89 BA/MA RW19/446, p. 14, 'Portugal'.
90 BA 09.01/68449, Huene to AA, 18 July 1944. Without giving his source of information Boelcke maintains that Portugal received seventy-two field cannon in July 1944; see Deutschland als Welthandelsmacht, 176–7.
91 Telo, Portugal na Segunda Guerra, vol. I, 190.
92 Wheeler, 'Price of Neutrality', part II, 98; Telo, Portugal na Segunda Guerra, vol. I, 191.
93 Leitz, Economic Relations, 171 n. 3.
94 IWM BA R13 XII/30 (previously Speer documents), Board of Trade German Division, statistics on steel improvers, 10 July 1946.
95 See, for instance, chapter X of Telo, Portugal na Segunda Guerra, vol. I.
96 Salazar presented these data in a letter to the British ambassador on 3 June 1944, the day he decided to introduce a wolfram embargo; see Nogueira, Salazar, 536 n. 1.
97 Boelcke, Deutschland als Welthandelsmacht, 176. During the whole of 1942 Portugal exported nearly Esc 4 billion worth of goods; BA/MA RW19/438, statistic 'Ausfuhr Portugals in Mill. Escudos', February 1944.
98 Wheeler regards the figure of 80,000 (as quoted by Salazar; see Nogueira, Salazar, 536 n. 1) as too low, as it does not include those non-mining jobs dependent upon the wolfram business, Wheeler, 'Price of Neutrality', part I, 113.
99 Nogueira, Salazar, 517. For detailed information on how Carmona became involved in trying to persuade Salazar to drop his opposition to a wolfram embargo, see ibid., 514–17.

100 We are again faced with Salazar's strong dislike of what he saw as 'imperialismo americano'.
101 Telo, *Portugal na Segunda Guerra*, vol. I, 229–30; Nogueira, *Salazar*, 505–6.
102 As Churchill had argued in a letter to Salazar in late March, the time when the Wehrmacht could have staged an attack on Portugal or Spain had definitely gone; Nogueira, *Salazar*, 507.
103 Nogueira, *Salazar*, 510.
104 BA 31.02/3352, table 5, 'Der deutsche Außenhandel mit wichtigen Ländern'. Despite the fact that trade relations virtually ceased in August 1944, Germany accounted for 8 per cent of Portugal's total imports and over 11 per cent of its exports for the whole of the year; Telo, *Portugal na Segunda Guerra*, vol. I, 240.
105 The figure for 1944, during which wolfram was imported only until June, was at least 315 mt, possibly even nearly 500 mt; for the first figure see Leitz, *Economic Relations*, 171 n. 3; for the second figure see BA/MA RW19/440, report on economic situation abroad April to June 1944, 14 July 1944.
106 A detailed overview of the developments between 24 May and 7 June is provided by Nogueira, *Salazar*, 533–9. As on the occasion of the announcement of the Azores accord, Huene again reacted with moderation to being informed of Salazar's decision; Telo, *Portugal na Segunda Guerra*, vol. II, 181.
107 While, in value terms, wolfram had by far exceeded any other Portuguese export item in 1942, during the period 1943–45 tinned fish occupied the primary position in Portugal's exports; Telo, *Portugal na Segunda Guerra*, vol. II, 39.
108 See BA/MA RW19/1555, letter 'Einfuhr von Ölsardinen aus Portugal', Schottky (RWM) to Radtke (OKW), 16 July 1941.
109 *Ibid.*, 182.
110 For detailed information on the secret war see Telo, *Propaganda e guerra secreta*.
111 Hans Wilhelm Eggen in a conversation with Swiss captain Paul Meyer, in Braunschweig, *Geheimer Draht*, 196. In early 1942 the Portuguese political police were infiltrated by German-paid agents with other agents spying for Germany from within the Ministry of Foreign Affairs, the harbour police and the custom guards; Wheeler, 'Price of Neutrality', part I, 121.
112 The Portuguese passenger liner *Serpa Pinto*, for instance, which carried thousands of refugees to North America, was also infamous for the many Allied and Axis-paid secret agents and smugglers among its crew; Wheeler, 'Price of Neutrality', part II, 101.
113 Eizenstat Report, 43.
114 For a detailed description of the odyssey of the Krupp guns see Willi A. Boelcke, 'Die Waffengeschäfte des Dritten Reiches mit Brasilien', *Tradition*, 16 (1971), 200, and particularly the second part of Boelcke's article, *ibid.*, 280–4.
115 Telo, *Portugal na Segunda Guerra*, vol. I, 249.
116 Telo, *Portugal na Segunda Guerra*, vol. II, 183.

7

CONCLUSION

In evaluating the wartime policies of the five European neutrals examined in this book, I was faced with various contrasting assessments made during and directly after the conflict, and again more recently. Ultimately, all these verdicts can be reduced to two conflicting points of view. On the one hand, we find statements firmly in defence of the actions of the neutrals during the war. In this vein, contemporaries such as Peter Tennant, British press attaché in Stockholm during the war, argued that

> Swedish neutrality was a means of survival which was successfully employed by a small cadre of extremely competent politicians and two brothers and bankers (Jakob and Marcus Wallenberg) ...[1]

Towards the end of the war, Winston Churchill echoed Tennant's view with regard to Switzerland:

> Of all the neutrals, Switzerland has the greatest right to distinction. She has been the sole international force linking the hideously sundered nations and ourselves. What does it matter whether she has been able to give us the commercial advantages we desire or has given too many to the Germans, to keep herself alive? She has been a democratic state, standing for freedom in self-defence among her mountains, and in thought, in spite of race, largely on our side.[2]

Post-war politicians and historians in the five countries have, of course, eagerly latched on to these laudatory comments when defending the wartime record of their respective *Heimat*. Winston Churchill's comment, for instance, was cited by Arnold Koller, Switzerland's Federal President in 1997, in a speech addressing the controversy over Switzerland's wartime policies.[3] Other examples abound. In the final paragraph of the English version of his seminal work on Swedish foreign policy during the Second World War, Wilhelm Carlgren insists that:

> in the Great Powers' scheme of things … respect for neutrality and the rules of neutrality carried far less weight than regard for their interests. A small country, which wished to live through a World War with its freedom and independence intact, was obliged to adopt in full measure a corresponding scale of values.[4]

In a collection of articles on Switzerland's and Sweden's neutrality, Carlgren's verdict is echoed in the concluding section. Switzerland's foreign economic relations were not

> as sometimes maintained – the result of a calculated quest for profit and as such a burden to the belligerents and those peoples affected by the war. Instead, Switzerland was concerned with the naked *economic survival* of its population.[5]

And, referring more broadly to all neutrals, the same authors conclude:

> The uppermost objective of the neutral had to be the *preservation of its existence and independence*. To achieve this, neutrality was a means, not a purpose in itself. If the belligerents did not observe the existing neutrality rights, the neutrals were also permitted, if necessary, to deviate from it.[6]

And finally, again on Switzerland but also applicable to the other four neutral states, 'Keeping Switzerland out of the war was certainly not a matter of angelic innocence, but survival in ruthless times is not child's play.'[7]

It is obvious that defenders of the policies of the neutrals have made good use of the complimentary comments expressed by various officials in the victorious governments. However, other remarks by some of the very same witnesses also stand as damning indictments of the policies of the neutrals. Winston Churchill is an obvious example. As with other Allied officials, the British Prime Minister repeatedly complained that the supply of vital materials to the Third Reich helped to prolong the war. Churchill expressed his objections most poignantly in a letter to Salazar in March 1944. Arguing for a cessation of wolfram supplies to the Nazis, Churchill referred to their

> influence on the duration of the war … without [wolfram] it would be impossible for Germany's war industry to function and to manufacture arms with which British soldiers were sent to their death.[8]

CONCLUSION

Three years previously, in September 1941, Anthony Eden had used precisely the same line of argument, though with reference to potential Turkish supplies of chrome to Germany.[9] And in May 1943, Switzerland was accused, again by Eden, of prolonging hostilities with the war material it was supplying to Germany.[10]

Severe Allied criticism of the adverse effects of the economic policies of the neutrals was thus applied to all five countries. In his famous address of 9 April 1944, Cordell Hull warned that

> [w]e can no longer acquiesce in these [neutral] nations drawing upon the resources of the allied world when they at the same time contribute to the death of troops whose sacrifice contributes to their salvation as well as ours. ... We have said to these countries that it is not longer necessary for them to purchase protection against aggression by nourishing aid to our enemy. ... We ask them only, but with insistence, to cease aiding our enemy.[11]

During the same month, the British ambassador at Ankara, Knatchbull-Hugessen, admonished the Turkish foreign minister, Menemencioglu, that

> in London thoughts of the future were outweighed by thoughts of the present. All countries were judged according to the part they had played in the war. At present Turkey was actually helping Germany by her negative attitude.[12]

Not always expressly stated was the accusation that the neutrals' wartime economic and financial relations policies with the Third Reich were not purely about survival, but about calculated gain. During the recent storm of publicity about the dealings of the neutrals with the Nazi regime, this accusation has been made very explicit. In the case of Switzerland, the country's own Independent Commission of Experts arrived at the damning conclusion that

> [o]nly in 1943 did the SNB begin citing dissuasion [of Germany from invading Switzerland] as an argument in favour of its policy of accepting German gold; this fact suggests that economic deterrence was an argument cobbled together *a posteriori* to justify the previous gold policy.[13]

While the commission also concluded that the 'profit motive was not the main reason for SNB's accepting delivery of gold from Germany', it conceded that it played a role in the sale of the 'German' gold to third parties.

While arriving at a similar conclusion, the 'Eizenstat Report' was even more outspoken in its rejection of the motive of self-preservation as the only explanation for the policies of the neutrals *vis-à-vis* the Third Reich:

> Many of the neutrals had a rational fear that their own independence was only a Panzer division away from extinction. But if self-defense and fear were factors in that rationale for neutrality, so too were profit in all neutral countries and outright Nazi sympathy in some. The neutrals ignored repeated Allied entreaties to end their dealings with Nazi Germany. Whatever their motivation, the fact that they pursued vigorous trade with the Third Reich had the clear effect of supporting and prolonging Nazi Germany's capacity to wage war.[14]

Ultimately, the five neutral countries survived the war without suffering any impairment of their sovereignty and independence. Seen in such terms, one might agree with those who argue that the policies of the neutrals were certainly successful and thus justified. Even more justified, indeed, if one considers that the people of the five states were spared the suffering experienced by millions of other Europeans. Neither 'Britain's oldest ally', Portugal, the 'non-belligerents' Spain and Turkey nor the 'strictly' neutral Sweden and Switzerland achieved this positive outcome by simply insisting on their status. In the early years of the war many other European countries were quickly and brutally reminded of the worthlessness of their neutral status by the invading Axis and Soviet troops.

Yet it is also clear that, during the same period, military capacity was not the decisive factor in the survival of the five countries. While the military capacities of the five countries improved to varying degrees during the war, prior to Germany's attack on the Soviet Union they would definitely not have deterred Hitler from ordering an attack on them. The answer needs to be sought elsewhere.

Neutral, or non-belligerent, the five states may have been, but they were never just passive bystanders in the destructive conflict around them. Ultimately, they survived actively, as vital components of the German war economy, and passively, as beneficiaries of the Allied war effort. In an ironic twist, the economic and financial services which the neutrals provided to the Third Reich helped to delay their own liberation from the threat of total integration into Axis Europe.

From the comments made by various members of the Nazi regime, including Hitler, it is clear that they well understood the importance of Germany's economic and financial relations with the neutral countries. Although the contributions to Germany's war effort varied in size –

Switzerland and Sweden were clearly more significant than Portugal, Spain and Turkey – each country catered to specific needs of the German economy. The use of the expression *kriegsentscheidend*, when referring to the import of Swedish iron ore, Iberian wolfram and Turkish chromite, and the use of Swiss financial services, did not constitute an example of the frequently hyperbolic language of the Nazis.

Despite the unresolved debate about the precise level of importance of Swedish iron ore, it cannot be doubted that its absence would have markedly restricted Germany's armaments production. An adequate supply of Iberian wolfram, so vital to various sectors of the German economy, proved to be of particular importance in the production of hardened steel. In view of the total absence of Turkish chromite supplies to Germany during 1940–42, their relevance to the German war effort appears less obvious than that of iron ore or wolfram. Yet even during that period, industrial users of chrome were able to draw part of their requirements from stocks accumulated in 1938 and 1939 from Turkish supplies while, in 1943 and 1944, Turkey regained its role as Germany's foremost source of chromite. Owing to its crucial role in Germany's currency and gold dealings Switzerland, finally, occupied a pivotal position in the Reich's trade relations. In addition, the country also furnished a variety of important products, including war material, to assist the German war effort.

Despite the significance of certain supplies and services to the German war effort, it appears, however, unlikely that their deliberate cessation would have led to the occupation of a particular neutral country. This is not to say that an attack by the Wehrmacht was not a possibility. In the longer term, after a successful conclusion of the war against the Soviet Union, the Nazi regime would have undoubtedly turned its attention to integrating the five countries more clearly into its sphere of control. In the short term, however, that is, particularly during the period 1940–1942/43, an attack on any of the five countries was much more likely for reasons of a non-economic nature.

In the case of Spain (and Portugal) and Turkey, military-strategic factors would have furnished the overriding motive for an attack. While Nazi Germany's war against Britain and later the United States provided a likely rationale for occupation of the Iberian countries, the war against the Soviet Union (and Britain and its empire) could well have made Turkey a target of German aggression. In view of Switzerland's position at the centre of Axis-controlled Europe, occupation of the country was not only unnecessary but, considering the certain loss of its financial services and the destruction of the transit tunnels to Italy, detrimental to Germany's war effort. Sweden, finally, appeared to be the most likely candidate for occupation for economic reasons. Its strategic position was clearly diminished after Germany's successful occupation of Norway and Denmark in 1940 (though increased again with the commencement of Operation Barbarossa and Finland's entry into the war). As Hitler had, in part, instigated his aggressive military campaign in Scandinavia to ensure Germany's access to Sweden's iron ore production, a deliberate cessation of these supplies could have led him to include the country in the Wehrmacht's operations. On the basis of this assessment it may therefore be concluded that, at least in 1940, the Swedish government was justified in continuing the exportation of vital supplies to Germany.

Throughout the war, however, not only Swedish officials but also representatives of the other four neutral governments repeatedly defended their countries' trade with the Nazis as an essential means of survival. This line of defence rings particularly hollow if one considers that the volume of trade continued at a substantial level, indeed increased at a time when Germany's military position was rapidly deteriorating. How can it be explained that, in 1943, none of the five neutrals reacted in the least to the obvious reversal of military fortunes? Instead, 1943 proved to be the high point of Germany's wartime trade with the neutrals. Turkey even resumed chromite supplies to Nazi Germany at the precise moment when the Wehrmacht was suffering a decisive military defeat at Stalingrad. Do we not need to look for other answers than the expedient 'survival justification'?

Ironically, officials of the three authoritarian regimes in Portugal, Spain and Turkey were frequently more honest about this issue than their counterparts in the two democracies, Switzerland and Sweden. In essence, Salazar, Franco and, to a lesser extent, Inönü admitted that they were exploiting the conflict between the Allies and the Axis to the (economic) advantage of their respective country. Industrialisation, modernisation and rearmament were the major objectives which the three leaders tried to drive forward with the help of both belligerent sides.

The results were, however, disappointing. In all three countries, the war years saw a dramatic slowing down of previous efforts at industrial development. Yet to blame this outcome solely on the disruptions and dislocations caused by the war would mean to ignore the policy mistakes committed by the three regimes. To varying degrees – in Spain more so than in Turkey and in Portugal – all three dictators dabbled in autarchic policies prior to and during the war.[15] Import substitution (and the restriction of foreign investment) became a favoured option, partly necessitated by the war, but applied for largely ideological reasons. In particular Franco's blind ideological commitment to this 'new economic path' led to shambolic results. Spain's

> industrial production shows a fall of 0.8 per cent a year between 1941 and 1945. ... There is little dispute that the fundamental cause of the undistinguished economic record of the New Order, particularly in the first decade of its existence, was the Francoist authorities' obsession with half-baked interventionist schemes aimed at bringing about some mythical form of self-sufficiency.[16]

The Nazi regime, which together with the Fascist regime in Italy had provided much of the model for the economic policies of its Spanish counterpart, proved to be of little practical help when it came to their implementation. Hitler (and Mussolini) were largely unwilling or unable to supply the capital goods necessary to modernise Spain (and Portugal and Turkey).[17] Nazi economic planners viewed the three neutral countries as convenient sources of raw materials and agricultural products. While a few major industrial projects were supported, for instance the development of the railway system and the construction of chemical factories, the ultimate aim was not to assist in the rapid industrialisation of any of the three countries. In the cynical words of a Turkish official, 'the Germans were willing to help us in every possible way – except to build factories for products which they could supply us with from their own plants'.[18] Instead, as I have concluded elsewhere with reference to Spain, 'National Socialist plans were inspired by the desire to fit [these countries] into the National Socialist *Großwirtschaftsraum.'*[19] In essence, national industrial development was to be encouraged only in areas that assisted the supply of those raw materials and agricultural products required by the German war economy.[20]

Despite the frequent disappointments which the Spanish regime experienced in its economic dealings with Germany (though the wolfram trade helped to lift the gold and foreign currency holdings of the Instituto Español de Moneda Extranjera to over Pts 1 billion by the end of 1943[21]) Franco remained committed to autarchic policies even after the demise of the Third Reich. Salazar, on the other hand, had always been more sceptical about the idea of autarchy than his more enthusiastic neighbour. Yet the Portuguese regime nonetheless applied some of the very same policies. Again, the results were discouraging, though, owing to Salazar's better 'handling' of the Allies, not quite as disastrous as in the Spanish case. Still, while Portugal came to 'literally swim in gold and foreign currency',[22] 'the evolution of national industry was practically nil ... The State used its control over foreign trade to obtain raw materials, but it did not manage to introduce new machinery and technology.'[23]

In Turkey, which had experienced an expansion of its small industrial sector in the 1930s,[24] the government's reaction to the outbreak of war in Europe very markedly slowed down the country's industrial modernisation. The second industrial plan of 1939 was shelved and the conscription of nearly a million men (of a population of over 17 million) into the country's armed forces left an insuperable gap in its agricultural and industrial work force. During the 1940s, Turkey's industrial production grew by only 1 per cent.[25]

Apart from helping to boost Turkey's gold and currency reserves to a value of US $ 262 million in 1946,[26] Turkey's wartime trade with Nazi Germany did little to alleviate the stalled modernisation efforts of the country's leaders – with the possible exception of one area. In terms of military modernisation, Inönü's 'middle course' between the two belligerent camps proved very successful, as Turkey was able to acquire modern equipment not only from Germany but even more so from the Allies. By the end of the war, Turkey's air force, for instance, had become `one of the largest and most powerful ... apart from the major powers, in the world'.[27]

In contrast, Franco's military establishment, while far more successful than that of any other neutral country in acquiring German military hardware, was to suffer from a complete absence of supplies from the Allies. Still, the substantial quantities of German war material received in 1943 and 1944 proved to be of considerable importance to the Francoist armed forces during the last stages of the Second World War and in its immediate aftermath when they utilised the equipment to repel Communist guerrilla incursions into Spain.

The anti-Communist campaign of the Franco regime was emulated, though not in military terms, by Salazar (and to a lesser extent by Inönü). In their domestic and foreign policies, the two Iberian dictators were guided by a virulent hatred (and fear) of Communism and the Soviet Union. In 1943, the Wehrmacht's rapid retreat in the east was clearly not to their liking. At least in part, Salazar and Franco regarded the supply of wolfram as their contribution to Hitler's anti-Communist campaign, if not even as a means to ensure the survival of their regimes. In this respect, Franco was in a particularly difficult position. While Portugal and Turkey were both allied to Britain and their regimes were not threatened by an Anglo-American victory, Franco had good reason to fear a victory of both the Soviets and the Western Allies. In contrast to the other four neutral states, Franco Spain's neutrality/non-belligerence had been blatantly pro-Axis for most of the war. It was clear to the Spanish dictator that he could expect very little sympathy from the Allies once the Axis had been defeated.

In contrast to the anxiety of the Franco regime, the established democracies of Switzerland and Sweden looked forward with great anticipation to an Anglo-American, though not to a Soviet, victory. Nevertheless, it required much Allied pressure and overwhelming evidence of an imminent Allied victory to induce all five neutral states to reduce substantially their economic relations with the Third Reich. In this context, the events of mid–1944 are particularly revealing. Commencing with Turkey's embargo on chromite exports in April 1944 – after further major German setbacks on the eastern front – the neutrals rapidly reduced their trade links with the Third Reich. The Allied invasion of France on 6 June coincided with Salazar's public announcement of a wolfram embargo and was immediately followed by the impounding of the German ship *Kassel* by the Turkish authorities. Turkey's 'conversion' became even more pronounced after the fall of Menemencioglu on 16 June. Even the conclusion of a new German–Turkish economic agreement on 16 July could not stop Turkey from turning completely towards the Allies and breaking off diplomatic relations with Germany on 2 August 1944.

The other four neutrals, however, maintained their relations with the Third Reich until the end. Their governments clearly proved to be slower in adapting to the new circumstances. While Portugal's wolfram embargo had deprived the country's economic relations with Germany of their vital component, the Franco regime continued to allow wolfram exports to the Third Reich in quantities exceeding those set out in the 2 May 1944 agreement with the Allies. Not even the Allied advance in France brought the Franco regime to its senses. Although Spain's economic relations with Germany were reduced to a minimum, the Franco regime saw no reason to abandon them completely.

Until July/August 1944, the trade between Sweden and Germany had been maintained at a level satisfactory to the Nazi regime. Even though, in contrast to the Iberian peninsula and Switzerland, Sweden was only indirectly affected by the landings in Normandy, the Hansson administration could not ignore the implications of the Allied advance. Initially, however, the Allies did not notice any radical departure from the Swedish government's previous economic policy. In July 1944, Churchill was again very critical of the Swedes. He demanded that they were to be 'pressed hard privately by us, and warned of the dangers if they come out of this war as non-contributory neutrals to our victory'.[28]

Churchill had good reason to be annoyed about the attitude of the Swedish government. Almost exactly one month after the Normandy landings, on 5 July 1944, Reich Economics Minister Funk was able to report to Hitler (via Martin Bormann) that the Riksbank had agreed to recommence its purchases of gold from Germany. According to Funk, this gave the Nazi regime the opportunity to purchase Swedish goods for Germany's armaments production outside the official trade clearing.[29] Reichsbank vice-president Emil Puhl subsequently managed to sell gold coins worth US $1.7 million to the Riksbank.[30]

This particular example of Sweden's reluctance to comply quickly with the demands of the Allies lends credence to Martin Fritz's conclusion that 'the alleged Swedish adoption of a less compliant posture towards Germany in the later phases of the war turns out to have been far more of a skilful deception and far less substantial than has previously been supposed.'[31] Nonetheless, British and US pressure, and the progress of the war, were slowly taking their toll of Sweden's economic relations with the Third Reich. Already during July, exports from Baltic harbours on the coast of north Sweden were reduced while coal, coke and cement shipments to Trondheim and Narvik were also decreased. During the following month, the gradual withdrawal of Swedish war-risk insurance for voyages to German ports had a detrimental effect on the shipping traffic between the two countries. Sweden continued, however, to export ball bearings to Germany until November and iron ore slightly longer.[32]

By mid-November, the Swedish government finally moved towards the total termination of the country's trade relations with the Third Reich. With its promise to the US government that all exports to Germany would end if and when about 3,000 mt of rubber products had arrived in Sweden, an end to the economic relationship with Germany seemed in sight. When the cargo eventually reached Göteborg on 1 January 1945, the Swedish government made a final attempt to persuade the Allies to permit at least the continuation of supplies of wood and paper to Germany. The uncompromising attitude of the Allies forced Sweden to finally cease its trade with the Third Reich, though diplomatic relations were maintained.

In Switzerland's case, the Allied landings had induced the Swiss government to modify its economic relations with Germany. Most notably, on 29 June 1944, war material exports were reduced to 20 per cent of their 1942 level. In general, however, Swiss political and business leadership did not feel the need to act with haste. In late August 1944, German councillor of state Lindemann correctly concluded that 'Switzerland was always completely prepared to arrive at an economic *modus vivendi* with Germany.'[33] For the time being, business continued largely as usual, so much so that, in July, a further SFr 30 million of gold was received from Germany.[34]

Even the arrival of US troops on its western border did not lead to dramatic steps, though the Federal Council acted with more haste than usual. On 7 September 1944, Switzerland abandoned its obligations to the German counter-blockade, though not, of course, its economic and financial links with the Reich. During the same month, an embargo on all exports of war material was introduced. Swiss bankers, also impressed by the Allied advance, finally decided to impose upon themselves a tougher code of behaviour.[35] Yet the import of gold from Germany did not stop. Not only did Switzerland take gold from Germany as late as April 1945, leading bankers and politicians also assured Emil Puhl that the country would maintain its good relations with Germany.[36]

In other areas also, the Swiss proved slow in reacting to Germany's imminent defeat. Even though the Allies had demanded a ban or, at least, reduction of through traffic to and from Italy as early as 1942, the Federal Council held out until late 1944 before it ordered a marked decrease of the goods transported across its country. The passage of coal was finally stopped on 9 February 1945, followed, two weeks later, by a ban on traffic from northern Italy. Only very belatedly did the Federal Council feel the need to comply with the demands of the Allies.[37] In effect, Switzerland and the other neutrals gave in only under duress. The behaviour of leading politicians and businessmen in the various neutral countries in 1944 (and even in 1945) revealed, above all, a shocking unwillingness to sever their economic links with the Third Reich.

To conduct its war of aggression and annihilation for six years, the Nazi regime required the economic and financial services of the five neutral states. Yet with the exception of the Franco regime, none of the five neutral governments desired a final German victory. Why then, did they struggle with all their might against the pressure of the Allies to reduce or even stop the export of important goods to Germany? With the threat of a German invasion removed since early to mid–1943, why, in late 1943 and early 1944, did the neutrals seemingly want to ignore the obvious reality of the rapidly growing military dominance of the Allies? Why did they ultimately wait until the military advance of the Allies in mid–1944 forced them into taking decisive action? Why were the five governments not affected by, in Werner Rings's words, 'great moral discomfort'?

In effect, profit considerations had long overridden or numbed moral concerns. To put it plainly, 'the neutrals continued to profit from their trading links with Germany and thus contributed to prolonging one of the bloodiest conflicts in history'.[38] By emphasising profit considerations neither the authors of the Eizenstat Report nor I imply some kind of Marxist interpretation of the policies of the neutrals. The governments of Portugal, Spain, Sweden, Switzerland and Turkey were not puppets controlled by their capitalist puppet masters. 'Profit' refers not solely to the balance sheets of individual businesses in the five countries, but extends to benefits obtained by the state (or, at least, certain state officials) in each country.

Of course, entrepreneurs in all five states profited from the war in general and from their countries' dealings with the Third Reich and the Allies in particular. The list, ranging from *volframistas* in Portugal[39] and Spain to large banks in Switzerland, is indeed long and has only marginally been touched upon in this book. In the well documented case of Switzerland it has been estimated that the war-time profits of Switzerland's companies amounted to several billion Swiss francs. An outstanding beneficiary of the trade with Germany was the country's main arms producer, Oerlikon-Bührle, with an estimated sales volume of about SFr 300 million to SFr 500 million.[40] Georg Emil Bührle, Oerlikon's owner, managed to increase his personal fortune from SFr 8.5 million in 1939 to 170 million in 1945. During the same period, total deposits in Switzerland's banking sector improved from SFr 18.297 billion to SFr 23.768 billion.[41]

Apart from the gains made by influential members of the business community, each of the five neutral states had other good reasons to participate actively in the economic side of the war. At the forefront of governmental considerations were undoubtedly fiscal and employment issues. Yet the reality differed at times quite markedly from the expectations of individual governments. Switzerland and Sweden were certainly more successful in making use of the war than the three south European dictatorships. In fiscal terms, the Swiss government managed, for instance, to attain SFr 772 million from a newly introduced war gains tax. In Spain, Portugal and Turkey, steps were also undertaken to find new sources of revenue, in particular through the introduction of a tax on wolfram purchases (Spain), a wolfram mining export tax (Portugal) and the imposition of the so-called Wealth Levy (Turkey).[42]

Portugal provides a good example of how the neutral countries benefited from the economic warfare between the belligerents. Undertaken both to satisfy Britain's own needs and to pre-empt German purchases of vital goods, British wartime procurement in Portugal turned the pre-war creditor into the debtor state when, at the end of the war, Britain owed its oldest ally £90 million.[43] Wolfram accounted for a substantial part of Britain's expenditure in Portugal. German acquisitions and Allied pre-emption meant that the first nine months of 1942 alone saw the export of wolfram to a value of over Esc 1 billion, or about 38 per cent of Portugal's total income from exports.[44] *In toto*, it has been estimated that the wolfram trade contributed about RM 100 million to RM 120 million annually to the Portuguese economy and about RM 25 million annually to the Portuguese treasury.[45]

In addition to certain fiscal advantages, trading with the belligerents also brought about changes in each neutral country's employment situation. In Switzerland's case, the change turned out to be for the better. Overall, Switzerland managed to reduce the number of its unemployed from 40,324 at the beginning of the war to 8,107 at the end.[46] A major contributory factor was clearly the trade with Germany. It has been estimated that 40 per cent of those occupied in engineering firms, half of those in the optical industry and 60 per cent of those in the arms industry 'worked' for Germany. In other industrial sectors (electrical, precision instruments) the numbers were even higher.[47]

Portugal also appears to have drawn major, though temporary, employment benefit from its trade with the Third Reich:

> While there are no accurate figures on the number of wolfram-related jobs, by 1943–44, the height of the 'wolfram fever,' the figures of 80,000–90,000 jobs, later 'lost' following the 1944 embargo, seem *low*, for they do not take into account the non-mining jobs in the commercial, supply, transportation, and clerical sectors both in the mining region and in Lisbon, Oporto and other towns where wolfram business was conducted.[48]

Chromite mining, on the other hand, did not achieve the same results for Turkey. As the organisation in control of Turkey's chromite production, the Etibank employed only 500 workers in its chromite mines at the end of the war – even though production had not actually decreased substantially from pre-embargo levels.[49] As a whole, Turkey's unemployment rate increased, in fact, from 25.3 per cent in 1935 to 40.2 per cent ten years later.[50]

In general terms, both industrial and rural workers benefited only marginally from their country's neutrality during the war – and certainly more in democratic Sweden and Switzerland than in dictatorial Portugal, Spain and Turkey. When political leaders in the latter three countries publicly defended their unneutral economic policies as of benefit to the 'ordinary' Portuguese, Spaniard or Turk, they were in reality often more interested in feathering their own nests. Despite official claims to the contrary, corruption and war profiteering ran rampant under Salazar, Franco and Inönü – though profiteering was, of course, also a reality in Sweden and Switzerland.

As I have already indicated, the benefits gained by members of the business community undoubtedly influenced their governments to pursue active trade relations with Nazi Germany. Particularly in Spain and Turkey this influence was frequently achieved through widespread corruption. Moreover, by being officially (or unofficially) involved in the running of both public and private companies members of the regimes were able to derive direct benefit from the war. In the case of Turkey,

> it is well known that a group of 30,000 to 40,000 people enriched themselves through wartime profiteering.[51] This group was comprised of military personnel who black-marketed army stocks, as well as importers and a group of industrialists. ... [H]oarders, black-marketeers, their allies in the public and military bureaucracies, importers and exporters, merchants, industrialists and employers exploiting their workers multiplied their assets and holdings.[52]

In Spain, the military elites both controlled and exploited the economy to a even greater and more transparent degree:

> Major economic decisions ... were largely entrusted to a coterie of army and naval officers and military engineers who tried to run the country like a military barracks. ... While the dictator himself displayed a crass ignorance of elementary economic principles, the incompetence and venality of his ministers and the army of underpaid civil servants who implemented policy became legendary. ... In an atmosphere of favouritism and extensive corruption, those entrepreneurs who maintained the most cordial relations with officialdom generally got what they wanted.[53]

In Portugal, finally, Salazar was frequently worried that the 'wolfram fever' might lead to severe social unrest, as it had enriched a minority at the cost of more difficult and more expensive living conditions for the majority of the population. Yet apart from taking greater control of the pricing and distribution of wolfram, Salazar's regime did not seriously intervene against the actual trading of the precious raw material – at least, not until the pressure of the Allies grew too strong.

As a whole, entertaining trade relations with the Third Reich was perceived as beneficial by all five neutral governments even though the socio-economic results across the five neutral states were in reality mixed. None of the neutral governments ever seriously questioned the continuation of trading with the Nazis until the growing pressure of the Allies forced them to do so. Ultimately, the economic bias – indeed, in some cases outright sympathy – the European neutrals displayed towards Nazi Germany lasted longer and was greater than necessary because, at least for some, it came at a good price. Strict neutrality, it may be argued, was not adhered to for reasons of self-preservation, yet its abandonment continued after the survival of each neutral was already assured. Ultimately, Antonio de Oliveira Salazar's conclusion applied to all five neutral countries: 'The desire for neutrality cannot be superior to the interests of the nation.'[54]

Notes

1 Peter Tennant's conclusion in Zetterberg, 'Neutralitet', 35 (quoting from Tennant's memoirs *Vid sidan av kriget, Diplomat i Sverige 1939–1945*, Stockholm, 1989, 304). On Jakob and Marcus Wallenberg's very controversial dealings with the Third Reich see the summary of a Henry Morgenthau letter of 7 February 1945 in LeBor, *Hitler's Secret Bankers*, 281–2, and, in particular, Aalders and Wiebes, *Die Kunst der Tarnung, passim*.

2 Excerpt from Churchill's letter to Anthony Eden, in Jonathan Mahler, 'Accounting Device', *New Republic*, 7 April 1997, 17.

3 Arnold Koller, 'Die Schweiz und die jüngere Zeitgeschichte', *Neue Zürcher Zeitung*, 6 March 1997, available at http://www.nzz.ch/online/02_dossiers/schatten/schatten970306a.htm. The Swiss historian Pierre Th. Braunschweig concludes his ardent defence of Switzerland's wartime record with precisely the same quote; see Pierre Th. Braunschweig, 'In the Eye of the Hurricane: Switzerland in World War II', *Whittier Law Review* 20 (1999), 659.

4 Carlgren, *Swedish Foreign Policy*, 229.

5 Bindschedler *et al.*, 'Schlußbetrachtungen', 437.

6 *Ibid.*, 439. Emphasis in original.

7 Braunschweig, 'In the Eye of the Hurricane', 659.

8 Nogueira, *Salazar*, 507. Churchill added that the British public could not understand why an ally supplied a raw material to Germany which helped the latter to destroy British arms, kill British troops and prolong the war.

9 'After all, what was this chrome to be used for? – to make munitions of war to kill our soldiers ...'; cited in Robertson, *Turkey and Allied Strategy*, 68.

10 Kamber, *Schüsse auf die Befreier*, 250.

11 Eizenstat Report, 25.

12 Weber, *Evasive Neutral*, 205.

13 Conclusion to May 1998 report by 'Independent Commission of Experts Switzerland – Second World War', http://www.uek.ch./e/m1/gold_ez.htm.

14 Eizenstat Report, V.

15 See, for instance, on Spain, José Antonio Biescas, 'El fracaso de la vía

nacionalista del capitalismo español: la inviabilidad de los intentos autárquicos', in José Antonio Biescas and Manuel Tuñón de Lara, *España bajo la dictadura Franquista 1939–1975* (Barcelona, 2nd edn, 1987), 21–54, on Turkey Yilmaz, 'Die wirtschaftliche Entwicklung', and, on Portugal, various contributions in *O Estado Novo; das origens ao fim da autarcia*, vol. I (Lisbon, 1987), in particular Sacuntala de Miranda, 'Crise económica, industrialização e autarcia na década de 30'.

16 Joseph Harrison, *The Spanish Economy; from the Civil War to the European Community* (Basingstoke and London, 1993), 17–18.

17 In 1958, 73 per cent of industrial enterprises were still equipped with machinery that antedated the Republic; Adrian Shubert, *A Social History of Modern Spain* (London, 1990), 207.

18 Max Weston Thornburg, Graham Spry and George Soule, *Turkey; an Economic Appraisal* (New York, 1949), 41.

19 Leitz, *Economic Relations*, 99.

20 To a certain extent, this approach even applied to an industrialised country such as Sweden. There, German officials intended to force the country's arms industry to become Germany's 'armaments workshop', that is, a supplier of spare parts and semi-manufactured products rather than a producer of war material in its own right; Wittmann, *Schwedens Wirtschaftsbeziehungen*, table A 18, 296–301.

21 Boelcke, *Deutschland als Welthandelsmacht*, 176.

22 Telo, *Portugal na Segunda Guerra*, vol. II, 253.

23 *Ibid.*, 29. Particularly owing to the speculative nature of many business transactions during the period 1938–1945 (wolfram!), industrial investment dropped markedly (by an annual average of 12.1 per cent); Rogério Roque Amario, 'A economia nos primórdios do Estado Novo – estagnação ou crescimento?', in *O Estado Novo; das origens ao fim da autarcia*, vol. I (Lisbon, 1987), 241.

24 As a share of Turkey's gross domestic product, its industrial production grew from 12 per cent to 18 per cent; Yilmaz, 'Die wirtschaftliche Entwicklung', 355.

25 *Ibid.*, 356.

26 *Ibid.* Turkey's gold reserves grew from 27.4 mt in 1939 to 216 mt in 1945; Jonathan Steinberg, *Die Deutsche Bank und ihre Goldtransaktionen während des Zweiten Weltkrieges* (Munich, 1999), 35.

27 Leiser, 'Turkish Air force', 393.

28 Levine, *From Indifference to Activism*, 69.

29 BA NS6/506, memo for Bormann, 5 July 1944.

30 Aalders and Wiebes, *Die Kunst der Tarnung*, 150.

31 Fritz, 'Swedish Ball-bearings', 35.

32 BA/MA RW4/v.653, WFst/Ag. Ausland II A 2 memo Germany – Sweden, 19 November 1944. While Swedish iron ore was still exported via Narvik, the major iron ore shipping traffic via Luleå had already ended on 27 September 1944; BA/MA RW19/3078; German consulate, Luleå, to AA, 4 October 1944.

33 IWM Speer Documents, Reel 26 FD3045/49, Sc. 146, file 1, protocol of a Four Year Plan Planning Office meeting, 29 August 1944.

34 Rings, *Raubgold aus Deutschland*, 164.

35 Bower, *Blood Money*, 70.
36 Rings, *Raubgold aus Deutschland*, 106–7.
37 Heiniger, *Dreizehn Gründe*, 63.
38 Eizenstat Report, V.
39 *Volframista* became a perjorative term describing 'an unscrupulous, double-dealing, fly-by-night, "get-rich-quick" entrepreneur'; Wheeler, 'Price of Neutrality', part I, 114.
40 Bourgeois, 'Les relations économiques', 60 n. 64.
41 Although the large commercial banks – with their particular involvement in foreign transactions – declined in number from seven to five, their share of the total deposits in all Swiss banking institutions grew from 24.5 per cent to 28.8 per cent; Jean-François Bergier, *Histoire èconomique de la Suisse* (Lausanne, 1984), table XXXVII, 314.
42 Introduced on 12 November 1942, the particular target of the Wealth Levy were Greek, Armenian and Jewish members of Turkey's business community. The levy is said to have raised at least US $137 million in its first year.
43 Wheeler, 'Price of Neutrality', part I, 112.
44 Boelcke, *Deutschland als Welthandelsmacht*, 176.
45 Nogueira, *Salazar*, 536 n. 1.
46 Bourgeois, 'Les relations économiques', 60.
47 Heiniger, *Dreizehn Gründe*, 80–1.
48 Wheeler, 'Price of Neutrality', part I, 113.
49 In contrast, a 29,000 strong work force laboured in the coal mines run by Etibank; Mehmet Sehmus Güzel, 'Capital and Labour during World War II', in Donald Quataert and Erik Jan Zürcher (eds), *Workers and the Working Class in the Ottoman Empire and the Turkish Republic 1839–1950* (London and New York, 1995), 130.
50 Erdal Yavuz, 'The State of the Industrial Workforce 1923–40', in *ibid.*, table 18, 124.
51 Deposits in the country's thirteen most important private banks doubled between 1940 and 1945 (from Ltq 275 million to Ltq 528 million); Thornburg *et al.*, *Turkey*, table 7, 158.
52 Güzel, 'Capital and Labour', 143–4.
53 Harrison, *Spanish Economy*, 18, 43.
54 In a radio broadcast on 25 June 1942; Wheeler, 'Price of Neutrality', part II, 108.

BIBLIOGRAPHY

German archives

German Federal Archive, Berlin

BA R25/53

BA 25.01/4913

BA 25.01/6334

BA 31.02/3352

BA 31.02/6040

BA R7/962

BA R901/68583

BA R901/68743

BA 09.01/68449

BA 09.01/68452

BA 09.01/68459

BA 09.01/68460

BA 09.01/68461

BA 09.01/68751

BA 09.01/68765

BA NS6/506

German Federal Archive, Freiburg

BA/MA RW4/v.653

BA/MA RW5/v.396

BA/MA RW5/v.430

BA/MA RW5/v. 643

BA/MA RW19/226

BA/MA RW19/433

BA/MA RW19/435

BA/MA RW19/438

BA/MA RW19/440

BA/MA RW19/441

BA/MA RW19/445

BA/MA RW19/446

BA/MA RW19/1555

BA/MA RW19/3078

BA/MA RW19/3195

BA/MA RW19/3326

BA/MA RWi/IB 2.3 (copy b)

German Foreign Ministry Archive, Bonn

PA-AA R106444

PA-AA R106445

PA-AA R106446

PA-AA R109462

PA-AA R114171

PA-AA R114172

British archives

Imperial War Museum, London

IWM BA R13 XII/30 (previously Speer documents)

IWM Krupp, file 15a

IWM Speer Docs. Reel 25, FD3045/49

IWM Speer Docs. Reel 26, FD3045/49

IWM Speer Docs. FD2620/45

Public Record Office, London

PRO FO837/721   PRO FO837/774
PRO FO837/735   PRO FO837/786
PRO FO837/743   PRO/AA89/102800-1
PRO FO837/767   PRO/AA89/103414-6,
PRO FO837/769   PRO PREM4, 21/1

University Library Archive, Cambridge

Templewood Papers Box XIII/7
Templewood Papers Box XIII/22
Templewood Papers Box XIII/24

US archives

National Archives II, College Park MD

RG59, box 2192

Franklin D. Roosevelt Library, Pougkeepsie NY

President's Secretary Files (PSF) Box 152.
PSF Box 50

Harry S. Truman Library, Independence MO

President's Secretary Files, supplement to Situation
Report (II) Spain, 15 November 1948.

Secondary sources

Aalders, Gerard and Cees Wiebes, *Die Kunst der Tarnung; Die geheime Kollaboration neutraler Staaten mit der deutschen Kriegsindustrie; Der Fall Schweden*, Frankfurt/Main, Sept. 1994.
Ahmad, Feroz, *The Making of Modern Turkey*, London, 1994.
Andolf, Göran, 'Interneringen av britter och tyskar 1943–1944', in Bo Huldt and Klaus-Richard Böhme (eds), *Vårstormar; 1944 – Krigsslutet skönjes*, Stockholm, 1995.
Andolf, Göran, 'De grå lapparna; Regeringen och pressen under andra världskriget', in Bo Hugemark (ed.), *Nya Fronter? 1943 – spänd väntan*, Stockholm, 1994.
Åhslund, Bengt, 'Det militärpolitiska läget vid krigsutbrottet 1939', in Carl-Axel Wangel (ed.), *Sveriges militära beredskap 1939–1945*, Stockholm, 1982.
Åström, Sverker, 'Swedish Neutrality: Credibility through Commitment and Consistency', in Bengt Sundelius (ed.), *The Committed Neutral; Sweden's Foreign Policy*, Boulder, Col., 1989.

Åström, Sverker, *Sweden's Policy of Neutrality*, Stockholm, 1977.

Bergier, Jean-François, *Histoire èconomique de la Suisse*, Lausanne, 1984.

Baynes, Norman H. (ed.), *The Speeches of Adolf Hitler, April 1922–August 1939*, vol. II, New York, 1969.

Bessa, Carlos, 'La neutralité Portugaise dans la Seconde Guerre Mondiale', in Louis-Edouard Roulet with Roland Blättler (eds) *Les états neutres européens et la seconde guerre mondiale*, Neuchâtel, 1985.

Biescas, José Antonio, 'El fracaso de la vía nacionalista del capitalismo español: la inviabilidad de los intentos autárquicos', in José Antonio Biescas, Manuel Tuñón de Lara, *España bajo la dictadura Franquista 1939–1975*, Barcelona, 2nd edn, 1987.

Bindschedler, Rudolf L., 'Die schweizerische Neutralität - Eine historische Übersicht', in Rudolf L. Bindschedler *et al.* (eds), *Schwedische und schweizerische Neutralität im Zweiten Weltkrieg*, Basel, Frankfurt/Main, 1985.

Bindschedler, Rudolf, Hans Rudolf Kurz, Wilhelm Carlgren and Sten Carlsson, 'Schlußbetrachtungen zu den Problemen der Kleinstaatneutralität im Großmachtkrieg', in Rudolf L. Bindschedler *et al.* (eds), *Schwedische und schweizerische Neutralität im Zweiten Weltkrieg*, Basel, Frankfurt/Main, 1985.

Björkman, Leif, *Sverige inför Operation Barbarossa; Svensk neutralitetspolitik 1940–1941*, Stockholm, 1971.

Boelcke, Willi A., *Deutschland als Welthandelsmacht 1930–1945*, Stuttgart, 1994.

Boelcke, Willi A., *Die deutsche Wirtschaft 1930–1945; Interna des Reichswirtschaftsministeriums*, Düsseldorf, 1983.

Boelcke, Willi A., 'Die Waffengeschäfte des Dritten Reiches mit Brasilien', *Tradition*, 16, 1971.

Boëthius, Maria-Pia, *Heder och Samvete; Sverige och andra världskriget*, Stockholm, 1991.

Böhme, Klaus-Richard, 'The Principal Features of Swedish Defence Policy 1925–1945', in Comité International des Sciences (ed.), *Neutrality and Defence: The Swedish Experience*, Stockholm, 1984.

Bonjour, Edgar, trans. Charles Oser, *Histoire de la neutralité Suisse; quatre siècles de politique extérieure fédérale*, vols. IV–VI, Neuchatel, 1970.

Bonjour, Edgar, 'Türkische und schweizerische Neutralität während des zweiten Weltkrieges', in Saul Friedländer, Harish Kapur, André Reszler (eds), *L'historien et les relations internationales; recueil d'études en hommage à Jacques Freymond*, Geneva, 1981.

Boog, Horst, Jürgen Förster, Joachim Hoffmann, Ernst Klink, Rolf-Dieter Müller, Gerd R. Ueberschär, *Der Angriff auf die Sowjetunion*, vol. 4 of *Das Deutsche Reich und der Zweite Weltkrieg*, ed. Militärgeschichtliches Forschungsamt, Stuttgart, 1983.

Bourgeois, Daniel, *Le Troisième Reich et la Suisse 1933–1941*, Neuchâtel, 1974.

Bourgeois, Daniel, 'Les relations èconomiques Germano-Suisses 1939–1945', *Revue d'histoire de la Deuxième Guerre Mondiale*, 121, 1981.

Bower, Tom, *Blood Money; The Swiss, the Nazis and the Looted Billions*, London, 1997.

Brandell, Ulf, 'Die Transitfrage in der schwedischen Außenpolitik während des Zweiten Weltkrieges', in Rudolf L. Bindschedler *et al.* (eds), *Schwedische und schweizerische Neutralität im Zweiten Weltkrieg*, Basel, Frankfurt/Main, 1985.

Braunschweig, Pierre-Th., *Geheimer Draht nach Berlin; Die Nachrichtenlinie Masson-Schellenberg und der schweizerische Nachrichtendienst im Zweiten Weltkrieg*, Zürich, 3rd edn, 1990.

Braunschweig, Pierre-Th., 'In the Eye of the Hurricane: Switzerland in World War II', *Whittier Law Review*, 20, 1999.

Brown Scott, James (ed.), *The Hague Conventions and Declarations of 1899 and 1907*, New York, 3rd edn, 1918.

Brügel, Johann Wolfgang, 'Dahlerus als Zwischenträger nach Kriegsausbruch', *Historische Zeitschrift*, 228, 1979.

Brundu Olla, Paolo, 'La neutralité du Portugal pendant la Seconde Guerre Mondiale', in Jukka Nevakivi (ed.), *Neutrality in History/La neutralité dans l'histoire*, Helsinki, 1993.

Burdick, Charles B., '"Moro": The Resupply of German Submarines in Spain, 1939–1942', *Central European History*, 3, 1970.

Carlgren, W. M., *Swedish Foreign Policy during the Second World War*, trans. Arthur Spencer, London and Tonbridge, 1977.

Carlsson, Sten, 'Die schwedische Neutralität – Eine historische Übersicht', in Rudolf L. Bindschedler *et al.* (eds), *Schwedische und schweizerische Neutralität im Zweiten Weltkrieg*, Basel, Frankfurt/Main, 1985.

Carreras, Albert, 'Depresión económica y cambio estructural durante el decenio bélico (1936–1945)', in J.L. García Delgado, *El primer Franquismo; España durante la Segunda Guerra Mundial*, Madrid, 1989.

Carrilho, Maria, 'Política de defesa e de rearmamento', in Mario Carrilho *et al.*, *Portugal na Segunda Guerra Mundial; contributos para uma reavaliação*, Lisbon, 1989.

Castelmur, Linus von, *Schweizerisch- Alliierte Finanzbeziehungen im Übergang vom Zweiten Weltkrieg zum Kalten Krieg. Die deutschen Guthaben in der Schweiz zwischen Zwangsliquidierung und Freigabe (1945–1952)*, Zürich, 1992.

Chevallaz, Georges-André, *Le défi de la neutralité; diplomatie et défense de la Suisse 1939–1945*, Vevey, 1995.

Cole, Robert, *Britain and the War of Words in Neutral Europe, 1939–45; The Art of the Possible*, Basingstoke, 1990.

Collado Seidel, Carlos, 'Zufluchtsstätte für Nationalsozialisten? Spanien, die Alliierten und die Behandlung deutscher Agenten 1944–1947', *Vierteljahreshefte für Zeitgeschichte*, 43, 1995.

Cronenberg, Arvid, '1936 års försvarsbeslut och upprustningen 1936–1939', in Carl-Axel Wangel (ed.), *Sveriges militära beredskap 1939–1945*, Stockholm, 1982.

Çalis, Saban, 'Pan-Turkism and Europeanism: a note on Turkey's "pro-German neutrality" during the Second World War', *Central Asian Survey*, 16, 1997.

David, Fred, 'Ein furchtbar neutraler Diplomat', *Die Zeit*, 29 May 1992.

Deringil, Selim, *Turkish Foreign Policy during the Second World War: an 'active' neutrality*, Cambridge, 1989.

Deringil, Selim, 'Turkish Reactions to European Crises: 1943', in Louis-Edouard Roulet with Roland Blättler (eds) *Les états neutres européens et la seconde guerre mondiale*, Neuchâtel, 1985.

Duggan, John P., *Neutral Ireland and the Third Reich*, Dublin, 1989.

Durrer, Marco, *Die schweizerisch-amerikanischen Finanzbeziehungen im Zweiten Weltkrieg. Von der Blockierung der schweizerischen Guthaben in den USA über die "Safehaven"-Politik zum Washingtoner Abkommen (1941–1946)*, Berne, 1984.

Durrer, Marco, 'Die Beziehungen zwischen Schweden und der Schweiz im Zweiten Weltkrieg aus schweizerischer Sicht: Informelle Solidarität', in Rudolf L. Bindschedler *et al.* (eds), *Schwedische und schweizerische Neutralität im Zweiten Weltkrieg*, Basel, Frankfurt/Main, 1985.

Espadas Burgos, Manuel, *Franquismo y política exterior*, Madrid, 1988.

Favez, Jean-Claude, *Das internationale Rote Kreuz und das Dritte Reich*, Zürich, 1989.

Fink, Jürg, *Die Schweiz aus der Sicht des Deutschen Reiches 1933–1945*, Zürich, 1985.

Fleury, Antoine, 'La neutralité suisse à l'épreuve de l'Union Européenne', in Jukka Nevakivi (ed.), *Neutrality in History*, Helsinki, 1993.

Fleury, Antoine, 'The Role of Switzerland and the Neutral States at the Genoa Conference', in Carole Fink, Axel Frohn, Jürgen Heideking (eds), *Genoa, Rapallo, and European Reconstruction in 1922*, Cambridge, 1986.

Freymond, Jean, 'Neutrality and Security Policy as Components of the Swiss Model', *Government and Opposition*, 23, 1988.

Fritz, Martin, 'Wirtschaftliche Neutralität während des Zweiten Weltkrieges', in Rudolf L. Bindschedler *et al.* (eds), *Schwedische und schweizerische Neutralität im Zweiten Weltkrieg*, Basel, Frankfurt/Main, 1985.

Fritz, Martin, 'Swedish Ball-Bearings and the German War Economy', *Scandinavian Economic History Review*, XXIII, 1975.

Fuhrer, Hans Rudolf, *Spionage gegen die Schweiz. Die geheimen deutschen Nachrichtendienste gegen die Schweiz im Zweiten Weltkrieg 1939–1945*, Frauenfeld, 1982.

Furtenbach, Börje, 'Sweden during the Second World War; Armament and Preparedness', *Revue internationale d'histoire militaire/International Review of Military History*, 26, 1967.

Gabriel, Jürg Martin, *The American Conception of Neutrality after 1941*, Basingstoke, 1988.

García Pérez, Rafael, *Franquismo y Tercer Reich: Las relaciones económicas hispano-alemanas durante la segunda guerra mundial*, Madrid, 1994.

García Pérez, Rafael, 'España en el Eje: La beligerencia y la opinión de los historiadores', in Stanley G. Payne, Delia Contreras (eds), *España y la Segunda Guerra Mundial*, Madrid, 1996.

García Pérez, Rafael, 'El envío de trabajadores españoles a Alemania durante la segunda guerra mundial', *Hispania*, 170, 1988.

Glasneck, Johannes and Inge Kircheisen, *Türkei und Afghanistan – Brennpunkte der Orientpolitik im zweiten Weltkrieg*, East Berlin, 1968.

Goda, Norman J. W., *Tomorrow the World; Hitler, Northwest Africa, and the Path toward America*, College Station, TX, 1998.

Goda, Norman J. W., 'Germany's Conception of Spain's Strategic Importance, 1940–1941', in Christian Leitz, David J. Dunthorn (eds), *Spain in an International Context; Civil War, Cold War, Early Cold War*, New York and Oxford, 1999.

Grafström, Anders, 'Svenska frivilligförband 1939–1944´, in Carl-Axel Wangel (ed.), *Sveriges militära beredskap 1939–1945*, Stockholm, 1982.

Gruchmann, Lothar, 'Schweden im Zweiten Weltkrieg; Ergebnisse eines Stockholmer Forschungsprojektes´, *Vierteljahreshefte für Zeitgeschichte*, 25, 1977.

Güzel, Mehmet Sehmus, 'Capital and Labour during World War II´, in Donald Quataert, Erik Jan Zürcher (eds), *Workers and the Working Class in the Ottoman Empire and the Turkish Republic 1839–1950*, London and New York, 1995.

Hadenius, Stig, *Swedish Politics during the 20th Century*, Stockholm, 3rd edn, 1990.

Hägglöf, Gunnar, 'A Test of Neutrality; Sweden in the Second World War´, *International Affairs*, 36, 1960.

Harrison, Joseph, *The Spanish Economy; from the Civil War to the European Community*, Basingstoke and London, 1993.

Heiniger, Markus, *Dreizehn Gründe. Warum die Schweiz im Zweiten Weltkrieg nicht erobert wurde*, Zurich, 2nd edn, 1989.

Hill, Leonidas E. (ed.), *Die Weizsäcker-Papiere 1933–1950*, Frankfurt/Main, Berlin, Vienna, 1974.

Hillgruber, Andreas (ed.), *Staatsmänner und Diplomaten bei Hitler. Vertrauliche Aufzeichnungen über Unterredungen mit Vertretern des Auslandes*, vol. I: 1939–1941, Frankfurt/Main, 1967.

Hitler´s Secret Book, intro. Telford Taylor, New York, 2nd edn. 1962.

Hitler´s Table Talk 1941–1944, intro. Hugh R. Trevor-Roper, London, 1953.

Hofer, Walther, 'Neutraler Kleinstaat im europäischen Konfliktfeld: Die Schweiz´, in Helmut Altrichter and Josef Becker (eds), *Kriegsausbruch 1939; Beteiligte, Betroffene, Neutrale*, Munich, 1989.

Hotz, Jean, 'Handelsabteilung und Handelspolitik in der Kriegszeit´, in *Die schweizerische Kriegswirtschaft 1939–1948*, Bern, 1950.

Hull, Cordell, *The Memoirs of Cordell Hull*, vol. II, London, 1948.

Ibáñez Hernández, Rafael, 'Españoles en las trincheras: la División Azul´, in Stanley G. Payne, Delia Contreras (eds), *España y la Segunda Guerra Mundial*, Madrid, 1996.

Inglin, Oswald, *Der stille Krieg. Der Wirtschaftskrieg zwischen Grossbritannien und der Schweiz im Zweiten Weltkrieg*, Zürich, 1991.

Jackson, Peter, 'French Strategy and the Spanish Civil War´, in Christian Leitz, David J. Dunthorn (eds), *Spain in an International Context; Civil War, Cold War, Early Cold War*, New York and Oxford, 1999.

Jäger, Jörg-Johannes, 'Sweden´s Iron Ore Exports to Germany, 1933–1944; A Reply to Rolf Karlbom´s Article on the Same Subject´, *Scandinavian Economic History Review*, XV, 1967.

Jaggi, Arnold, *Bedrohte Schweiz; Unser Land in der Zeit Mussolinis, Hitlers und des Zweiten Weltkrieges*, Berne, 1978.

Jochmann, Werner (ed.), *Adolf Hitler; Monologe im Führerhauptquartier 1941–1944*, Bindlach, 1988.

Johansson, Alf W., *Finlands sak; Swensk politik och opinion under vinterkriget 1939–1940*, Stockholm, 1973.

Johansson, Alf W., 'I skuggan av operation Barbarossa; Attityder och stämningar 1940/1941´, in Bo Hugemark (ed.), *I Orkanens Öga; 1941 – osäker neutralitet*, Stockholm, 1992.

Johansson, Alf W., 'Per Albin Hansson och utrikespolitiken under andra världskriget', in B. Huldt and K. Misgeld (eds), *Socialdemokratin och svensk utrikespolitik; Från Branting till Palme*, Stockholm, 1990.

Johansson, Alf W., 'La neutralité suédoise et les puissances occidentales entre 1939 et 1945', *Revue d'histoire de la deuxième guerre mondiale*, 109, 1978.

Kamber, Peter, *Schüsse auf die Befreier. Die "Luftguerilla" der Schweiz gegen die Alliierten 1943–1945*, Zürich, 1991.

Karlbom, Rolf, 'Sweden's Iron Ore Exports to Germany, 1933–1944', *Scandinavian Economic History Review*, XIII, 1965.

Karlsson, Rune, *Så stoppades tysktågen; den tyska transiteringstrafiken i svensk politik 1942–1943*, Stockholm, 1974.

Kay, Hugh, *Salazar and Modern Portugal*, London, 1970.

Kleinfeld, Gerald and Lewis Tambs, *Hitler's Spanish Legion: The Blue Division in Russia*, Carbondale and Edwardsville, 1979.

Koblik, Steven, 'Sweden's Attempts to Aid Jews, 1939–1945', *Scandinavian Studies*, 56, 1984.

Koçak, Cemil, *Türkiye'de Milli Sef Dönemi (1938–1945); Dönemin Iç ve Dis Politikasi Üzerine Bir Arastirma*, Ankara, 1986.

Koller, Arnold, 'Die Schweiz und die jüngere Zeitgeschichte', *Neue Zürcher Zeitung*, 6 March 1997.

Kreis, Georg, 'Die schweizerische Neutralität während des Zweiten Weltkrieges in der historischen Forschung', in Louis-Edouard Roulet with Roland Blättler (eds) *Les états neutres européens et la seconde guerre mondiale*, Neuchâtel, 1985.

Kurz, Hans Rudolf, *Nachrichtenzentrum Schweiz. Die Schweiz im Nachrichtendienst des Zweiten Weltkriegs*, Frauenfeld, 1972.

Kurz, Hans Rudolf, *Die Schweiz in der Planung der kriegführenden Mächte während des Zweiten Weltkrieges*, Biel, 1957.

LeBor, Adam, *Hitler's Secret Bankers; How Switzerland profited from Nazi genocide*, London, 1997.

Landau, Jacob M., *Pan-Turkism; From Irredentism to Cooperation*, London, 2nd edn., 1995.

Leiser, Gary, 'The Turkish Air Force, 1939–45: the Rise of a Minor Power', *Middle Eastern Studies*, 26, 1990.

Leitão de Barros, Júlia, 'Anglofilia e Germanofilia em Portugal durante a Segunda Guerra Mundial', in Mario Carrilho *et al.*, *Portugal na Segunda Guerra Mundial; contributos para uma reavaliação*, Lisbon, 1989.

Leitz, Christian, *Economic Relations between Nazi Germany and Franco's Spain 1936–1945*, Oxford, 1996.

Leitz, Christian, 'Arms Exports in the Third Reich, 1933–1939: The Example of Krupp', *Economic History Review*, LI, 1998.

Leitz, Christian, 'Nazi Germany and the Threat of an Allied Invasion of Spain, 1942–1943', in Peter Monteath, Frederic S. Zuckerman (eds), *Modern Europe, Histories and Identities*, Adelaide, 1998.

Leitz, Christian, '"More carrot than stick", British Economic Warfare and Spain, 1941–1944', *Twentieth Century British History* 9, 1998.

Leitz, Christian, 'Nazi Germany's Intervention in the Spanish Civil War and the Foundation of HISMA/ROWAK', in Paul Preston and Ann L. Mackenzie (eds), *The Republic Besieged; Civil War in Spain 1936–1939*, Edinburgh, 1996.

Leitz, Christian, 'Hermann Göring and Nazi Germany's Economic Exploitation of Nationalist Spain, 1936–1939', *German History* 14, 1996.

Leitz, Christian, 'Nazi Germany's Struggle for Spanish Wolfram during the Second World War', *European History Quarterly* 25, 1995.

Levene, Paul A., *From Indifference to Activism; Swedish Diplomacy and the Holocaust, 1938–1944*, Uppsala, 1996.

Logue, John, 'The Legacy of Swedish Neutrality', in Bengt Sundelius (ed.), *The Committed Neutral; Sweden's Foreign Policy*, Boulder, Col., 1989.

Lönnroth, Erik, 'Sweden's Ambiguous Neutrality', *Scandinavian Journal of History*, 2, 1977, (special issue on 'The Great Powers and the Nordic Countries 1939–1940').

Lutzhöft, Hans-Jürgen, *Deutsche Militärpolitik und schwedische Neutralität 1939–1942*, Neumünster, 1981.

Lutzhöft, Hans-Jürgen, 'Deutschland und Schweden während des Norwegenfeldzuges (9. April–10. Juni 1940), *Vierteljahreshefte für Zeitgeschichte*, 22, 1974.

Mahler, Jonathan, 'Accounting Device', *The New Republic*, 7 Apr. 1997.

Maier, Klaus A., Horst Rohde, Bernd Stegemann, Hans Umbreit, *Die Errichtung der Hegemonie auf dem europäischen Kontinent*, vol. 2 of *Das Deutsche Reich und der Zweite Weltkrieg*, ed. Militärgeschichtliches Forschungsamt, Stuttgart, 1979.

Manninen, Ohto, 'Operation Barbarossa and the Nordic Countries', in Henrik S. Nissen (ed.), *Scandinavia during the Second World War*, Minneapolis, 1983.

Marguerat, Philippe, 'La Suisse et la neutralité dans le domaine économique pendant la Seconde Guerre mondiale: 1940–fin 1944', in Louis-Edouard Roulet with Roland Blättler (eds) *Les états neutres européens et la seconde guerre mondiale*, Neuchâtel, 1985.

Martin, Bernd, 'Deutschland und die neutralen Staaten Europas im zweiten Weltkrieg', in Louis-Edouard Roulet with Roland Blättler (eds) *Les états neutres européens et la seconde guerre mondiale*, Neuchâtel, 1985.

McGeary, Johanna, 'Echoes of the Holocaust', *Time*, 24 Feb. 1997.

McKay, C. G., 'Iron Ore and Section D: The Oxelösund Operation', *Historical Journal*, 29, 1986.

Medlicott, W. N., *The Economic Blockade*, vol. II, London, 1959.

Millman, Brock, 'Turkish Foreign and Strategic Policy 1934–42', *Middle Eastern Studies*, 31, 1995.

Millman, Brock, 'Credit and Supply in Turkish Foreign Policy and the Tripartite Alliance of October 1939: A Note', *International History Review*, XVI, 1994.

Milward, Alan S., 'The Reichsmark Bloc and the International Economy', in Gerhard Hirschfeld, Lothar Kettenacker (eds), *Der "Führerstaat": Mythos und Realität; Studien zur Struktur und Politik des Dritten Reiches*, Stuttgart, 1981.

Milward, Alan S., 'Could Sweden have stopped the Second World War?', *Scandinavian Economic History Review*, XV, 1967.

Miranda, Sacuntala de, 'Crise económica, industrialização e autarcia na década de 30', in *O Estado Novo; das origens ao fim da autarcia*, vol. I, Lisbon, 1987.

Moyzisch, Ludwig C., trans. Constantine Fitzgibbon, Heinrich Fraenkel, *Operation Cicero*, London and New York, 1950.

Munch-Petersen, Thomas, *The Strategy of Phoney War; Britain, Sweden, and the Iron Ore Question, 1939–40*, Stockholm, 1981.

Neves, Mário, 'A diplomacia portuguesa nas duas guerras do século', in Mario Carrilho *et al.*, *Portugal na Segunda Guerra Mundial; contributos para uma reavaliação*, Lisbon, 1989.

Nogueira, Franco, *Salazar*, vol. III, *As grandes crises (1936–1945)*, Coimbra, 1978.

Nilsson, Anne, *De Allierade och Sverige; Sveriges roll i de allierades ekonomiska krigföring under andra världskriget*, Stockholm, 1988.

Nissen , Henrik S., 'Adjusting to German Domination', in Nissen (ed.), *Scandinavia during the Second World War*, Minneapolis, 1983.

Nøkleby, Berit, 'Adjusting to Allied Victory', in H. S. Nissen (ed.), *Scandinavia during the Second World War*, Minneapolis, 1983.

Ogley, Roderick, *The Theory and Practice of Neutrality in the Twentieth Century*, London, 1970.

Oliveira, César, 'A sobrevivência das ditaduras e a neutralidade peninsular na Segunda Guerra Mundial', in *O Estado Novo; das origens ao fim da autarcia*, vol. I, Lisbon, 1987.

Olmert, Y., 'Britain, Turkey and the Levant Question during the Second World War', *Middle Eastern Studies*, 23, 1987.

Overy, Richard J., *War and Economy in the Third Reich*, Oxford, 1994.

Önder, Zehra, *Die türkische Außenpolitik im Zweiten Weltkrieg*, Munich, 1977.

Ørvik, Nils, *The Decline of Neutrality 1914–1941*, London, 2nd edn, 1971.

Payne, Stanley G., *The Franco Regime, 1939–1975*, Madison, Wis., 1987.

Petersen, Neal H. (ed.), *From Hitler's Doorstep; The Wartime Intelligence Reports of Allen Dulles, 1942–1945*, University Park, PA, 1996.

Picard, Jacques, *Die Schweiz und die Juden 1933–1945; Schweizerischer Antisemitismus, jüdische Abwehr und internationale Migrations- und Flüchtlingspolitik*, Zürich, 2nd edn, 1994.

Piekalkiewicz, Janusz, *Schweiz 39–45; Krieg in einem neutralen Land*, Stuttgart and Zug, 2nd edn, 1979.

Pike, David Wingeate, 'Franco and the Axis Stigma', *Journal of Contemporary History* 17, 1982.

Praz, Anne-Françoise, *Du Réduit à l'ouverture; La Suisse de 1940 à 1949*, Prilly, 1995.

Preston, Paul, *Franco: a biography*, London, 1995.

Preston, Paul, 'Franco's Foreign Policy 1939–1953', in Christian Leitz, David J. Dunthorn (eds), *Spain in an International Context; Civil War, Cold War, Early Cold War*, New York and Oxford, 1999.

Preston, Paul, 'Franco and his Generals, 1939–1945', in Paul Preston, *The Politics of Revenge; Fascism and the Military in Twentieth-century Spain*, London and New York, 1995.

Preston, Paul, 'Franco and the Axis Temptation', in Paul Preston, *The Politics of Revenge; Fascism and the Military in Twentieth-century Spain*, London and New York, 1995.

Preston, Paul, 'Franco and Hitler: The Myth of Hendaye 1940', *Contemporary European History*, 1, 1992.

Proctor, Raymond L., *Agonía de un neutral*, Madrid, 1972.

Proctor, Raymond L., 'La Division Azul', *Guerres mondiales et conflits contemporaines*, 162, 1991.

Richardson, Gunnar, *Beundran och fruktan; Sverige inför Tyskland 1940–1942*, Stockholm, 1996.

Rings, Werner, *Schweiz im Krieg 1933–1945*, Zürich, 9th exp. edn, 1997.

Rings, Werner, *Raubgold aus Deutschland. Die "Golddrehscheibe" Schweiz im Zweiten Weltkrieg*, Munich, 2nd edn, 1996.

Robertson, John, *Turkey and Allied Strategy 1941–1945*, New York and London, 1986.

Roque Amario, Rogério, 'A economia nos primórdios do Estado Novo – estagnação ou crescimento?', in *O Estado Novo; das origens ao fim da autarcia*, vol. I, Lisbon, 1987.

Rosas, Fernando, 'O Pacto Ibérico e a neutralização da Península', in Fernando Rosas, *O Salazarismo e a Alliança Luso-Britânica; estudos sobre a política externa do Estado Novo nos anos 30 e 40*, Lisbon, 1988.

Roth, Thomas, 'Schweden erwache! Tysk propaganda mot Sverige 1942', in Bo Hugemark (ed.), *Vindkantring; 1942 – politisk kursändring*, Stockholm, 1993.

Ruhl, Klaus-Jörg, *Spanien im Zweiten Weltkrieg: Franco, die Falange und das 'Dritte Reich'*, Hamburg, 1975.

Rustow, Dankwart A., 'Politics and Development Policy', in Frederic C. Shorter (ed.), *Four Studies on the Economic Development of Turkey*, London, 1967.

Rutley's Elements of Mineralogy, London, 27th edn., 1988, rev. C. D. Gribble.

Salmon, Patrick, 'British Plans for Economic Warfare against Germany 1937–1939: The Problem of Swedish Iron Ore', *Journal of Contemporary History*, 16, 1981.

Schönherr, Klaus, 'Neutrality, "Non-Belligerence", or War; Turkey and the European Powers' Conflict of Interests, 1939–1941', in Bernd Wegner (ed.), *From Peace to War; Germany, Soviet Russia and the World, 1939–1941*, Providence, RI and Oxford, 1997.

Schönherr, Klaus, 'Die türkische Außenpolitik vom Vorabend des Zweiten Weltkrieges bis 1941', *Österreichische Osthefte*, 36, 1994.

Senn, Hans, 'Militärische Aspekte der Neutralität', in Louis-Edouard Roulet with Roland Blättler (eds) *Les états neutres européens et la seconde guerre mondiale*, Neuchâtel, 1985.

Serrano Suñer, Ramón, 'Política de España; amistad y resistencia con Alemania durante la Segunda Guerra Mundial', in Stanley G. Payne, Delia Contreras (eds), *España y la Segunda Guerra Mundial*, Madrid, 1996.

Shubert, Adrian, *A Social History of Modern Spain*, London, 1990.

Smyth, Denis, *Diplomacy and Strategy of Survival: British Policy and Franco's Spain, 1940–1941*, Cambridge, 1986.

Smyth, Denis, 'The Dispatch of the Spanish Blue Division to the Russian Front: Reasons and Repercussions', *European History Quarterly*, 24, 1994.

Smyth, Denis, 'Screening "Torch": Allied Counter-Intelligence and the Spanish Threat to the Secrecy of the Allied Invasion of French North Africa in November, 1942', *Intelligence and National Security*, 4, 1989.

Steinberg, Jonathan, *Die Deutsche Bank und ihre Goldtransaktionen während des Zweiten Weltkrieges*, Munich, 1999.

Stone, Glyn, *The Oldest Ally: Britain and the Portuguese Connection, 1936–1941*, Woodbridge, 1994.

Stone, Glyn, 'Britain, France and Franco's Spain in the Aftermath of the Spanish Civil War', *Diplomacy and Statecraft*, 6, 1995.

Telo, António José, *Portugal na Segunda Guerra (1941–1945)*, vols I and II, Lisbon, 1991.

Telo, António José, *Propaganda e guerra secreta em Portugal (1939–45)*, Lisbon, 1990.

Telo, António José, 'Relações Portugal-EUA 1940–1941', in *O Estado Novo; das origens ao fim da autarcia*, vol. I, Lisbon, 1987.

Tennant, Peter, *Vid sidan av kriget, Diplomat i Sverige 1939–45*, Stockholm, 1989.

Tennstedt, Ernst, *Die türkischen Meerengen unter der Konvention von Montreux im Zweiten Weltkrieg*, Hamburg, 1981.

Thomas, Martin, 'French Morocco – Spanish Morocco: Vichy French Strategic Planning against the "Threat from the North", 1940–1942', in Christian Leitz, David J. Dunthorn (eds), *Spain in an International Context; Civil War, Cold War, Early Cold War*, New York and Oxford, 1999.

Thornburg, Max Weston, Graham Spry, George Soule, *Turkey; an Economic Appraisal*, New York, 1949.

Toynbee, Arnold and Veronica M. Toynbee (eds), *Hitler's Europe* (Survey of International Affairs 1939–1946), London *et al.*, 1954.

Trepp, Gian, *Die Bank für Internationalen Zahlungsausgleich im Zweiten Weltkrieg: Bankgeschäfte mit dem Feind. Von Hitlers Europabank zum Instrument des Marshallplans*, Zürich, 3rd edn, May 1997.

Trevor-Roper, Hugh R. (ed.), *Hitler's War Directives 1939–1945*, London, 1966.

Trommer, Aage, 'Scandinavia and the Turn of the Tide', in H. S. Nissen (ed.), *Scandinavia during the Second World War*, Minneapolis, 1983.

Tusell, Javier and Genoveva García Queipo de Llano, *Franco y Mussolini: La política española durante la segunda guerra mundial*, Barcelona, 1985.

Urner, Klaus, 'Neutralität und Wirtschaftskrieg: Zur schweizerischen Außenhandelspolitik 1939–1945', in Rudolf L. Bindschedler *et al.* (eds), *Schwedische und schweizerische Neutralität im Zweiten Weltkrieg*, Basel, Frankfurt/Main, 1985.

U.S. and Allied Efforts to recover and restore Gold and other Assets stolen or hidden by Germany during World War II, preliminary study coordinated by Stuart E. Eizenstat, prepared by William Z. Slany, Washington D.C., May 1997.

US Department of State (ed.), *The Spanish Government and the Axis; Documents*, Washington, 1946.

Viñas, Angel, 'Franco's Dreams of Autarky Shattered; Foreign Policy Aspects in the Run-up to the 1959 Change in Spanish Economic Strategy', in Christian Leitz, David J. Dunthorn (eds), *Spain in an International Context; Civil War, Cold War, Early Cold War*, New York and Oxford, 1999.

Vogler, Robert Urs, *Die Wirtschaftsverhandlungen zwischen der Schweiz und Deutschland 1940 und 1941*, Zürich, 1983.

Volkmann, Hans-Erich, 'Außenhandel und Aufrüstung in Deutschland 1933 bis 1939', in Volkmann and Friedrich Forstmeier (eds), *Wirtschaft und Rüstung am Vorabend des Zweiten Weltkrieges*, Düsseldorf, 1975.

Wahlbäck, Krister, *The Roots of Swedish Neutrality*, Stockholm, 1986.

Wahlbäck, Krister and Göran Boberg (eds), *Sveriges sak är vår; Svensk utrikespolitik 1939–45 i dokument*, Stockholm, 1967.

Wangel, Carl-Axel, 'Verteidigung gegen den Krieg', in Rudolf L. Bindschedler *et al.* (eds), *Schwedische und schweizerische Neutralität im Zweiten Weltkrieg,* Basel and Frankfurt/Main, 1985.

Weber, Frank G., *The Evasive Neutral; Germany, Britain and the Quest for a Turkish Alliance in the Second World War,* Columbia Miss., 1979.

Weisband, Edward, *Turkish Foreign Policy 1943–1945; Small State Diplomacy and Great Power Politics,* Princeton, 1973.

West, John M., 'The German-Swedish Transit Agreement of 1940', *Scandinavian Studies,* 50, 1978.

Wheeler, Douglas L., 'The Price of Neutrality: Portugal, the Wolfram Question, and World War II', parts I and II, *Luso-Brazilian Review,* XXIII, 1986.

Wheeler, Douglas L., 'In the Service of Order: The Portuguese Political Police and the British, German and Spanish Intelligence Services, 1932–1945', *Journal of Contemporary History,* 18, 1983.

Wildhaber, Luzius, 'Neutralität und Gute Dienste', in Louis-Edouard Roulet with Roland Blättler (eds) *Les états neutres européens et la seconde guerre mondiale,* Neuchâtel, 1985.

Wilhelmus, Wolfgang, 'Zu den Beziehungen zwischen dem faschistischen Deutschland und Schweden nach dem Überfall auf die Sowjetunion (Juni bis Dezember 1941)', *Zeitschrift für Geschichtswissenschaft,* 26, 1978.

Wittmann, Klaus, *Schwedens Wirtschaftsbeziehungen zum Dritten Reich 1933–1945,* Munich and Vienna, 1978.

Wittmann, Klaus, 'Deutsch-schwedische Wirtschaftsbeziehungen im Zweiten Weltkrieg', in Friedrich Forstmeier and Hans-Erich Volkmann (eds), *Kriegswirtschaft und Rüstung 1939–1945,* Düsseldorf, 1977.

Wylie, Neville, '"Life between the Volcanoes." Switzerland during the Second World War', *Historical Journal,* 38, 1995.

Yavuz, Erdal, 'The State of the Industrial Workforce, 1923–40', in Donald Quataert, Erik Jan Zürcher (eds), *Workers and the Working Class in the Ottoman Empire and the Turkish Republic 1839–1950,* London and New York, 1995.

Yilmaz, Bahri, 'Die wirtschaftliche Entwicklung der Türkei von 1923 bis 1980', *Südosteuropa Mitteilungen,* 33, 1993.

Zetterberg, Kent, '1942 – Storkriget vänder, Sveriges utsatta läge består', in Bo Hugemark (ed.), *Vindkantring; 1942 – politisk kursändring,* Stockholm, 1993.

Zetterberg, Kent, 'Neutralitet till varje pris? Till frågan om den svenska säkerhetspolitiken 1940–42 och eftergifterna till Tyskland', in Bo Hugemark (ed.), *I Orkanens Öga; 1941 – osäker neutralitet,* Stockholm, 1992.

Zetterberg, Kent, 'Le transit allemand par la Suède de 1940 à 1943', *Revue d'histoire de la deuxième guerre mondiale,* 109, 1978.

Zimmermann, Horst, 'Die "Nebenfrage Schweiz" in der Außenpolitik des Dritten Reiches', in Manfred Funke (ed.), *Hitler, Deutschland und die Mächte; Materialien zur Außenpolitik des Dritten Reiches,* Düsseldorf, 1976.

Web sites

http://www.switzerland.taskforce.ch
http://www.uek.ch
http://www.uek.ch./e/m1/gold_ez.htm (Conclusion to Interim Report on Gold
    Transactions, 'Independent Commission of Experts: Switzerland – Second
    World War', May 1998).

INDEX

intelligence operations in 167–8,
174n.111–12
military position 9n.11, 140n.48,
149–50, 153–4, 162, 166, 178
press and censorship 146, 151
and Spain 145–8, 153–4
Portuguese Legion (Legião
Portuguesa) 151, 153, 170n.36
Preston, Paul 128, 137
propaganda 7, 29, 80n.66, 97, 107,
120, 150, 152
Puhl, Emil 184, 185
Pyrenees 119, 150, 153

Raeder, Erich 9n.11, 91, 124
Red Army 95, 99, 128
Red Cross 39
Reichsbank 28–9, 37, 39, 69, 184
Rheinfelden 47n.132
Rheinmetall 105
Ribbentrop, Joachim von 14, 46n.97,
55–6, 90–2, 94, 96–7, 100,
122–3, 130, 140n.40, 140n.44,
142n.71, 169n.16
Richert, Arvid 55–6, 78n.41
Riksbank 70, 184
Rings, Werner 11, 15, 21, 41n.11,
47n.130, 185
Rio de Janeiro 168
Ritter, Karl 27
Romania 28, 88, 93
Rome 117, 119, 121
Roosevelt, Franklin D. 72, 83n.126,
99, 121, 135, 154
Rosenberg, Alfred 97
Rowak 132, 157
Ruhr 64

Salazar, António de Oliveira 144–56,
159, 163–4, 168–9, 171n.42,
174n.102, 176, 180–3, 188–9
Sandler, Rickard 52
Santander 119

Saracoglu, Sükrü 90–2, 94–6, 98,
110n.50, 110n.54, 112n.83
Sargent, Orme 110n.41
Saydam, Refik 90
Schellenberg, Walter 23–5
Schnurre, Karl 57, 60–1
Schulenburg, Friedrich Werner von
97
Schultheß, Edmund 14
Schweinfurt 83n.129
Schwendemann, Karl 145
Senegal 124
Senn, Hans 21–2
Serrano Suñer, Ramón 114, 119,
122–3, 127, 129, 138n.7,
140n.40, 140n.44, 141n.55,
169n.16
Seyboth, Gottfried 32
Sicily 154
Simplon tunnel 35
Skaggerak 53, 66, 82n.106
SKF (Svenska Kullagerfabriken) 73
Slovakia 45n.90, 52
SNB (Swiss National Bank) 28–9,
46n.98, 161, 177
Söderblom, Staffan 83n.128
SOE (Special Operations Executive)
66
Sonderstab HWK (Special Staff for
Trade and Economic Warfare)
31
Sonimi group 158
Soviet Union 18, 23, 34, 36, 49, 50–
1, 56–9, 68, 72, 79n.47,
80n.64, 84n.135, 86, 87, 89,
90–1, 93–9, 103, 109n.27,
109n.35, 109n.37, 111n.79,
113n.104, 117, 125–9, 145,
149, 151–2, 154, 156, 165–6,
178, 179, 182–3
Spain 1, 3
and Allies 116, 119, 131–7, 165,
182–3